METER IN MUSIC,

1600–1800

Music: Scholarship and Performance
Thomas Binkley, General Editor

METER
in Music,
1600–1800

⌘

Performance, Perception, and Notation

GEORGE HOULE

Indiana
University
Press

BLOOMINGTON & INDIANAPOLIS

Library of Congress Cataloging-in-Publication Data

Houle, George.
  Meter in music, 1600–1800.

  (Music—scholarship and performance)
  Bibliography: p.
  Includes index.
  1. Musical meter and rhythm. 2. Musical notation.
  3. Music—17th century—Performance. 4. Music—
  18th century—Performance. I. Title. II. Series.
  MT75.H7   1987   781.6'2'09032   86-45789
  ISBN 0-253-33792-5
  ISBN 0-253-33793-3 companion cassette

  1 2 3 4 5 91 90 89 88 87

Contents

❧

PLATES

INTRODUCTION

The notation of seventeenth- and eighteenth-century music is often a puzzle to performers. The symbols of notation appear tantalizingly similar to modern ones, but their meanings are not, a fact that can lead to bewilderment and misinterpretation. Yet when the original notes are translated into their equivalents in modern notation, as in any phonetic pronunciation scheme, something vital is lost. By learning to read the original notation correctly, one can enter more closely into the composer's thoughts and his performers' traditions.

The right musical pronunciation is sought avidly today by scholars and performers because the music is so rewarding when the language is spoken correctly, and also because there is an increasingly demanding modern audience. Understanding the language makes it possible both to perform from and to edit the original notation; a knowledge of musical meter is crucial to this understanding.

Meter is considered to be the regular flow of the beat, its subdivisions or pulses, and the organization of the beat into bars or measures. Larger rhythmic units, phrases and periods, which encompass many measures, are usually not regular. They are perceived as the resolution of tensions produced when some of the smaller metrical units are rendered more prominent than others, but the dynamic artistic irregularity in the construction of phrases and periods is founded on a substructure of regular pulses, beats, and measures.

Although little attention to larger rhythmic units is found among theorists and writers until the late eighteenth century, the notation, perception, and performance articulation of meter is a topic few omit from their discussions and instructions. The reason for this interest may have been their heightened consciousness of music's metrical flow.

During the seventeenth and eighteenth centuries, musicians frequently discussed meter in terms that are obscure to us, such as *quantitas notarum intrinseca,* or "good" and "bad" notes, but these terms have the virtue of defining the beat and measure without reference to accent or any other articulation. Performers were left free to enhance the listener's perception of meter by using a variety of articulation techniques, according to the medium of performance and the style of the music.

As the mensural *tactus* was replaced by a beat that could be slower or faster in response to diverse notation symbols, the beats and measures became units of notation upon which articulation formulas were based. These formulas were learned by instrumentalists as part of an elementary performance technique and were the basis of articulation and phrasing, akin to a singer's use of pronunciation. The effect of the various degrees of separate articulation that could be used for each note is lively and clear and establishes a basic continuity through the music's varied rhetorical figures.

Accent, defined as dynamic stress by seventeenth- and eighteenth-century writers, was one of the means of enhancing the perception of meter, but it became predominant only in the last half of the eighteenth century. The idea that the measure is a pattern of accents is so widely held today that it is difficult to imagine that notation that looks modern does not have regular accentual patterns. Quite a number of serious scholarly studies of this music make this assumption almost unconsciously by translating the (sometimes difficult) early descriptions of meter into equivalent descriptions of the modern accentual measure.

Articulation of meter and melodic figures in nineteenth- and twentieth-century music is carefully specified by the composer in his score, and if he has been lax in this regard, the deficiency is remedied by the editor of his collected works. The music's public appearance is, so to speak, with hair combed, buttons fastened, and tie straight. Notation in the seventeenth and eighteenth centuries appears to be not so well groomed because of its greater reliance on the performer's traditional articulation formulas.

Notation summarizes the composer's individual vision of music as well as the performance traditions of his time. Fortunately, seventeenth- and eighteenth-century music is generally allowed to appear in modern editions without transcription, so that the composer's vision and hints are preserved and the performer can learn to read them.

The performer must come to this music with more than just the right attitude, right historical understanding, and right instrument. Without proper performance technique, a vision of the inspiration of this music cannot be found. This achievement can only result from careful, informed preparation, founded on the directions and comments in the technical manuals of the time. It is not a simple matter to replace modern habits and techniques, themselves painfully learned and joyfully mastered, with others that may seem awkward and clumsy until they are mastered as well.

A performer who can impart to music the lilt, grace, and drive of the underlying structure of seventeenth- and eighteenth-century music has command of a powerful force. Creating a persuasive beat in performance requires a paradoxical mixture of precision and flexibility that avoids both mechanical regularity and incoherence. Otherwise, the music can seem to be either machinelike or a series of small music-rhetorical figures, lacking architectural integrity. With an understanding of seventeenth- and eighteenth-century perceptions of meter and a mastery of the musical techniques of the time, we will be better able to perform this music with the verve, passion, and authority it deserves.

METER IN MUSIC,

1600–1800

I

❧

The Origins of the Measure
in the Seventeenth Century

THE CONCEPT OF the musical measure, time signatures, and bar lines evolved gradually from sixteenth-century mensural notation. Some symbols of modern notation are derived from the mensural system, though we may be unaware of their original significance. Some new symbols were accepted into seventeenth-century notation, but most of those in use were familiar to musicians for over a century.

The semicircle C and its diminution ₵, for example, are mensural symbols, for which 4/4 or 2/2 time signatures were later invented as substitutions. Time signatures using numerical fractions, such as 3/2 or 9/8, evolved from proportions into meter signs. Basic changes in the way musical time and notation were perceived occurred when tempo significance was added to mensural symbols.

The mensural system related all notes to a down-and-up gesture of moderate speed, called the *tactus* (meaning "beat"). Bar lines were used occasionally to indicate note values equivalent to one or two *tactus,* but they did not necessarily define a metrical hierarchy. The *tactus* gradually came to measure a longer span of time, although it continued to be indicated by the same note value; this general trend, perceptible to us through hindsight, was too gradual to occasion comment by theorists and performers in the seventeenth century. Performers became accustomed to reading smaller note values, for several reasons, and the note value associated with a comfortable beat became the quarter note, rather than the semibreve (whole note) or minim (half note) as in the sixteenth century.

The "measure," or time value of the *tactus,* was conducted with an equal down-and-up motion for duple meters, even though it came to include two or four beats instead of one. Triple proportions (triple meters) were conducted by a *tactus* beat with a downstroke double the duration of the upstroke. Seventeenth-century musicians came to interpret mensural signs and proportions themselves as indicating a slower or faster *tactus,* although the change in the speed of the *tactus* was slight—less than the change occasioned by employing another proportion or diminution. Proportions with large-numbered denominators were interpreted to indicate faster tempos and those with small-numbered denominators to indicate slower ones. Because of this, the number of beats included in *tactus* measures varied, and musicians became interested in the practical question of how many beats were included in the measure of the *tactus.*

Another inheritance from mensural notation was the convention that smaller notes were performed faster and larger notes were performed slower; therefore, tempo was indicated not only by the sign or proportion but also by the size of the notes. Compositions written in 3/2 and ₵ generally equated the half note or minim with the beat and were slower in tempo than those in 3/4 and ₵, where the quarter note represented the beat. Some late seventeenth-century explanations of meter began to equate all quarter notes, for example, even when comparing them in ₵ and 3/4 measures. Mensural theory would regard quarter notes in these different measures as different values because 3/4 was a proportion and its three quarters were equivalent in value to the four quarters in ₵. As a result, these two logical extensions of mensural principles were sometimes in conflict.

Words to indicate tempo served to mediate the conflicts and uncertainties of note values, signs, and proportions. In the early seventeenth century, *tarde, velociter, adagio,* and *presto* distinguished between fast and slow, that is, degrees of change intermediate to those determined by diminution (2:1) or proportion (usually 2:1, 3:1, or 3:2). As the vocabulary of tempo words became richer and more precise later in the century, the terms gained in authority and were able to indicate finer degrees in the change of speed.

Italian music seems to have been the first to use mensural signs and proportions as time signatures. The most frequently used proportions came to describe how many notes of what size were found in a measure, and 3/4, 6/8, and 12/8 became very popular. 3/1 and 3/2 were still associated with proportions and were less used. Tempo words were Italian; they traveled with Italian music and musicians and gradually converted most of the rest of Europe to Italian practice. At the least, they blended the Italian conversions of mensural signs into time signatures with the more conservative German or English practices.

Note Values and the Tactus

Perhaps the most important change in the evolution from mensural to measure notation was in the relation of notes to the *tactus* beat. In mensural notation the *tactus* governed the performance of "fast" and "slow" music alike: faster music was written in smaller note values and slower music in larger ones, or else a numerical proportion was written in the score to change the value of notes in relation to the *tactus*.

The treatise of Sebald Heyden has influenced many twentieth-century scholars to believe that the *tactus* of the sixteenth century represented an unvarying beat:

> In the examples of these two men [Iohannes Ghiselinus and Iacobus Obrecht] a definite relationship of signs would always be evident if the hidden meaning of the signs were revealed by a prescribed limit in the art, not by the accidental introduction of varying kinds of *tactus*.
>
> Through this accident of changing the *tactus* the relationship and nature of all proportions having mutually dissimilar signs are confused and defective. Indeed how unnecessary it was to invent so many different kinds of *tactus* that even now we endure unwillingly! For when we see many kinds of *tactus* invented simply to change the tempo of a composition frequently, making it now slower, now faster, and now very fast, then I ask, what are we to think later composers understood by proportions, augmentations and diminutions? From the art itself it is absolutely certain that they wanted to show through various kinds of *tactus* the same thing that early composers had indicated more correctly and artistically either by a diminution of signs or by proportions.[1]

Heyden taught that the unvarying *tactus* was a necessary part of mensural notation, although it is clear from this quotation that it was not the only practice of sixteenth-century musicians. J. A. Bank shows that many twentieth-century scholars also believe that an invariable *tactus*-tempo was the basis of sixteenth-century notation, and that they quote Heyden, Ornithoparchus (1517), Listenius (1549), H. Finck (1556), Lanfranco (1533), Schneegasz (1596), and Thomas Morley (1597) in support of this belief.[2] The practice of mensural notation was taught to young musicians then as well as now as if the *tactus* were invariable in speed, a pedagogical technique that simplifies many complexities of actual practice.

The *tactus* was ordinarily equated with the semibreve, as John Dowland's translation of Ornithoparchus's *Micrologus* makes clear: "A *Semibreefe* in all Signes (excepting the Signes of Diminution, augmentation and proportion) is measured by a whole *tact*."[3]

The speed of the *tactus* in the sixteenth and seventeenth centuries was often described in general terms and sometimes identified with the body's pulse.[4] Of course, the pulse can be quite variable, but it does have the advantage of being instantly available. The *tactus* was designated either as *tactus maior* or *tactus minor,* the latter being twice as fast as the former. Ornithoparchus, in John Dowland's translation, adds a third, *tactus proportionatus,* which will be discussed later in this chapter:

Of the Division of *tact*

Tact is three fold, the greater, the lesser and the proportionate. The greater is a Measure made by a slow, and as it were reciprocall motion. The writers call this *tact* the whole, or totall *tact*. And, because it is the true *tact* of all Songs, it comprehends in his motion a semibreefe not diminished: or a Breefe diminished in a duple.

The lesser *Tact,* is the half of the greater, which they call a *Semitact.* Because it measures by it [*sic*] motion a Semibreefe, diminished in a duple: This is allowed onely by the Unlearned.

The Proportionate is that, whereby three Semibreefes are uttered against one, (as in a Triple) or against two, as in a *Sesquialtera.*[5]

Therefore, although the *tactus* in mensural notation was usually equated with the semibreve, it could be identified with other note values. The speed of the music appears not to be changed by choosing *tactus maior* or *minor* since *tactus maior* was equal to a note value twice as large as that of the *tactus minor.* The choice between them depended upon which was the more convenient in clarifying the *tactus* in performance.

Ornithoparchus-Dowland says, "Wherefore *tact* is a successive motion in singing, directing the equalitie of the measure: or it is a certaine motion, made by the hand of the chiefe singer, according to the nature of the marks, which directs a Song according to measure."[6] The *tactus* beat was given by a down-and-up motion that was either even or uneven. If even, it indicated pulses of duple meter and if uneven, triple meter (two pulses measured on the downstroke and one on the up).

In a diagram, Dowland gives the number of *tactus* equated with various note values in different mensurations and under several proportion signs. Two minims go in the time of a *tactus,* the semiminim (quarter note) goes "4. to one stroake," the eighth note, "8. to one stroake" and the sixteenth note, "16. to one stroake."[7]

Zarlino links the *tactus* with mensural signs: "To indicate equal *battute* (*tactus*) in writing, musicians used these four [mensuration] signs: O, C or Ɔ, ₵; and to indicate unequal *battute* these four signs: ⊙, C, or Ɔ, ₵. They could also indicate unequal *battute* with the sign 3/2 preceded by the mensuration sign."[8] "Equal *battute*" means that the *tactus* is conducted with a gesture divided into two equal pulses, one down and one up. "Unequal *battute*" means that the downstroke is given two pulses and the upstroke one. The *tactus* is the interval between two downbeats, so that its length is not changed by the method of beating.

There are physiological limits to the speed of a conductor's beat. If the beat is too slow to be followed easily, the conductor subdivides the gesture, thereby doubling its speed. If too fast, then he or she consolidates two beats in one, halving the speed. In metronome indications, the beat becomes too slow around MM 40, and too fast around MM 130–35. This provides a range of tempo of more than triple the speed of the slowest beat. The *tactus* was near the center of this range, since the body's resting pulse generally corresponds to MM 60–80. The *tactus maior* was equated with this speed, and *tactus minor*, therefore, with MM 120–40. Since MM 140 is uncomfortably fast, it would seem that *tactus maior* might be restricted to the range of MM 60–66.

Marin Mersenne confirms this speculation by equating the *tactus* with a second in time, one-sixtieth of a minute, therefore with MM 60. He also explains that the *tactus* is related to the body's pulse, but the pulse is faster than the *tactus*. In addition he describes how to construct a pendulum with a musket-ball suspended from a string 3½ feet long that will swing back and forth precisely in one second. The string may be shortened by mathematical formulas to correspond to the tempo of different proportions, or "faire prendre l'accoustumance aux Maistres qui font chanter, de batre réglement la mesure de telle vitesse qu'ils voudront" (to suit the custom of singing-masters to beat the measure at whatever speed they wish).[9]

Mersenne discusses how the speed of the *tactus* is frequently quickened or slowed, "suivant la lettre & les paroles, ou les passions differentes du sujet dont ils traitent" (following the characters, words, or the various emotions they evoke). He states that different tempos, like the speeds of different wheels in a clock, may be used to determine the beat of the measure. It may be given by the movement of a torch at night, a piece of wood, or a piece of paper in the day, although "ceux qui conduisent maintenant les concerts, marquent la mesure par le mouvement du manche des Luths ou des Tuorbes, dont ils ioüët" (those who conduct at concerts nowadays mark the measure by the movement of the necks of the lutes or theorboes on which they play). However, the manner of giving the beat is of no importance if the singers are accurate, and in some concerts the beat is not conducted at all.[10] From Mersenne's discussion it would seem that there was a normative *tactus* speed, perhaps an old-fashioned or traditional way of regarding the governance of tempo, but that the ordinary practice of performers varied in the matter of speed as well as in the way of indicating the beat.

In the sixteenth century, theorists described the *tactus* in relation to notation rather than as an independent topic. In the seventeenth century, both Agostino Pisa and Pier Francesco Valentini wrote treatises entirely devoted to the *tactus*. Their meticulous consideration of every detail of the *tactus* gesture, a matter that was apparently too obvious to be considered in the sixteenth century, is a sign of change in the meaning of the *tactus*.

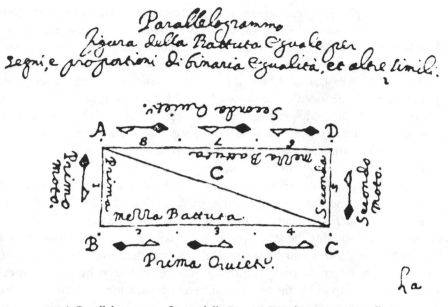

PLATE 1. Parallelogrammo figura della Battuta Eguale. (*Trattato Della Battuta Mvsicale di Pier Francesco Valentini Romano*, para. 154, p. 76.)

Pisa considered these problems: (1) What motion does the hand make when rising to begin the stroke? (2) Does the *tactus* begin at the instant the hand moves or when the hand reaches the bottom of the stroke? (3) Are notes (subdivisions of the *tactus*) performed while the hand moves in the air? (4) Is there an interval of time while the hand stops at the bottom or top of the stroke during which notes are being performed? (5) Is the final note of a piece to be stopped when the hand reaches the top of its last stroke? [11]

Valentini's treatise alludes to Pisa's discussion and often disagrees with it (he refers to Pisa as Asip). In his description of beating the *tactus*, Valentini speaks of a downstroke that is succeeded by "quiete" or reposes, then an upstroke followed by reposes. He also discusses which notes, as divisions of the *tactus*, are performed when the hand is moving, and which when in repose. He includes diagrams to illustrate the relation of notes to the "battuta eguale" and to the "battuta ineguale," which are reproduced in plates 1 and 2. [12]

In the "parallelogrammo" illustrating the equal beat (plate 1), the first eighth-note occupies the time of the first motion, from A down to B, the second, third, and fourth eighth-notes occupy the first repose at the bottom of the stroke, B to C. The fifth eighth-note occupies the time of the second motion, from C up to D, and the sixth, seventh, and eighth eighth-notes occupy the time of the second repose, D to A, at the top of the stroke. [13] The "circolo" (plate 2) demonstrates the method of giving an unequal (triple) beat. The first motion accompanies the first of the twelve seminimins, from A to B, the

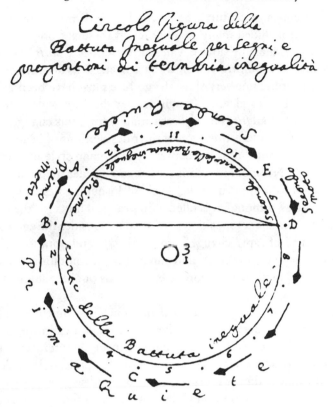

PLATE 2. Circolo figura della Battuta Ineguale. (*Trattato Della Battuta Mvsicale di Pier Francesco Valentini Romano*, para. 156, p. 78.)

first repose accompanies the additional seven semiminims constituting the remainder of the first part of the beat, depicted by the line B to D. The second motion accompanies the ninth semiminim, line D to E, and the second repose accompanies the remaining three semiminims. If one counts semibreves, the first takes the circumference of the circle from A to C, the second from C to D, and the third from D to A, but the beat is still given as before.

The speed of the *tactus* was quite variable, "tal volta adagio, e tal volta presto, e tal volta tra'l presto e l'adagio mediocremente, secondo richiedono li stile delle compositioni, et il scale delle parole" (sometimes slow, sometimes quick, and sometimes between quick and moderately slow, according to the styles of compositions and the indication of the words).[14]

The *tactus* can be represented by various note values: "oltre la Breve et oltre la Semibreve, si nella eguale come anco nella inegual Battuta, qual si voglia nota musicale, per mezzo delle date proportioni può esser misurata, et abbracciata dal tempo et intervallo di una Battuta" (besides the breve and the semibreve under the duple or triple *tactus,* any note value may be equated and embraced by the time interval of a *tactus,* by means of the proportions).[15]

In the seventeenth century, the *tactus* required minute investigation because it so often included many small notes; if these are not to be performed quickly, the *tactus* must be slower. Valentini describes a *Battuta larga*, a "slow beat," [16] as well as a *Battuta veloce*, a "fast beat," [17] to accommodate various speeds. If the beat became very slow, the gesture must have been more difficult to follow as well as to give. Although neither Pisa nor Valentini specifically states that the usual *tactus* is now slower than before, this change could be deduced from the meticulous precision of their descriptions of beating the *tactus*.

Valentini was faithful to the conservative Roman style of composition of his teacher, G. B. Nanino. His treatise seems to consider the *tactus* and its relation to notation as it applied to the music of Josquin, Palestrina, and the Roman conservatives, although it is filled with practical hints for the performance of seventeenth-century compositions. We tend to consider the early seventeenth century as a time of rapid change in musical style and notation, yet the force of tradition was very powerful, and innovations in notation competed with strong habits of practice and vigorous expositions of old-fashioned theoretical concepts.

In contrast to the notation of vocal and much instrumental music, smaller note values predominate in lute and keyboard tablatures in the late sixteenth and seventeenth centuries. In consequence, mensurally interpreted note values (*longa, breve,* and *semibreve*) are not usual, and minims and smaller notes are always subdivided by duples unless specially marked as triple, just as in modern notation. The *tactus* remains nominally equal to the value of the semibreve, but the semibreve moves much slower than the beat. William Barley's *A new booke of tabliture* of 1598 explained only the useful small notes, and didn't bother with the *longa* and *breve* at all: "Finally there are certaine figures or characters used in the tabliture, which likewise of necessite must bee known unto you. . . . The figures are thus marked | ⌐ ⌐ ⌐ ⌐, a semibriefe |, A Minom ⌐, a Crotchet ⌐, a Quaver ⌐, a Semiquaver ⌐." [18]

This change of notation is mentioned by Thomas Ravenscroft, who, like Valentini, was a conservative in regard to notation and considered the new practices to be corruptions. Ravenscroft's exposition of notation is by no means without its confusions, but he is clear about the fact that the notes in common use are of smaller values than those in older notation. "But in regard the *Notes* now in use are not of so long a quantity, as when the *Perfect Moodes* were used, the most part of the *Notes Ligatured,* & *Ligatures* themselves are layd aside, except the *Breve* and *Semibreve,* which are yet retayned." [19]

Evidence that the *tactus* was generally slower in the seventeenth century is circumstantial since we lack written comparisons between the sixteenth- and seventeenth-century *tactus.* Both John Playford and Christopher Simpson describe the "measure of the *tactus*" to musical beginners so as to suggest that it is quite slow:

To which I answer (in case you have none to guide your Hand at the first measuring of Notes) I would have you pronounce these words (*one, two, three, four*) in an equal length, as you would (leisurely) read them: Then fancy those four words to be four *Crotchets,* which make up the quantity or length of a Semibreve, and consequently of a *Time* or *Measure:* In which, let these two words (*One, Two*) be pronounced with the Hand Down; and (*Three, Four*) with it up.[20]

A number of seventeenth-century writers describe beating the *tactus* with four motions of the hand or arm rather than the two-part down-and-up gesture of the sixteenth-century *tactus.* Carl Dahlhaus considers a treatise of 1627 as possibly the first to describe the *tactus* as a four-part beat:

> La Compositione di poi della battuta è de due parti, la prima delle quali è il battere, e la seconda l'elevar della mano: di più in cadauna di queste parti sono duoi Tempi, di modo che in tutto sono quatro: in questi si distribuiscono in questo modo: cioè, nell'istesso tempo dell'abbassat' uno, e nel fermar la mano a basso, un'altro vien distribuito: nell'elevar poi similmente si applica il terzo, e nel fermar la mano in alto, il quarto: il qual modo di distribuir questi tempi è il vero, e reale.[21]

> The *tactus* contains two parts, the downbeat and the upbeat of the hand. These are further divided into two parts each, so that the whole consists of four parts, as follows: The first part is lowering the hand, the second is the stop at the bottom of the gesture, the third is raising the hand (analogous to lowering the hand), and the fourth is the stop at the top of the gesture. This is the true and proper way of dividing these beats.

Lorenzo Penna describes the four-part *tactus* beat, adding an "ondeggiare la mano," or wavering of the hand, to the up-and-down motion:

> Hà la Battuta quattro parti, la prima è battere, e la seconda è fermare in giù, la terza è alzare, e la quarta è fermare in sù; Nelle Note nere spiccana benissimo queste quattro parti di Battuta, perche la prima è nel percuotere, la seconda è nel levare un poco ondeggiando la mano, la terza è nell'alzata, e la quarta è nel fermare in sù.[22]

> If the *tactus* has four parts, the first is on the beat, the second is while the beat is down, the third is on the rise, and the fourth is while the beat is up. For black [quarter] notes, mark each part of the *tactus* well, with the first on the downstroke, the second while raising by wavering the hand a little, the third on the upstroke, and the fourth on ending at the top.

Johann Quirsfeld draws diagrams in the shape of a square and a diamond to guide the hand in beating the *tactus:*[23]

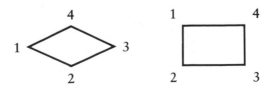

PLATE 3. Conducting with the hand: title illustration from *Musikalischen Arien* by Johann Martin Ruberts (Stralsund, 1647). (*Musikgeschichte in Bildern: Haus und Kammermusik,* ed. Walter Salmen.)

Each stroke of the diagram is equivalent to a quarter part of the *tactus* in these conducting patterns.

At the end of the century, Daniel Merck describes the duple meters as follows:

> Der *Tact,* welcher in vier Theil gerechnet wird/ ist an nachfolgenden Zeichen zu Erkennen. (1) 𝄴 (2) 𝄵 (3) 2. Stehet das Zeichen wie Num. 1. wird der *Tact* in 4. Theil langsam geschlagen. Wo das Zeichen Num. 2. sich findet noch so geschwind/ bey den Italianern stehet darbey *alla breve,* und wird der *Tact* mit auf- und Niderschlag gegeben in zwey Theil/ da doch 4. Viertel können aussgetheilet werden. Ist das Zeichen Num. 3. befindlich so wird der *Tact* etwas langsamers geschlagen als bey Num. 2.[24]

> The *tact,* which is counted in four parts, is indicated by the following signs: (1) 𝄴 (2) 𝄵 (3) 2. If the sign is as no. 1 (𝄴), the beat is given in four slow parts. If the sign is as no. 2 (𝄵), it is half again as fast, as when the Italians mark "alla breve," and the up and down beat of the measure is given in two parts, which can be divided into four quarters. If the sign is as no. 3 (2), the beat is given somewhat slower than with no. 2.

The translation of *Tact* as "measure," rather than as "beat" or *tactus,* seems justified in this context, as it establishes that the duration of the *tactus*-semibreve is that of four slow quarter notes in 𝄴. These are counted either in

PLATE 4. Conducting with a stick: frontal tile of a stove (1705) in the music room of the Winterthur Heimatmuseum, Lindengut Winterthur. (*Musikgeschichte in Bildern: Haus und Kammermusik*, ed. Walter Salmen.)

PLATE 5. Conducting with a roll of paper: copper-plate engraving of the rehearsal of a chamber cantata by Johann Christoph Steudner, after Paul Decker the elder, in the Handel-Haus, Halle. (*Musikgeschichte in Bildern: Haus und Kammermusik*, ed. Walter Salmen.)

two or in four when it is taken faster (*alla breve*). The sign 2 is intermediate to these. The measure of ₵ has become virtually a 4/4 measure that lacks only a few details of verbal description, which will soon be added by eighteenth-century writers.

Many pictures show ensembles of the seventeenth and eighteenth centuries being directed by time beaters, and among them three variations in method are found. Plate 3 shows a group of singers and instrumentalists being conducted by the hand gesture of one of the singers. Plate 4 shows a similar group of musicians being led by a singer wielding a rather stout baton. If this stick were struck against a table, it could make a hearty sound, but in this picture the table is covered by a rich cloth that would mute any percussive effect. Plate 5 depicts a rehearsal of a chamber cantata that includes a singing conductor who conducts with a roll of paper in his left hand while holding his score (apparently a vocal part) in his right hand.

The technique of the modern conductor is not yet seen in the seventeenth century, but theorists tell us that the *tactus* was not always a simple beat of one stroke down and the other up. It had become a gesture subdivided into enough segments to allow each part of the *tactus* to be represented by a comfortable beat.

Signs for Duple Meter

Mensuration signs indicated duple or triple metrical relationships and were measured by the *tactus*. Duple subdivision of large note values was indicated by imperfect *tempus* and *prolation*. *Tempus* governed the relationship of the breve to the semibreve and was perfect if three semibreves were included in the breve, imperfect if there were two. *Prolation* governed the relation of the semibreve to the minim; perfection indicated three minims and imperfection two in each semibreve. Additional signs indicated different note relationships to the *tactus*. Signs of diminution, equating larger note values than the semibreve with the *tactus*, were more frequently employed than signs of augmentation. Diminution signs included a vertical line through a mensural symbol, such as ₵, and numbers indicating a proportion, such as 3/2.

Mensuration signs, diminutions, and proportions had a secondary, somewhat illogical use in the sixteenth-century practice of notation: they could be used to indicate a change in the speed of the *tactus*. This change seems to have been less than that brought by the proportions in common use, such as 2:1, 3:1, or 3:2. Glareanus states:

> When musicians are afraid [that] the audience might get tired, they hasten the *tactus* by crossing the circle or semicircle and calling it a diminution. Actually they do not diminish the value or the number of the notes; they just quicken the beat, *quod tactus fiat velocior.* Thus the three sections in a Kyrie in a Mass (Kyrie I, Christe, Kyrie II) are often signed O ₵ ∅ to avoid boredom.[25]

Thomas Ravenscroft connected a change of speech of the *tactus* to diminution signs:

> [Diminution] is a certaine Decreasing of the *Quality* (and not of the Quantity) of the *Notes* and *Rests,* by *Internall* and *External Signes:* or when the Element is abated in the *Greater* or *Lesser* of the Nature of it; and it was invented to hasten the *Tact,* for a reviving of the *Eare,* when it is dul'd and wearied with a slow *Motion;* not that the *Number* or value of the Notes is thereby Diminished, but only that the *Tact* for the *Motion* of it is hastened, both in the *Perfect* and *Imperfect* measure.[26]

This interpretation of mensural signs as indicating tempo change continued into the seventeenth century. According to Wolfgang Caspar Printz:

> 2. Die Zeichen/ so die Hurtigkeit oder Langsamkeit des Tactes andeuten/ werden *Signa quantitatis mensuralis* genennet/ und seyn derselben vier: C, ₵, ∅, Θ. Deren erstes einen sehr langsamen/ das andere einen mittelmässigen/ das dritte einen geschwinden/ und das vierdte einen sehr geschwinden Tact andeutet. 3. Die letzten beyde seyn fast gar abkommen: Wäre aber zu wünschen/ dass sie wieder auffgebracht würden/ . . .[27]

The signs that designate the swiftness or slowness of the *tact* are called *signa quantitatis mensuralis,* and there are four of these: C, ¢, Ø, and Φ. The first denotes a very slow *tact,* the second a medium, the third a fast, and the fourth a very fast *tact.* The last two have fallen into disuse, but it is to be wished that they were still in use.

In 1656, De La Voye-Mignot writes that O, ⊙, O2/3, and Φ2/3 have become obsolete.[28] Only the more conservative and old-fashioned notation of the mid-seventeenth century makes use of these signs.

Henry Purcell confirms Printz's statement regarding the first three of these signs, but has nothing to say about the fourth: "Yᵉ first is a very slow movement yᵉ next a little faster, and last to brisk and airy time, & each of them has allways to yᵉ length of one semibrief in a barr."[29]

Bononcini advocates the use of mensural signs with proportions in order to specify the mensuration to which a proportion relates, but his contemporary Lorenzo Penna gives examples of proportions used as meter signs without mensuration signs. Although C and ¢ were much used, the other mensural signs, O, ⊙, and Ø, became rare in musical notation in the later seventeenth century.

In the early seventeenth century, the performance of music written under the signs C and ¢ was governed by the traditions of mensural notation, but there was some uncertainty about the exact proportion indicated by ¢, as it could be either twice as fast as C or one-third faster. This issue can be resolved only by considering ¢ in the context of the genre of composition and note values used.

The proportion of 2:1 governs ¢ when used simultaneously with C in other contrapuntal voices. However, a 2:1 ratio between C and ¢ does not necessarily indicate a change of speed or of rhythmic quality, since notes of double size are usually found when the *tactus* is twice as fast. A perceptible change in the speed of the music does occur if the *tactus* is "somewhat faster." In order to be precise, this change would need to be represented by a ratio more mathematically complex than 2:1, the proportion specified by many writers for the diminution of ¢.

Proportion and mensuration signs were sometimes interpreted to indicate such mathematically complex, perceptible changes of speed. The relation between the usual *tactus* and one somewhat faster is illustrated by the performance of "note negre" madrigals of the mid-sixteenth century. These are written in C (*tempus imperfectum non diminutum*) and use many minims and semiminims, for which the *tactus* (*maior alla semibreve*) must be given approximately one-third to one-half slower than for the conventional C (also *tempus imperfectum non diminutum*) that uses mostly semibreves and minims. *Note negre* madrigals were considered to be in a new style in the mid-sixteenth century, and their sprightly pace, due to the fast note values, contributed to their freshness.[30]

J. A. Bank comments that

> During the last quarter of the 16th century—certainly not earlier—when the madrigal-style has filtered through everywhere and the black notation has become common property, a specific terminology came into being, giving expression to it: *tactus simplex protractior* opposite to *tactus correptior;* according to Christoph Praetorius at ϕ, ϕ, the *tactus* must be shortened together with the notes (*Erotemata*, 1574, lib. II, cap. 4). V. Goetting speaks of *tactus tardior* C, as opposed to *tactus celerior* ϕ (*Compendium musicae modulativae*, 1586, fol. C 11). G. Schneegasz (1591) and S. Calvisius (1594) use the same terminology, together with Michael Praetorius (1607–19), A. Banchieri (1609), A. Brunelli (1606).[31]

From this we can see that Michael Praetorius's explanation of the tempo relation of C and ϕ reflects a tradition of notation rather than a new practice.[32] He differentiates between "Tactu aequali Tardiore, C, quo signantur Madrigalia" (slow duple *tactus*, C, used in madrigals) and "Tactu aequali Celeriore, ϕ, quo signantur Motetae" (quick duple *tactus*, ϕ, used in motets).[33]

Although C is generally used in madrigals and ϕ in motets, Praetorius explains that the tempo is determined by the note values and the genre of composition as well:

> Jetzigerzeit aber werden diese beyde *Signa* meistentheils also *observiret*, dass das C fürnelich in *Madrigalien*, das ϕ aber in *Motetten* gebraucht wird. Quia Madrigalia & alia Cantiones, quae sub signo C, Semiminimas & Fusis abundant, celeriori progrediuntur motu; Motectae autem, quae sub signo ϕ Brevibus & Semibrevibus abundant, tardiori: Ideo hîc celeriori, illic tardiori opus est Tactu, quò medium inter duo extrema servetur, ne tardior Progressus auditorum auribus pariat fastidium, aut celerior in Praecipitium ducat, veluti Solis equi Phaëtontem abripuerunt, ubi currus nullas audivit habenas.
> Darvmb deuchtet mich nicht vbel gethan seyn/ wenn man die *Motecten*, vnd andere geistliche Gesänge/ welche mit vielen schwarzen Noten gesetzt seyn/ mit diesem *Signo* C zeichnet; anzuzeigen/ dass alsdann der *Tact* etwas langsamer vnd gravitetischer müsse gehalten werden: Wie dann *Orlandus* in seinen *Magnificat 4 Vocum* vnd *Marentius* in vorgedachten *Spiritualibus* vnd andern *Madrigalibus* solches in acht genommen. Es kan aber ein jeder den Sachen selbsten nachdenken/ vnd *ex consideratione Textus & Harmoniae observiren*, wo ein langsamer oder geschwinder *Tact* gehalten werden müsse.
> Dann das ist einmal gewis vnd hochnötig/ das in *Concerten per Choros* ein gar langsamer gravitetischer *Tact* müsse gehalten werden. Weil aber in solchen *Concerten* bald Madrigalische/ bald *Motetten* Art vnter einander vermenget vnd vmbgewechselt befunden wird/ muss man sich auch im *Tactiren* darnach richten: Darvmb dann gar ein nötig *inventum*, das bisweilen/ (wie drunten im I Capittel des Dritten Theils) die *Vocabula* von den Wälschen *adagio, presto. h.e. tardè, Velociter,* in den Stimmen darbey *notiret* vnd vnterzeichnet werden/ denn es sonsten mit den

beýden *Signis* C vnd ₵ so offtmals vmbzuwechseln/ mehr *Confusiones* vnd verhin-
derungen geben vnd erregen möchte.[34]

At the present time these two signs [C and ₵] are used; C usually in madrigals
and ₵ in motets. Madrigals and other *cantiones* that abound in quarters and
eighths under the sign C, move with a faster motion; motets, on the other hand,
that abound in breves and semibreves under the sign ₵, [move with a] slower
[motion]; therefore the *tactus* is here faster, and there slower, by which a mean
between two extremes is kept, lest too slow a speed produce displeasure in the ears
of the listener, or too fast a speed lead to a precipice, just as the horses of the sun
snatched away Phaeton, when the chariot obeyed no reins.

This indicates to me that motets and other sacred music written with many
black notes and given the sign C must be performed with a *tactus* that is somewhat
grave and slow. This can be seen in Orlando [di Lasso]'s four-voiced Magnificat
and Marenzio's early sacred and other madrigals. Each person can consider these
matters for himself and, considering the text and harmony, take the *tactus* more
slowly or more quickly.

It is certain, and important to note, that choral concertos must be taken with
a slow, grave *tactus*. Sometimes in such concertos, madrigal and motet styles are
found mixed together and alternated, and these must be regulated through conducting the *tactus*. From this comes an important invention. Sometimes . . . the
Italian words *adagio* and *presto,* meaning slow and fast, are written in the parts,
since otherwise when the signs C and ₵ so often alternate, confusion and problems
may arise.

Praetorius continues with brief descriptions of the use of C and ₵ by Orlando di Lasso, Giovanni Gabrieli, Monteverdi, and Viadana. From these it is
clear that C used with smaller notes indicates a slower *tactus,* and ₵ used with
larger notes, a quicker *tactus.* The signs C and ₵ were the primary indications of
the speed of the *tactus.* The text, the frequency of harmonic change, and the
use of Italian terms provided additional information to the performer.[35]

A 2 : 1 ratio between the signs C and ₵ is avoided by using fast notes with
the slow *tactus* C, and slow notes with the fast *tactus* ₵; this combination results in an intermediate but appreciable tempo change appropriate to the style
of the madrigal or the motet. Therefore, only a slight slowing of the speed of
the music is indicated by *Adagio* or *tardè,* and a slight quickening by *presto*
or *velociter.* This change would be in the same proportion as that between
madrigal and motet styles, as indicated by C or ₵ and the appropriate note
values.

Georg Quitschreiber offers a simpler interpretation of the relations of C to
₵. In chapter IV of his *Musikbüchlein für die Jugend* he states that C is the sign
of the great *tact* of the *tempus,* frequently used by the previous generation and
still in use in his time. In C there are two slow beats (*Schläge*), one down and
one up. In ₵, the sign of the small or common *tact,* there is one complete beat
(*Schlage*) or two half-beats that move quickly down and up. This was invented,

he says, for students who found it easier to beat ₵ with four one-quarter beats in a *tact* rather than eight in ℂ. This indicates that the *tact* of ℂ is twice the duration of that of ₵, but in chapter VII, Quitschreiber states that the beat of ℂ is given "somewhat slower" than ₵, or by "singing" two beats (*Schläge*) instead of one in a *tact*. Perhaps different tempo relationships were observed in different circumstances.[36]

Most school manuals and books for the musical amateur in the seventeenth century are as brief as Quitschreiber's in their descriptions of the mensural or meter signs. They agree that, in general, the note values are twice as fast in ₵ as they are in ℂ, and that the beat is faster in ₵.[37]

Near the end of the seventeenth century, Daniel Speer confirmed and expanded Praetorius's interpretation of the various speeds of the *tactus*. Speer gave three possible speeds for the *tactus* in ₵, with the proper one to be determined by the performer on the basis of the genre of the composition, the tempo words, and the note values. By using three different tempo words for "fast," Speer may be suggesting that these words now indicate different gradations of speed.

> 1. Ein ganz langsamer/ welcher zur gravität/ und zur jetzigen Manier geschwind gesetzten und schweren Sachen/ hochstnotig zu gebrauchen. 2. Ein mittelmässiger *Tact* der fast am gemeinstens üblich. 3. Ein geschwinder *Tact*, so zu langsamen gesetzten alten *Moteten*, und zu dem jetzt überschriebenen *alla breve, presto*, und *allegro* zu gebrauchen.[38]

> 1. It is very important to use quite a slow beat in slow, grave, and difficult pieces, that are written in fast notes, according to the present custom. 2. A moderate beat is the most commonly used today. 3. A faster beat is used for old motets written in slow notes, and for the modern designations of *alla breve, presto*, and *allegro*.

Daniel Merck states that ₵ is one-half faster than ℂ, in the proportion of 3 : 2, rather than twice as fast.

> Stehet das Zeichen wie Num. 1 (ℂ) wird der *Tact* in 4. Theil langsam geschlagen. Wo das Zeichen Num. 2 (₵) sich findet noch so geschwind/ bey den Italianern stehet darbey *alla breve*, und wird der *Tact* mit Auf- und Niederschlag gegeben in zwey Theil/ da doch 4. Viertel können aussgetheilet werden. Ist das Zeichen Num. 3. befindlich/ so wird der *Tact* etwas langsamers geschlagen/ als bey Num. 2.[39]

> If the sign ℂ is used, the beat (*tact*) is given in four slow parts. If the sign ₵ is used, the beat is given in two parts, which may be divided into four quarters. It is faster by half, as the Italians perform *alla breve*. If the sign 2 is used, the beat is given somewhat slower than under ₵.

Merck describes the quarter notes of the *tact* as beats, and *tact* also describes their association in one unit. The word *tact* has therefore taken on the meaning of "measure" rather than "beat," yet it is still used as if it meant a *tactus* that could be indicated with a down-and-up motion of the hand.

Some seventeenth-century theorists continue to define the relation of C to ₵ as 2 : 1. Saint Lambert uses the phrase *une fois plus vîte* to describe the relation of ₵ to C in a context that defines the relationship as "two in the time of one."

> Les deux mouvemens qu'on fait de la main en battant cette mesure [₵], doivent être dans leur duré pareils à ceux de la Mesure à quatre temps [C]; c'est-à-dire, ny plus lents, ny plus pressez, & cecy doit faire comprendre que dans les Pieces marquées du Signe mineur, les notes vont une fois plus vîte que dans celles qui sont marquées du Signe majeur; puisque dans la même durée d'un temps, on met deux Noires au lieu d'une.

> The two movements of the hand made in beating this measure [₵] should be the same in their duration as those of the measure of four beats [C]; that is, neither slower nor faster. This means that in pieces with the minor time signature [₵] the notes are twice as fast as those in the major time signature, since (in ₵) two quarter notes instead of one are put in the time of one beat.[40]

The sign of 2 was adopted from the diminution 2/1 by French musicians and was used primarily by them. When it is encountered outside of France, it identifies the French style. French signs that designate duple meters included C and ₵ as well, the latter being explained by most writers as equivalent to 2. De LaVoye-Mignot in 1657 was the first to mention 2, but he gave no tempo indication for the sign. He stated that it could replace either C or ₵.[41]

Antoine Du Cousu, a musical conservative, says that 2, *le binaire*, is a proportion indicating diminution in the ratio of 2 : 1. His examples show ₵ and 2 used simultaneously in counterpoint with another voice in C, a musical situation requiring all tempo relationships to be in the ratio of 2 : 1.[42] Thus he agrees with Saint Lambert's mensural interpretation of the sign.

The musical context of the third entrée from Lully's ballet *L'amour malade* (LWV 8/13), suggests that the three signs, C, ₵, and 2, must indicate three different tempos (Ex. 1.1).[43]

EX. 1.1. *L'amour malade*, 3ᵉ entrée, 2 chercheurs de trésors.

If a tempo relationship of 2 : 1 is adopted, the various sections contrast sharply. If "une fois plus vite" is taken to mean "once again as fast" (3 : 2), the contrasts between sections are reduced. Both interpretations are tenable according to theoretical evidence, but the artistic effect is strikingly different.

According to Jean Rousseau, 2 was marked with two quick strokes, down and up, and indicated a faster tempo than ¢.[44] Perrine identified 2 as a substitute for ¢ but not for C.[45] Etienne Loulié included 2 with ¢ and 2/4 as the only duple measures he discussed (C was defined as a quadruple measure), and he marked it with two pulses, down and up.[46] Masson said that it was used in bourées and rigaudons, "with a fast beat."[47] Georg Muffat stated that 2 was given "rather slowly" when used in "ouvertures, preludes and symphonies," but was faster when used in "balets," and generally it was to be taken slower than ¢.[48] This appears to be opposite to the usual French practice.

The doubling of tempo between C and ¢, ¢ and 2, and 2 and 4/8, as defined by Saint Lambert, seems not to be in accord with these theorists. Etienne Loulié indicates that ¢ is twice as fast as C and appears to equate the tempo of 2 with ¢.[49] Peter Wolf has shown that the notation of French recitatives, from those of Lully's *tragedies lyriques* to those of Rameau's operas, generally equates ¢ with 2.[50] Poetic diction is given an equivalent rhythm in music when the quarter note in C equals the quarter note in 3 as well as the half note of both ¢ and 2. It appears that, at least in recitatives, this practice was established late in the seventeenth century.

Mensural signs are the most frequently used indications of duple meter in the seventeenth century, but some numerical duple proportions are also used. According to Georg Falck, in all duple proportions, such as 2/1, 4/2, and 8/4, the ratio of 2 : 1 is preserved in tempo relationships.[51]

As proportions, 2/1, 4/2, and 8/4 are alike, but according to Wolfgang Caspar Printz, the larger the number in the denominator of the sign, the faster the speed of the *tactus*.[52] Charles Masson confirms the quick speed of the *tactus* in 8/4: "Elle se bat fort vîte dans les autres marquez ainsi 8/4, come l'Entrée des Bergers & Bergères dans l'Opéra de Roland" (It is given very fast in the other [measures] marked 8/4, as in the Entrée des Bergers & Bergères in the opera *Roland*).[53]

In the seventeenth century duple meters were indicated by mensural signs, which kept much of their traditional significance, and some proportions. Because the *tactus* became slower, performance was regulated by subdivisions of the *tactus*-measure, that is, beats. The speed of various duple meters was indicated by measure signs, aided by the note values and the genre of the composition. Tempo words were used on occasion to supplement or clarify the meaning of mensural signs.

Signs for Triple Meter

Triple mensural proportion signs, while still used in both conservative and newer-style seventeenth-century notation, were gradually transformed into the fractional numbers of modern time signatures.

Pier Francesco Valentini devotes over 150 pages of closely written manuscript to proportions in his "Trattato del tempo, e del modo, e della prolatione." [54] His discussion is devoted largely to the theorists and composers of the sixteenth-century, although valuable insights into seventeenth-century practice can be found.

> La sesquialtera qui apparente 3/2 (la quale nel canto figurato per il 3 numero superiore non denota altro, che in luogo delle due note de egual quantità, indicato per il 2, numero inferiore, che andavano primo cantate nell'intervallo di una battuta; tre mandar se ne deuono) non dà, nè può perfectione ad alcuna nota, ancor che ella mandi tre note in luogo di due a battuta.

> The sesquialtera that is marked by 3/2 (the numerator 3 shows that instead of two notes of equal quantity, indicated by the denominator 2, three are required in the time of one *tactus*) does not confer perfection on any note, but places three notes instead of two to the *tactus*.

Whatever number and size of notes replace those previous to the proportion, they occupy the same amount of time. The proportions of 3/2 and 3/4 differ only in the size of the notes used, not in their speed.

One system of proportions is based on the equivalence of notes;·in 3/2, three of any note value become equivalent to two. In ₵3/2, three semibreves become equivalent to two semibreves, and under C3/2, three minims to two minims. In another system, the *tactus* is the unit of equivalence: in 3/2, the note values of three halves of a *tactus* become equivalent to two halves. The results are not altered, but Dahlhaus points out that the second system is closer to establishing the semibreve as the "whole note," the equivalent of a measure. [55] Valentini combines these two views.

Valentini gives examples of many numerical proportions, both duple and triple, and shows the value of every note in relation to the *tactus*. Each proportion is preceded by a mensuration sign that allows the performer to know the relationship of notes to the *tactus* both before and after the proportional change.

Valentini explores every possible proportion regardless of whether or not it had any practical use. He discusses more numerical signs than any other theorist of the time, including superparticular proportions such as 5/4, 7/6, and 10/9, multiple proportions such as 5/1 and 7/1, and submultiple proportions such as 1/5 and 1/7. [56] Among the plethora of fractions cited are those that subsequently became time signatures.

The speed of notes in this mensural proportion system is dependent upon the mensural sign placed before the proportion. For example, the value of a minim under these different signs is as follows:

C3/2 = one-third *tactus*

C3/1 = one-sixth *tactus*

¢3/2 = one-sixth *tactus*

¢3/2 = one-twelfth *tactus*

O3/2 = one-third *tactus*

C   = one *tactus* (if in counterpoint
       with parts under other signs)

C   = one-third *tactus* (if in counterpoint
       with parts under dotted C)

C3/2 = one *tactus*

O3/2 = one *tactus*

Valentini considers 6/4, 12/8, and 24/16 to be equivalent to the proportion of 3/2.

Proportion signs were sometimes used alone, without the sanction of the established practice of mensural notation. Bononcini wrote: "Per ultimo si deue auuertire, che l'introdurre le proporzioni ne i canti, senza segno del Tempo e (come dice Valerio Bona nelle sue *Regole di musica*) come mettere i soldati in Campo senza Capitano" (Finally it must be said that to use the proportions without mensural signs is [as Valerio Bona says in his *Regole di musica*] like sending soldiers on the field without a captain).[57]

The speed of notes, therefore, was dependent upon the mensural *tempus* signs C and O, which governed the subdivision of the breve into either two or three semibreves. In Italian, *tempus* becomes *tempo,* a word that evolved in the seventeenth century from a mensural term to one meaning the speed of notes. It was subsequently accepted into English, as designating the speed of the musical beat.

Michael Praetorius explains "Signis proportionatis in Tactu Inaequali."[58] The *tactus inaequalis* is divided into *majore* ¢3/2, called "proportio tripla," and *minore* C3/2, called "proportio sesquialtera." In the works of "Orlando [di Lasso], Marentio, Fel. Anerio & aliis," the signs for "proportio tripla" include 3+, 3/1, ¢3, Ø3+, ◊3/1, and Ø3/2+. Under these signs three semibreves are equal to one *tactus*. The signs for sesquialtera include C3, O3, Ø3, C3/2+, O3/2+, and ⊙. Praetorius writes that under *tactus inaequalis minore,* three semibreves are equal to two *tactus,* and his musical example shows three minims equal to one *tactus*.

Tripla majore, ¢3/1, is used in slow and serious pieces, "Motetis & Concertis." *Tripla minore,* sesquialtera C3/2, is used in "Madrigalibus, praesertim autem in Galliardis, Courantis, Voltis & aliis id generis Cantionibus." Triplas

(3 and 3/1) that use breves and semibreves are performed with *tactus inaequalis tardior;* and sesquialteras (3/2) using semibreves and minims are performed with *tactus inaequalis celerior.*[59] Therefore, the use of ₵ to designate *tactus* speed is exactly reversed from that of duple notation. There ₵ was equated with *tactus celerior* and ℂ with *tactus tardior.*

Carl Dahlhaus offers an explanation of this reversal:

> Die Tripla maior ₵3/1 setzt einen Tactus alla breve voraus und ist nach der Regel des Christoph Praetorius zu interpretieren, bedeudet also, dass drei Semibreven einen Tactus alla breve ausfüllen. Und da ein tactus ₵ alla breve um ungefähr die Hälfte langsamer ist als ein Tactus ℂ alla semibreve, repräsentiert die Tripla maior ₵3/1 einen Tactus tardior und die Tripla minor ℂ3/2 einen Tactus celerior. Dass das ₵ im zweizeitigen Tempus einen Tactus celerior, in der Proportion ₵3/1 dagegen einen Tactus tardior bezeichnet, ist im Wechsel zwischen Semibrevis und Brevis als Bezugseinheit begründet.[60]

> The *tripla maior* ₵3/1 presupposes a *tactus alla breve* and is to be interpreted according to the rule of Christoph Praetorius, therefore three semibreves are contained in one *tactus alla breve.* Since a *tactus* ₵ *alla breve* is about one-half slower than the *tactus* ℂ *alla semibreve,* the *tripla maior* ₵3/1 represents a *tactus tardior* and the *tripla minor* ℂ3/2 a *tactus celerior.* That the ₵ in duple tempus signifies a *tactus celerior,* but in the proportion ₵3/1 a *tactus tardior,* is founded on the change between semibrevis and brevis as the unit of reference.

₵ signifies a faster *tactus* (*celerior*) as a duple sign, but a slower one (₵3/1 *tardior*) as a triple sign; under ₵ large note values are used. Duple ℂ *tardior* changes to ℂ3/2 *celerior,* and under ℂ small note values are used. Therefore under triple signs the large notes are slower and the small notes faster than they would be in a strict proportion. Perhaps the most important element in Praetorius's explanation is that the sign itself signifies the speed of the *tactus,* although the genre of composition and the size of the notes must also be considered.

Praetorius adds one more kind of triple meter, the "Sextupla, seu Tactu Trochaico Diminuta";[61] it is measured with a *tactus aequalis mediocris,* the ordinary duple *tactus.* The name "sextupla," Praetorius writes, means that there are six semiminims in one *tactus.* These are sometimes written with the number 3 over groups of three notes. The sextupla can be notated in three ways. (1) In *hemiolia minore* (all black notes under the sign ₵), there are three black minims or "Semibrevis cum Minima" on the downstroke, and three on the upstroke. If the sign 6/1 is used for *hemiolia minore,* it indicates a proportion equating six semiminims or black minims with the *tactus.* (2) The second sextupla is used by the French and Italians in "Courranten, Sarabanden," and other similar pieces. Minims and semiminims are used in place of the semibreves and black minims of the first sextupla. The sign 6/4 indicates that six semiminims equal four of those before the sign. (3) The third way, Praetorius cautions, has proved so difficult for performers that he is uncertain whether it should be used. The sign sesquialtera, 3/2, is used with semibreves and minims, but the *tactus* must be taken very fast, which often causes confusion. Therefore he has written a ₵ before the 3/2 proportion to indicate this fast speed.

Valentini would not approve of this third alternative, for the strict mensural interpretation of this sign, ₵3/2, makes the minim one-twelfth of the *tactus,* not one-sixth; therefore, it is twice as fast as Praetorius tells us the notes should be taken in relation to the *tactus.* Perhaps this is why Praetorius's performers were puzzled by his use of the sign.

In the triple meter signatures of Giovanni Maria Bononcini and Lorenzo Penna, we begin to recognize the familiar time signatures of modern measures. Penna calls them signs of "tripola," not proportions.

According to Bononcini,[62] they are:

tripla maggiore: O3/1, C3/1, ₵3/2, ₵3/2, with three semibreves to the *tactus,* two on the downstroke, one on the upstroke.

tripla minore: C3/2, O3/1, C3/1, C3/2, with two minims on the downstroke, one on the upstroke.

C3/4, *tripla di semiminime.*

C3/8, *tripla di crome.*

C6/4, *sestupla di semiminime.*

C6/8, *sestuple di crome.*

C12/8, *dodecupla di crome.*

C12/16, *dodecupla di semicrome.*

According to Penna,[63] they are:

3/1, *tripola maggiore,* formerly indicated by ₵3/2, three semibreves to the *tactus,* two on the downstroke, one on the upstroke.

3/2, *tripola minore,* formerly indicated by O3/2, three minims to the *tactus,* two on the downstroke, one on the upstroke.

3/4, *la tripola picciola, ò quadrupla, ò semiminore, ò di semiminime,* semiminims and minims, two semiminims on the downstroke, one on the upstroke.

3/8, *la tripola crometta, ò ottina, ò di crome.*

3/16, *la semicrometta.*

6/4, *la sestupla maggiore.*

6/8, *la sestupla minore.*

12/8, *la dosdupla.*

Meter signatures with six in the numerator indicate three notes on the downstroke and three on the up; with twelve in the numerator, there are six on the downstroke and six on the upstroke.

The number of signs is small compared to those given by Valentini, and Penna mentions that he is explaining only those most frequently used. Penna includes a few additional proportions, the *hemiolia maggiore* and *minore,* that were "formerly used," and also the proportions 5/2 and 7/2, included as "tripola." This seems to faintly echo Valentini's odd mensural proportions. Penna's explanation is brief, and he mentions that there "are others in other forms."

Penna explains some traditional uses of a proportional sign, for example, turning it upside-down signifies a return to the notation before the proportion was introduced.

> Tutte le Note delle data Tripole vanno cantate, come si è insegnato, sino al fine della Composizione, e nelli modi auisati in ciascheduna Tripola, douendosi poi per qualche accidente tornare à cantare frà la Composizione col valore ordinario nel Tempo, ini farà dato, e posto dal Compositore il segno, ò col porui il Tempo, ouero con riuoltare li numeri della Tripola corrente al rouerscio, come l'esempio.[64]

> All the notes under each triple sign should be sung according to their proper signs until the end of the composition in the way prescribed. Should it be necessary, in some circumstances, to sing the composition in the ordinary values of *tempo* [i.e., "common time" or ₵], the composer writes the sign for *Tempo*, or turns the numbers of the current tripola upside down, as in the example [Ex. 1.2].

EX. 1.2

Bononcini also comments on "turning the numbers contrary," for example, following 3/1 with 1/3, which "destroys" the first proportion. This remnant of the old-fashioned interpretation of proportions explains some signatures that are puzzling to musicians today, such as the 2/3 signature used by François Couperin in the second section of the "Grande Ritournéle" in the Huitiéme Concert of *Les goûts réunies*. It must be understood as a proportion, not a time signature (Ex. 1.3).

EX. 1.3

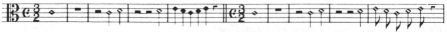

This unusual notation, in which the eighth notes are left white,[65] is mentioned by both Penna and Bononcini. The one-flagged or beamed "white" eighth notes replace ordinary quarter notes (semiminims) (Ex. 1.4).

EX. 1.4

Penna omits the mensural sign (*tempo*) before the numerical proportion in his signatures. He mentions its former use but gives no reason for its exclusion. In 1714, Printz comments on the omission of the mensural sign with a time signature:

Wenn der Gesang mit einer *irrationalem Proportion* anfängt/ lassen die meisten neuen *Musici* das *Signum quantitatis mensuralis* weg/ und setzen unter die Zahlen/ so die *Proportion* andeuten/ allein: und zwar nicht ohne Ursache. Denn weil die untere Zahl der vorgeschriebenen *Irrationalen Proportion* schon die Krafft hat die Länge des Tactes anzudeuten/ so ist das *Signum quantitatis mensuralis* uberflüssig/ unnöthig/ und also/ vermöge . . . abzuschaffen.[66]

If the music begins with an irrational proportion [3/1, 3/2, 3/4, 3/8], most of the new musicians omit the mensural sign, and use only the numbers that show the proportion. This is not without cause, as the denominator of the indicated proportion already has the ability to show the length of the *tactus:* therefore the mensural sign is superfluous, unnecessary, and should be abolished.

Even in 1714, the fractional number of the time signature is explained as a proportion, but the omission of the mensural sign is explained as if it did not affect the proportional interpretation of the signature.

Bononcini retains the mensural **C**. His general explanation of triple signs involves comparing the notes before with those after the proportion sign that changes their relation to the *tactus:* "De gli altri poi che seguono, per maggiore brevità si da questo regola generale, che il numero sotto posto denota quante figure andavano, ò s'intende, che andastero alla battuta, & il sopra posto, quante ne vadino per l'avenire" (Of the others indicated, for greater brevity, they follow this general rule: the lower number indicates which note values went or were understood to go to the beat, and the upper number how many notes will go in the future [i.e., after the sign]).[67]

It seems that the proportion sign is still recognized in its traditional meaning by Bononcini, but he has this to say about the beat that regulates the speed of notes according to the various meter signs:

Si deue auuertire, che tutte le proporzione di battuta eguale, si deuono constituire sotto l'istessa battuta eguale, e tutte le proporzione di battuta ineguale si deuono anch'esse constituire sotto la medesima battuta ineguale, non variandosi altro che alle volte il moto in questa maniera, cioè facendolo hora ordinario, hora adagio; & hora presto, secondo il voler del Compositore; per il che si possono far composizione, nelle quali le parti siano segnate diuersamente, purche i segni possano essere gouernate facilmente da una istesia battuta, come in diuerse Opere de Frescobaldi, e di molt' altri dotti Compositore si può vedere, & eziando nella sesta mia opera.[68]

It should be noted that all of the proportions corresponding to an equal beat are given by the same equal beat, and all the proportions of the unequal beat by the identical unequal beat. The motion does not vary except—occasionally—in speed, now an ordinary pace, now slow, and now fast, according to the wish of the composer, for this reason the parts of a composition are given different signs. Under these signs the same beat easily regulates [the music], as may be seen in the works of Frescobaldi and other learned composers, and in my own opera sesta.

Bononcini does not explain what signs these are, and the first to come in mind today, tempo words such as *allegro* and *adagio,* may not have been in his mind. Frescobaldi was one of the first to specify that the "proportion" itself indicates the speed of the beat. The interpretation he offers contradicts mensural theory and practice: "E nelle trippole, ò sesquialtere, se saranno maggiori, si portino adagio, se/ minori alquâto più allegre, se di tre semiminime, più allegre se saranno sei per quattro si di/ a illor tempo con far caminare la battuta allegra" (In the triplas, or sesquialteras, if they are major let them be played slowly, if minor somewhat more quickly, if of three semiminims more rapidly, if 6/4, move the beat fast).[69]

Frescobaldi's interpretation of proportion signs is repeated by many performers and writers in the seventeenth century. The amount of tempo change is difficult to estimate, but following Praetorius's explanation of *tactus celerior* and *tardior* for duple meters, a slight variation from the norm seems to be what is intended. This would heighten the emotional quality of performance by the use of a mathematically more complex proportion than is usually specified in mensural notation.

Carissimi amplifies Frescobaldi's directions:

> Es befinden sich zwar nicht wenig/ welche in allen *triplis* ohne Unterschied einerley *Tact* und *Mensur* gebrauchen/ geben darbey vor/ die vilfältige Veränderung der Zahlen seye nur von den *Componisten* erfunden/ die *Musicos* dardurch zu vexiren/ aber weit gefehlt/ dass die *triplae* alle in der *Quantitaet* Ausstheilung oder *Proportion* überein kommen/ gestehet man gern/ aber in der *Qualitaet* Langsam- oder Geschwindigkeit/ oder wie es die Italiäner *Tempo,* und die Frantzosen *Mouvement* nennen/ wird *rorundè negirt*/ und gäntzlich widersprochen.[70]

> It is frequently thought that only one beat and measure, without any distinction, is used for all [simple] triples, and asserted at the same time that the many varieties of signs are invented by composers only to vex the performers. This is quite wrong. The triples all agree with regard to quantity, division and proportion, as everyone easily understands, but in the slow or fast quality, called *tempo* by the Italians and *mouvement* by the French, this agreement is roundly negated and contradicted.

Carissimi includes the numerical signature and the genre of the composition as determinants of the tempo. 3/1, for example, is used in "slow compositions and serious works in the *Stylo Ecclesiastico*"; 3/2 is "used somewhat more briskly than the former, particularly in the serious style, and therefore the beat must be given somewhat faster." 3/4 "requires a faster beat than the last as this tripla is used mostly in ariettes and happy pieces."[71]

Wolfgang Caspar Printz formulates a general rule to govern the speed of the *tactus* as indicated by proportional signatures:

> Die Länge des Trochaischen Tactes wird angedeutet durch die untere Zahl der vorgeschriebenen Proportion, davon diese Regul is Acht zu nehmen: Je kleiner die untere Zahl der Proportion ist/ je langsamer soll der Tact geschlagen werden; und je grösser dieselbe Zahl ist/ je geschwinder soll der Tact geschlagen werden.[72]

The length of the trochaic beat is indicated by the lower number of the pro-portion, therefore this rule should be observed: the smaller the lower number of the proportion, the slower the beat; and the larger the number, the faster the beat.

Loulié agrees with this formulation.[73]

We can now return to Bononcini's statement that the composer's wishes about the speed of notes must guide the performer under all meter signs. Mensural signs, which formerly indicated the speed of notes only through their relation to the *tactus,* have come to indicate the speed of the *tactus* in themselves.

Printz did not approve of numerical signatures set in the middle of pieces to alter the tempo, and advocated the use of Italian terms instead:

> In der Mitte eines Gesanges/ damit die *Signa quantitatis mensuralis* nicht gar zu offt gesetzt werden dürffen/ werden gewisse Wörter unter oder uber die *Systemata* geschrieben/ und zwar *Adagio, lento,* oder *largo,* wenn der Tact langsam; *allegro* oder *vivace* wenn er lustig/ hurtig munter; *presto* wenn er sehr geschwinde soll geschlagen werden.[74]

> The *signa quantitatis mensuralis* should not be permitted to be set in the middle of a piece of music very often, instead, certain words should be written under or over the staff: *adagio, lento,* or *largo* if the beat is slow, *allegro* or *vivace* when it is merry, swift, and lively, and *presto* when the beat is very fast.

This statement is one of the first to make explicit comparison of the speed indicated by tempo words. Time signatures and tempo words have become equivalent ways of indicating the speed of the *tactus.*

Jean Rousseau derives the speed of some of his triple time-signatures from individual note values that are equivalent before and after the fractional sign. He explains first that there are six varieties of ordinary signs, i.e., C, ₵, 2, C3, 3, and 3/2; then that there are four more, 3/4, 3/8, 6/4, and 6/8, which are "new signs used for only a certain time." Later, he mentions the origin of the "new signs" when he states that "the Italians" also used 12/4, 12/8, 9/4, and 9/8, signs that he does not discuss.[75] French music of this period that is written in imitation of the Italian style often uses Italian meter signs.

> Au signe de Trois pour Quatre, ainsi nommé, parce qu'au lieu que la Mesure au signe Majeur [C] est composée de quatre Noires, celle-cy n'en a que Trois, la Mesure se bat a trois temps plus vîtes que le Triple simple [3]; mais comme la vitesse de ces temps les rend difficiles a marquer, on le bat a deux temps inégaux; deux Noires pour le frappé & une Noire pour le levé. Au Signe de trois pour Huit composé de trois croches, au lieu que le Majeur en a Huit, la Mesure se bat comme au Trois pour Quatre, mais beaucoup plus Vîte.[76]

> Under the sign of 3/4 (called thus because in place of the four quarter notes of C this measure has only three), the beat is given with three strokes, faster than under the *triple simple,* 3. As the quickness of these strokes makes them difficult to

beat, each gesture is made by two unequal strokes, two quarter notes on the down-, and one quarter on the upstroke. Under the sign of 3/8, there are three eighth notes instead of eight in C. The beat is given as it is under the sign of 3/4, but much faster.

Daniel Merck offers the same explanation of 3/4: "Die *Proportio Tripla* ist/ wann die Zeichen dess gewöhnlichen vier Viertel *Tacte*s nicht gefunden werden/ und an statt deren vornen/ oder anderstwo/ Ziffern darfür gesetzt sind/ so verliehret der *Tact*-Schlag ein Theil/ also/ dass nur 3. Theil geschlagen werden" (The triple proportion is used when the sign of the usual four-quarter measure is not found, but in its place one or two figures are placed at the beginning or elsewhere; then, as the *tact*-beat loses a part, it is given in only three parts).[77]

But he also says that "tripla sesquialtera 6/4" is "mit dem 3. Viertel Tripel gantz gleich/ aussgenommen/ dass der Tact in 6. Theil eingetheilet wird" (entirely like the three-quarter triple except that the *tact* is divided into six parts). This statement seems to contradict the concept of note equivalence and to restate the proportional interpretation of subdividing equivalent *tactus* units. However, a change in the meaning of the word *tact* has occurred: It is no longer equivalent to *tactus*. Merck has previously shown that the *tact* C is to be considered four beats.[78] His description of the triple meters needs further translation in order to become entirely comprehensible: "*Tripla Major* wird diser genennet/ . . . in welchem drey gantze *Tact* erst einen *Tact* ausmachen" (Tripla Major, as it is called, . . . is when three whole notes make one measure).

The German sentence literally states that three whole *tact* make one *tact;* this is verbal nonsense. *Tact* traditionally means a semibreve, the note value equal to the *tact;* now it has come to mean a measure, a group of beats making a unit. Thus one whole note in 3/1 is equal to a beat, and three of these beats are equal to the measure. Merck's meaning was undoubtedly clear to his readers, as they were aware of the word's derivation from *tactus*, but it can now be clarified only by using two terms for the word *tact*, which encompasses the concepts of both *tactus* and measure.

In the second half of the seventeenth century, French musicians continued to use the combination of mensuration and proportion signs that we have seen in use by Italians and Germans (C, ¢, 3/1, and 3/2). The French also adopted the fractional numbers derived from proportion signs that Penna and Bononcini explained (3/4, 3/8, 3/16, 6/4, 6/8, 6/16, 9/4, 9/8, 9/16, 12/4, 12/8, and 12/16), but they did not use the accompanying mensural signs. In addition, they developed other signs that were used only in French music and were closely associated with French genres of composition, particularly dances.

The signs 3 (*Triple simple*) and 2 (*le Binaire*) are frequently used in tablatures to indicate a basic triple or duple metrical organization. 3 was conducted with two downbeats and one up for slow tempos, one downbeat of two pulses and an upbeat of one pulse for faster tempos, or one downbeat (or upbeat) of three pulses for very fast tempos.[79] Loulié states that 3 is the same as 3/4; Rousseau indicates that it is conducted by three quick strokes (*trois temps légers*), in contrast to C3, which is conducted by three slow strokes. Under all the meter signs of French notation, the genre of the piece determines the speed of the music. Georg Muffat remarks that "gigues and canaries need to be played the fastest of all, no matter what the time signature."[80]

However, there are problems in indicating the tempo of music through meter signs. Saint Lambert comments on the liberties taken by musicians contrary to the rules of tempo implied by meter signatures, and gives an example from the practice of the most eminent musician of the day:

> Often the same man marks two airs of completely differing tempo with the same time signature, as for example M. de Lully, who has the reprise of the overture to *Armide* played very fast and the air on page 93 of the same opera played very slowly, even though this air and the reprise of the overture are both marked with the time signature 6/4, and both have six quarter notes per measure distributed in the same way.[81]

Saint Lambert gives a number of other examples of the uncertainty of the tempo significance of meter signs, and comments that "musicians who recognize this drawback often add one of the following words to the time signature in the pieces they compose: *Lentement, Gravement, Légèrement, Gayement, Vîte, Fort Vîte,* and the like, in order to compensate for the inability of the time signatures to express their intention."[82]

Note values and time signatures often needed the help of tempo words in order to transmit fully the composer's choice of tempo to performers, but these words were still only secondary indications in the late seventeenth century.

Simplifications and Individual Interpretations

Notation in the early seventeenth century was a highly learned art, dependent on a complex tradition and governed by intricate rules. Expert knowledge of the system was part of the education of a complete musician. He or she would need to know historical as well as current interpretations of old notation. It is not surprising that method books offered simplifications as well as individual interpretations of notation to amateurs and beginners. Simplifications were also found in specialized notation, such as tablatures for the lute and the lyra viol.

William Bathe's *Briefe introduction,* published in the last decade of the sixteenth century, gives practical elementary instruction to performers. The *tactus* is reduced to a simple formula:

For Time, Cap. 3.

There be 2. kindes of time, Semibreefe time, and three minim time. Semibreefe time is the striking up and downe of the hand equally in length continuing. Three minim time is the striking downe and then up of the hand, equally in length, making each latter stroke, iust halfe the former [in time].

The marke of the former kinde of time is ¢

The marke of the latter is ℂ

In tuning Songs of Semibreefe time, you must put of the notes, as much as maketh a minim length to euery moving of the hand, likewise in the minim time, saue that to euery stroke there goeth but a minim length.

Heere note that these two kindes of time, may be deuided into minim time by keeping all strokes equall in length, putting a minim length to euery whole stroke.[83]

The simplest system therefore required only two signs, one for the equal *tactus* and the other for the unequal *tactus*. There was one change of note value in relation to the *tactus* for each sign that was intended to indicate a change in the speed of the beat. An anonymous method book published in 1686 kept to this simplified scheme as its only explanation of "time."[84]

John Playford's *An introduction to the skill of musick* retained a version of mensural notation in the 1662 and 1674 editions, but the edition of 1697 abandoned the "four moods" in favor of only two:

That there is but *two Moods* or *Characters* by which *Time* is distinguished, (Viz.) *Common-Time* and *Tripla-Time*, all other Variations and Distinctions of *Time* (like so many Rivulets) take their Original from these *Two*; the Marks of which are always placed at the beginning of your *Song* or *Lesson*.[85]

Thomas Mace used only two signs of "time" in *Musick's monument*, ¢ and 3, and explained neither. Tablatures for the lyra-viol are equally simple; for example, the "Manchester Gamba Book" uses only ¢ and ℂ.[86]

Charles Butler uses the same simplified indications recognized by Bathe and Ravenscroft. His discussion of meter begins with duple "proportion," for which the sign is ¢, and triple "proportion," for which the sign is ℂ. Butler was a man of an unusual turn of mind. He was a beekeeper who published a book about the lore of bees, *The feminine monarchie*, and an experimenter with the orthography of the English language—his book on music is printed in a combination of phonetic spelling plus special symbols. Butler's discussion of the time signatures proposes some novelties.

Using the semibreve as the "measure note" or unit of time to be subdivided in different manners, he invents new signs: 2.1 (duple), 6.1 (sextupla), 3.1 (triple), and 9.1 (noncupla). The number one (1) signifies the semibreve, and the first number of each sign declares the number of notes into which the semibreve is to be divided:

Sextupla is đe *Triple* of đe *Minim* in *Duple* Proportion: Ꝟen to eae *Minim* in

Duple Tim⁶, is sung 3 blak Minims [or a blak Sembrief and a Minim,] (and consequently 6 croeets, wie must hav⁶, for differen⁶, de form of Qavers) 3 to de Fall, and 3 to de Ris⁶ of de Hand [or if you will keep⁶ + Minim-Tim⁶, 3 to on⁶ Strok⁶, and 3 to an oder:] wie *Triple* is der⁶for⁶ called *Sextupla;* becaus 6 of des⁶ blak Minims go⁶ to on⁶ Sembrief-Tim⁶.

Noncupla is de *Triple* of de Minim in *Triple* Proportion: wen to eae Minim in *Triple* Tim⁶, is sung 3 blak Minims, 6 to de Fall, and 3 to de Ris⁶ of de Hand: wie *Triple* is der⁶for⁶ called *Noncupla;* becaus nin⁶ of des⁶ blak Minims go⁶ to on⁶ Sembrief-tim⁶.

De Sign⁶ of *Sextupla* is, Wit de blak Not⁶s, his figured Number 6.1: and of de *Noncupla,* it is wit de lik⁶ blak not⁶s, his figured Number 9.1.[87]

The signs 6.1 and 9.1 are neither proportions (in any conventional sense) nor modern time signatures, and are unique to Butler. Butler divided the minim into duple or triple parts, as if it were subject to mensuration.

One of Butler's most interesting statements occurs in the following paragraph.[88] It explains the relationship of notes in the various "proportions":

Not⁶ heer⁶ dat de blak Minim in *Sextupla* Proportion, beeing 1/2 of a *Duple* Minim, and de Croeet in *Triple* Proportion, beeing 1/2 of a *Triple* Minim, are bod⁶, as on⁶ form, so of on⁶ tim⁶; der going 6 of eae sort to a Sembrief-Strok⁶: but der is dis differenc⁶, dat of de six blak Minims, de fowrt beginnet de Ris⁶ of de Hand, and is der⁶for⁶ mor⁶ notably accented; as de First is, wie beginnet de Fall: and of de six croeets, de First beginnet de Ris⁶, and is der⁶for⁶ mor⁶ notably accented: as lik⁶wis⁶ de First and third is: so dat de blak Minims go⁶ jumping by Three's, and de croeets by two⁶'s: wer⁶by de Melodi of de sam⁶ Not⁶s becoomet divers: as in dis Example [Ex. 1.5].

EX. 1.5

This is the first mention, as far as I know, of how a performer or listener distinguishes groupings of notes in musical meter. It is one of very few seventeenth-century identifications of metrical grouping by "accent." It introduces a subject, to be fully discussed elsewhere in this study, that fascinated musicians in the later seventeenth and eighteenth centuries.

The division of *tactus* into duple and triple, or even and uneven strokes, became the basis of many explanations of "time signatures" in the eighteenth century, particularly for German writers. Subclassifications were added, but for both notation and conducting techniques the essential distinction remained that of duple or triple beats.

Summary

The origins of the modern measure are found in the changes that occurred in mensural notation in the seventeenth century. The speed of the *tactus* varied under different circumstances during the sixteenth century; however, variations of speed were systematically indicated in seventeenth-century notation by new interpretations of mensural signs and proportions. A new interpretation of mensural notation was made necessary by the increasing use of small note values that were not governed by mensuration.

The *tactus* was identified with the note value of the semibreve in mensural notation, and the *tactus* continued to be equated with the semibreve even when the musical beat came to be represented by smaller note values. The *tactus-*semibreve in the seventeenth century became a metrical unit containing either two or four beats. Although this change is evident in musical notation, it took place so gradually that we can perceive it only by viewing the notation and the theorists' comments within the time perspective of the entire century. In the lifetime of an individual musician, the speed of the ideal *tactus* probably was one element of musical performance that seemed quite stable.

A change of speed in the *tactus* in the ratio of 2:1 was usually accompanied by a change to larger or smaller note values; therefore, it was imperceptible to the listener. It would be perceptible only if the ratio of change were a little less (or more) than 2:1. Generally, seventeenth-century note values, in conjunction with their mensural and proportion signs, conveyed a reliable image of the speed of the music they represented, but the irrational changes of tempo associated with new signs and new interpretations of old ones began to shake this certainty.

The speed of the music could be determined by measuring note values against the *tactus,* keeping in mind that the *tactus* itself was sometimes altered to go faster or slower than the norm. Proportion signs altered note values in relation to the *tactus,* but they also indicated an increase or decrease in the speed of the *tactus.* From the great number of proportions theoretically possible in mensural notation, the few actually used in seventeenth-century notation became the basis of the fractional numbers of modern time signatures.

This system required composers to use meter signs uniformly to indicate both metrical structures and tempos, but sometimes compositions with the same metrical structure were not intended to be performed at the same tempo. This caused some uncertainty, which was resolved increasingly by the use of words such as *allegro, adagio, celerior,* and *tardior,* which first came into use early in the seventeenth century. Tempo words were also used to indicate changes of speed when the word-music relationship, note values, and the rate of harmonic change signaled a different genre of composition in the absence of a mensural sign or proportion. Irmgard Herrmann-Bengen's study of tempo indications shows that degrees of speed were seldom indicated, other than "fast" or "slow," before the middle of the seventeenth century.[89]

The vocabulary of tempo words gradually expanded to allow a comparison of speeds. Daniel Merck offers the following terms: "*Grave,* gravitätisch, . . . *Adagio, largo,* langsam; wie auch *lentement,* sanfft; *presto, allegro,* geschwind/ frölich; *vivace,* lebhaft; *prestissimo, viste,* gar geschwind; *più allegro, più adagio,* mehr hurtig/ oder mehr langsamer."[90] At the end of the seventeenth century most diminutives of tempo words and adjectives indicating an emotional character had not yet become popular.

The speed of a piece of music could not be judged solely by its time signature and tempo words, as it depended upon the note values and the genre of composition as well. The speed of dance music was necessarily determined by the dance, and the speed of motets by ecclesiastical musical tradition. Both the composer and the performer were aware of those requirements which overrode the indications of the notation itself.

The notation of meter in the seventeenth century is not yet that of measure notation, in which the speed of an individual note is largely dependent upon a tempo word. In modern notation relatively small note values may represent slow notes and large note values fast notes, although this is an apparent contradiction. It is only in the late seventeenth century that the concept of slow and fast movements emerges in musical forms.

"Slow movements" are fundamentally differentiated from "fast movements" not by the one being made up of slow notes and the other by fast notes, but rather by the listener's perception of metrical hierarchy. If quick notes are grouped in regular metrical units, which in turn are perceived as part of larger units, and so on to even larger ones, we recognize a "slow movement." The beat given to conduct such a piece may be faster or slower, in a proportion of 2 : 1, without changing our sense of the "tempo" of the music. Hierarchical metrical structure in a piece conveys peace and order through regularity.

If the beat does not arrange itself in a regular pattern but seems to shift in its groupings or to give rise to phrases of irregular length, we sense that we are hearing a "fast movement." Quick shifts of metrical grouping provide excitement and energy.

Modern notation visually represents a "slow movement" to a performer when small notes are written with flags or beams that show metrical grouping. The best notation uses the smallest size note values possible to convey many levels of meter in slow movements. In fast movements, large notes are used that are not visually subordinated to one another, and, being large, they claim our attention as being separate and individual. These qualities make slow movements in small notes and fast movements in large notes logical and useful to performers.

The convention of the mensural *tactus* was a very important guide to con-

ductors in the seventeenth and even the eighteenth century. The rise of the virtuoso conductor in the nineteenth century brought with it a technique far re-
moved from the apparently simple down-and-up gesture of the *tactus* beater.
The modern conductor has a powerful and efficient technique, commanding
meter, rhythm, dynamics, accentuation, tempo, and nuances of performance
that were formerly controlled only by individual performers. A *tactus* conductor is necessarily more of a coordinator or a colleague of the other musicians,
rather than the commanding leader that the modern virtuoso conductor has
become.

The *tactus* beat of a seventeenth-century conductor supported an awareness of a larger span of time than a conductor's gestures usually do today. Although many individual conductors today strive for this awareness, the basic
technique of *tactus* beating in the seventeenth century was centered on it. Even
if the *tactus* might be too slow-moving to be comfortably represented by a
single down-and-up gesture, we know from theorists' detailed discussions that
the conductor's beat was derived from the *tactus*. The modest alterations of the
tactus suggested by Penna and Quirsfeld show that some slight adjustments
were thought to be useful.

It would be interesting to hear fine musicians playing seventeenth-century
music conducted according to techniques of that period. It is possible to imagine that the performers would be less rigorously controlled, and therefore more
responsible for the metrical coherence of their own performances. We simply
do not know what effect such a re-creation of conducting technique might have.

Seventeenth-century notation of meter modified mensural notation in important ways and signaled the shifts of movement, grouping, and speed typical
of the music of the period. It is usually disastrous to disregard the original
"time signatures" of seventeenth-century music, or to modify them according
to a more modern idea of notation, as one loses the precise yet subtle meanings
they are able to convey.

II

⤙⤚

Time Signatures
in the Eighteenth Century

TIME SIGNATURES in the eighteenth century were generally recognized as signifying how many notes of what value were included in a measure, although the signature sometimes indicated this information only indirectly. Signatures became associated with genres of music; for example, music in the *stile antico* used mensural signs, such as C and ₵, and simple proportions, such as 3/1 and 3/2. Music in the theatrical style used the new Italian or French signs that were associated with particular dances, character pieces, or even emotional affects.

Theorists in the eighteenth century were concerned with logical classifications of time signatures—simple and compound duple and triple meters. The notational systems that they attempted to classify, however, challenged the logical mind, since mensural signs and proportions (reinterpreted as they were) were mixed with new time signatures (even though they were derived from proportions). Composers as well as performers needed to tread carefully between traditional and newly fashionable interpretations of notation.

Changes in notation in the eighteenth century stimulated some theorists to suggest additional innovations, in the hope that a logical system could be found. Reforms of notation were avidly discussed in eighteenth-century France; some theorists advocated note values as the best indicator of tempo, and others (Italianate, and perhaps more forward-looking) preferred the use of tempo words. Various reforms were proposed, but none were accepted in practice.

Theorists also discussed new techniques of conducting musical meter, and the relationship of time signatures to the expressive content of the music.

French Theorists

In the late seventeenth century, a few French theorists abandoned the traditional categories under which the signs of mensural notation were discussed, and to which the new signs were appended. The traditional order began with the mensural signs C and ₵, followed (in old-fashioned treatises) by O, ⌽, and perhaps ☉. In practice, all of these signified duple metrical organization. Next were "proportions," whether they were actually used as proportions or as fractional numbers; these were primarily signs for triple meter. A final category included "sextuplae," or compound triples that were based on a mixture of mensural signs and proportions. The new signs 3/4, 6/4, 3/8, 6/8, 9/8, 12/8, and so on, were placed and defined in one of the two latter categories.

Etienne Loulié's *Elements* is, perhaps, the first treatise to base categories for meter signs on the number and kind of beats included in the measure; this became the method by which almost all eighteenth-century theorists classified the notation of meter. Loulié defined six types of measures: duple, triple, quadruple, compound duple, compound triple, and compound quadruple. Duple measures were 2, ₵, and 2/4 (he was the only seventeenth-century theorist to include 2/4). C was considered to be a *mesure à quatre temps,* as well as ₵ (which was included in two categories) and 4/8. The *mesure à trois temps* was signified by 3/1, 3/2, 3/4, 3/8, 3/16, and 3 (*triple simple,* which he stated was the same as 3/4). Compound duple meters included 6/4, 6/8, and 6/16, and compound triple meters 9/4, 9/8, and 9/16. Compound quadruple meters were 12/4, 12/8, and 12/16.

Loulié further explained meter signs in a section of his treatise written for those "capable of reasoning on the principles of music." C before a numerical sign or fraction identified the beat as slow quadruple time, and ₵ before a numerical sign identified the beat as fast quadruple time. However, Loulié did not favor the use of C and ₵ in conjunction with fractional numbers; he remarked that "foreigners have retained some of them in their works, but their practice is not very certain; some use them in one manner, some in another."

Loulié criticized the use of mensural signs and other outmoded forms of notation, such as coloration (*triple noire*) and void notation (*triple blanc,* or white ternary), "where there is more caprice than reason." According to him, reason groups meter signs only by the number of beats in a measure.[1]

Michel Pignolet de Montéclair reduced the number of categories to two, stating that "essentially there are only two kinds of measures to which all others are related—the duple and the triple."[2] With the simple duple and triple, the hand beats every note in the measure. When the beat is very fast, the hand compensates by omitting every other stroke or, in the case of the triple beat, omitting two strokes. If it is not possible to beat every note in a bar, measures are classified as compound (*composée*). Even though 6/4 is fundamentally related to the triple beat, it is called compound because it equals two 3/4 measures, a downbeat for one and an upbeat for the other.[3]

French classifications of meter signs make almost no reference to the *tactus*, choosing instead to recognize the number of beats (*temps*) in a measure. Since *temps* can be translated "beat," "pulse," or "time," English equivalents must be chosen with caution. The system of classification for meter signatures most favored by French theorists was by duple, triple, and compound measures (with two, three, or four beats). C came to be considered a compound of two measures of 2/4, and it was sometimes replaced by 4/4. The number 2 was used as well as ₵. Saint Lambert classified signatures as duple (C, ₵, 2, 4/8), triple (3/2, 3, 3/4, 3/8), and compound (6/4, 6/8, 12/4, 12/8, 9/4, 9/8). Dupont[4] and David[5] followed this classification, as did Rousseau.[6] An Italian, Manfredini, also used this duple-triple-compound classification.[7]

Borin and J. F. Démotz de la Salle advocated another system that classified signatures as simple or complex. The *signes simples* were 2, 3, C, and ₵, and the *signes composées* indicated measures with two, three, or four beats:

De deux tems 2/4, 4/8, 4/16, 6/4, 6/8, 6/16
De trois tems 3/2, 3/4, 3/8, 3/16, 9/4, 9/8, 9/16
De quatre tems 12/4, 12/8, 12/16.[8]

This system therefore retained something of the seventeenth-century groupings of mensural signs (duple) and proportions (triple). Borin[9] and Corrette[10] adhered to this classification, and Rousseau offered it as an alternative in his *Dictionnaire* article "Mesure."

The tempo significance of meter signs and note values was still recognized. In general, quarter notes in measures of 6/4 and 9/4 (but not 2/4 and 3/4) were to be taken *graves* (slowly); eighths in measures of 6/8, 9/8, and 12/8 (but not 4/8 or 3/8) were *légers* (*vivace*), the slowest of quick tempos; and sixteenths in 6/16, 9/16, 12/16 (but not 3/16) were *vîtes* (fast). 2/4 and 3/4 were to be taken *léger*; 3/8 and 4/8 *vîte*; 3/16 and 4/16, *très vîte*.[11]

Borin classified all measures as having two, three, or four beats. He based five categories of tempo on "airs de characteres," listing three tempos for four-beat measures, four tempos for two-beat measures, and five tempos for three-beat measures:[12]

Lent: Four-beat measures in recitatives of operas, cantatas, and motets, two-beat measures in the "first part of an opera" (ouvertures, perhaps?). Three-beat measures are "fort grave" in recitatives.
Grave: Three-beat measures in sarabandes, passecailles, and courantes.
Leger: Four-beat measures in allemandes. Two-beat measures in gavottes and gaillardes. Three-beat measures in chaconnes.

Vite: Four-beat measures in "entrées des furies." Two-beat measures in bourées and rigaudons. Three-beat measures in menuets.

Très-vite: Two-beat measures such as in the "entrée des bergères et bergers de l'opera de Roland" by Lully. Three-beat measures in passepieds.

Saint Lambert's *Principes du Clavecin* described several different conducting patterns. For the triple measure, instead of down (two beats) and up (one beat), he gave one beat down, one beat to the right, and one beat up. For common time of four beats, instead of two down then two up, Saint Lambert gave one beat down, one beat to the right, one beat across to the left, and then one beat up. Other theorists advocated different patterns; Dupont gave a *tactus inaequalis* figure of one down, then two up instead of the more usual two down, one up. French writers continued to discuss different ways of beating the measure throughout the eighteenth century.

New ways of beating time give additional evidence of the changed status of the measure. The *tactus*-beat was an anachronism when musicians no longer thought of the measure as a beat, even a very slow beat. The French theorists describe conducting techniques that are similar to modern ones.

English Theorists

According to Alexander Malcolm, an English theorist:

Things that are designed to affect our Senses must bear a due Proportion with them; and so where the Parts of any Object are numerous, and their Relations perplext, and not easily perceived, they can raise no agreeable Ideas; nor can we easily judge of the Difference of Parts where it is great; therefore that the Proportion of the *Time* of Notes may afford us Pleasure, they must be such as are not difficultly perceived: For this Reason the only Ratios fit for *Musick,* besides those of Equality, are the double and triple, or the Ratios of 2 : 1 and 3 : 1; of greater Differences we could not judge, without a painful Attention.[13]

Further on he returned to this topic:

The Measures are only subdivided into 2 or 3 equal Parts; and if there are more, they must be Multiples of these Numbers as 4 to 6 is composed of 2 and 3; again *observe,* the measures of several Songs may agree in the total Quantity, yet differ in the Subdivision and combination of the lesser Notes that fill up the measure. . . .

Of Common and Triple Time

1. Common Time is of Two Species: the first where every *measure* is equal to a semibreve . . . The second where every measure is equal to a Minim. The movements are very various, but there are three common Distinctions, *slow* signified by ₵, brisk—₵, very quick—₵, but what that slow, brisk and quick is, is very uncertain, and must be learned by Practice. . . .

Triple time
1. Simple triple measure: 3𝅝, 3𝅗𝅥, 3♩, or 3♪ (two notes are beat down and one up)
2. Mixt triple measure: 6𝅗𝅥, 6♩, or 6♪
3. Compound Triple: 9♪
4. Compound mixt triple: 12♪ [14]

Malcolm distinguished between measures with the same total number of notes but with a different structure. His method of recognizing this distinction was akin to Butler's (1636). The word "accented" was used to describe the aural perception of measure organization:

> Of the several Species of Triple, there are some that are of the same *relative measure*, as 3/2, 6/4, 12/8, and 3/4, 6/8. These are so far of the same *mode* as the Measure of each contains the same total quantity   but the different *constitutions* of the *Measure* with respect to the Subdivisions and connections of the Notes, make a most remarkable Difference in the Air: For example, the Time of 3/2 consists generally of Minims, and these sometimes mixt with *Semibreves* or with *Crotchets,* and some *Bars* will be all Crotchets: but 3/2 is contrived so that the Air requires the *Measure* to be divided and is beat by three times, and will not do another Way without manifestly changing and spoiling the Humour of the Song: Suppose we would beat it by two *Times,* the first Half will always (except when the *Measure* is actually divided into 6 Crotchets, which is very seldom) end in the Middle, or within the *Time* of some note; and tho' this is admitted sometimes for Variety . . . yet it is rare compared with the general Rule, which is to contrive the Division of the *Measure* so that every Down and Up of the *Beating* shall end with a particular Note; for upon this depends very much the Distinctness and, as it were, the Sense of the *Melody;* and therefore the Beginning of every *Time* or *Beating* in the *Measure* is reckoned the accented Part thereof. [15]

Malcolm placed a greater reliance for tempo on Italian tempo words than on time signatures. He wrote:

> Because the *Italian* Compositions are the Standard and Model of the better Kind of *Musick,* I shall explain the Words by which they mark their Movements, and which are generally used by all others in Imitation of them: They have 6 common Distinctions of *Time,* expressed by these Words, *grave, adagio, largo, vivace, allegro, presto,* and sometimes *prestissimo.* [16]

The first was the slowest, the rest were gradually faster, but Malcolm warned that only practice would allow a musician to know precisely how much faster or slower one was from another.

The same tempo word used with a triple meter sign indicated a faster speed than when used with common time. Common time could be accompanied by any of the tempo words, but some triple signs were associated with certain tempos. 3/2 was ordinarily adagio but could be taken vivace, 3/4 could have any tempo, 3/8 was allegro or vivace. 6/4, 6/8, and 9/8 were usually allegro. 12/8 was usually allegro, but could sometimes be adagio.

Malcolm suggested that meter signs had lost their precise tempo significance, but complained that tempo words were much too variable. Meter signs such as 3/2, 3/4, and 3/8 indicated the same basic meter, and if the tempo were left entirely to "the arbitrary Direction of these words, *adagio, allegro*, &c.," the difference between such meter signs was "more Caprice than Reason." His discussion leaves the reader aware of the problems but not of solutions.[17]

William Turner offered an equally detailed discussion of time signatures; he was less concerned with fundamental principles but carefully weighed each signature for its meaning. The signs for common time, according to Turner, indicated tempo, with ₵ being "somewhat faster" than ₵. For triple time, however,

> The only Rule that is to be given for the Length of *Notes* in this *Case*, is that where the *Movement* is *Slow;* they will always write the word *Slow* at the Beginning of each Lesson: or at least ought always to do so, the *Moods* in *Triple-Time* not at all denoting now, (though formerly they did) what is to be sung *Slow* or *Fast*, as they do in *Common-Time*.[18]

Turner's logical conclusion from the lack of tempo significance of triple signs is that 6/4 and 6/8, 9/4 and 9/8 are unnecessary. However, he does not object to the duplications of simple triples such as 3/1, 3/2, 3/4, and 3/8.

In a later remark about 12/8, Turner made it clear that he considered that tempo was indicated by note values in conjunction with time signatures, not by the signatures alone:

> I will not be so Ill-natur'd as to dispute the Reasonableness of this *Mood*, where it is aptly applied; which is in very swift *Movements*, as Jiggs, etc. but why it should be made use of in slow (sometimes very slow) *Movements*, I cannot conceive; since the Mood of 3/8 (which takes in but one of these four Measures) may do much better, especially for the convenience of *Scholars*, or rather, the Mood of 3/4 or that of 3/2; which barrs in three *Minims*, they seeming to me, to be much more Proper than *Quavers*, to denote slow Movements: For if such a Method were put in Practice, there would be no manner of Occasion to write (at the beginning of Lessons) the *Italian* words, *Adagio, Grave, Largo* &c. (which are put before slow *Movements*) or *Allegro, Presto, Vivace*, &c. (which are applied to swift *Movements;* and which they do in all the *Moods* hitherto spoken of, without Exception) there being Variety sufficient in the different Species of the *Notes* themselves, to shew what movement is slow, and what brisk; without putting our *Pupils* or our selves, to the trouble of learning Foreign Languages.[19]

This statement verifies a dependence on tempo words even though Turner regrets their necessity. Using large notes for slow tempos and small notes for quick tempos was a conservative practice that was advocated by a number of theorists.

Turner's classification of triple measures stated how many beats were included in each measure and indicated that these individual beats were of triple subdivision:

3 × 1 (one beat of triple subdivision)—3/2, 3/4, 3/8;
3 × 2 (two beats of triple subdivision)—6/4, 6/8;
3 × 3—9/4, 9/8;
3 × 4—12/8.[20]

William Tans'ur was very old-fashioned in wanting the sign C or ₵ placed before the fractional number of triple signatures. Tans'ur preserved an ideal *tactus* beat as the norm, indicated by the old mensural signs and varied by "proportions." Most other theorists of the eighteenth century paid no attention to this vestige of mensural notation.

> Or better would it be, if our Tripla-Time-Moods had the Common-Time-Moods always assigned just before them thus: C3/2 &c., or at least, the terms *Adagio, Largo,* or *Allegro,* set over the Cliff, at the Beginning of a Piece of *Music,* or when the Time differs; for them you might at one view know what sort of *Binary Movement* your Ternary is compared unto; and how *quick* or slow the Movement was intended by the Author. This, I say, would make *Time* very easy to every Practitioner, and take away many obscurities that have heretofore Confounded the Ignorant: for when things are *falsely compared together,* the absurdity thereof greatly darkeneth the Understanding.[21]

Tans'ur's idea that tempo words convey equivalent information to the mensural signs ⊙ O, and ₵ echoes Printz's statement of 1689. He seems badly out of date.

The *Dictionnaire* of Brossard, translated into English and expanded by James Grassineau, gave a thorough exposition of early eighteenth-century meter signatures. Five duple time signatures were described in the article on "time," in which Alexander Malcolm's words quoted above are repeated, and tempo is considered as follows:

> But then what that slow, brisk, and quick is, is very uncertain, and only to be learned by practice; the nearest measure we know of it, is to make a quaver the length of a pulse of a good watch; then a crotchet will be equal to two pulses, a minim four, and the whole bar or measure eight; this may be reputed the measure of brisk *Time,* for slow 'tis as long again, and for the quick only half as long.[22]

The subject was not complete until the reader was informed of how to keep *time:*

> Now to keep *time* equally, we make use of a motion of the hand or foot; knowing the time of the crotchet, we shall suppose the measure actually divided into four crotchets, for the first species of common time; then half the measure will

be two crotchets; therefore the hand or foot being up, if we put it down with the very beginning of the first note or crotchet, and then raise it with a third, and then down again to begin with the next measure; this is what we call beating of *Time*.[23]

The implication of his discussion is that time signatures were gauged in reference to a standard tempo.

Concerning *Measure*, Grassineau said:

> Ternary or triple measure is that wherin the fall is double the rise, or *è contra;* or where two minims are played during a rise and but one in a fall; and *vice versa;* to this purpose the number three, or 3/8 &c. are placed at the beginning of the lines when the measure is intended to be triple, and a semicircle **C** when it is to be common.[24]

Under *Triple,* Grassineau's translation refers to "the Italians," although Brossard specifically mentioned Bononcini and Penna. "The common name of *Triple time* is taken hence, that the whole or half of the bar is divisible into three parts, and beat accordingly, the first time down, the second time with the return of the hand, and at last with the hand quite up, and it is this motion that makes what the Italians mean by the phrase *Ondeggiare la mano*."[25]

Grassineau discussed some twenty different triple meter signs, including some identified as obsolete or obsolescent. He mentioned four species of triple signs, the first being simple triple: 3/1, 3/2, 3/4, 3/8, and 3/16. "The ancients had, and the *Italians* at present have four different signs for triple major [the first sign, 3/1, is 'triple major']: ⊕ 3/1♮, ¢ 3/1♮, ⊕ 3/2♮, ¢ 3/2♮."[26] These were not of practical importance to Grassineau, however, since he considered them obsolete. The second species of triple was *compound triple:* 9/1, 9/2, 9/4, 9/8, and 9/16. The third species of triple was *mixed triple* or *binary triple:* 6/4, 6/8, or 6/16. The fourth species was called *dodecupla:* 12/1, 12/2, 12/4, 12/8, and 12/16.

Finally Grassineau mentioned the 5/2 and 7/2 meters discussed by Penna, but commented, "These raising some difficulty and confusion were rejected, and not admitted into the number of *mixed triples*."

The classification of meter signs according to duple and triple was used by Prelleur,[27] Tans'ur, Holden,[28] Steele,[29] and, in New England, by John Stickney.[30]

More complicated classifications are found in increasing number in the second half of the century. The English translation of Rameau's *Traité* omitted the radical proposals of the French version (to be discussed with Rameau's proposed reforms of notation) and established four categories: common time (**C**, ¢, 𝄵, 2, and 2/4); triple time (3/2, 3/4, 3/8); composed triple time (9/4, 9/8); and common time composed of triple time (6/4, 12/8).[31] This categorization, in essence, was used by Antoniotto[32] and Callcott[33] as well.

Kollmann[34] and Elias Mann[35] relied on a simple-compound classification, as follows:

	Compound or
Simple Measures	Tripled Measures
2 part: 2/2, 2/4, 2/8	6/4, 6/8, 6/16
3 part: 3/2, 3/4, 3/8	9/4, 9/8, 9/16
4 part: 4/2, 4/4, 4/8	12/4, 12/8, 12/16

Note that 4/4 has replaced ¢.

German Theorists

Early in the eighteenth century, Johann Peter Sperling used the word *Zeichung* (signatures), rather than "proportions," for meter signs. This change in terminology recognized a new function of the fractional numbers that were inherited from mensural notation. By not coupling fractional number signatures with ¢, he marked them as independent signs rather than proportions:

> Zu wissen ist nur/ dass wann eine unbekannte/ und in diesem dritten Capitel nicht vorgestellte Zeichung des *Tacts* vorkommet/ man zu betrachten habe solche aus zweyen über einander gesetzten *numeris* bestehende Zeichung; und zwar erstlich den obern *Numerum,* welcher anzeiget die *Quantität,* wieviel nemlich noten aufm *Tact* gehen: Und hernacher den untern *Numerum,* welcher anzeiget die *Qualität/* was nemlich für noten es seyn/ deren so viel auffm *Tact* gehen; Ist nun solcher unterer *Numerus/* 1. so gehen so viel eintheilige Noten/ das ist gantze/ auffm *Tact:* Ist dieser *Numerus* 2. so gehen so viel zweytheilige Noten, das ist halbe/ auffm tact.[36]

> When an unknown figure, one not explained in this third chapter, is encountered, consider the two numbers written one above the other. First, the upper number shows the quantity or how many notes are in the measure. Next, the bottom number shows the quality or what kind of note makes up the number counted in the measure. If this bottom number is 1, so many single-part notes or whole notes go to a *tact.* If the number is 2, so many two-part notes or half notes go to a *tact.*

Sperling's names for notes correspond to the fraction of the *tactus*-beat that the note occupies. *Ein halbschlagig Note,* "a half-beat note," is half of a semibreve, as one semibreve is equal to a *tactus* beat. The terms "half note," "whole note," etc., appear in Sperling's *Principia* because of the identification of the *tactus* with the semibreve, or whole note.

Sperling's third chapter explains a total of fifty-nine time signatures. These are systematically considered: all possible combinations of 1, 2, 4, 8, and 16 are used as numerators and 1, 2, 4, 8, and 16 as denominators for "four-part measures"; and 3, 6, 9, 12, and 24 are used as numerators and 1, 2, 4, 8, and 16 as denominators for "three-part measures." Sperling included 12/8 and 6/8 as three-part measures or *trippel-Tacts,* as he was following a classification system established in the seventeenth century, even though it is clear that these are four-part and two-part measures of triple subdivision.

Sperling included five other signs that he said could be found in the works of Schmelzer (d. 1680) and Walther (possibly Johann Jacob Walther, a late seventeenth-century violinist-composer, or perhaps the sixteenth-century Lutheran composer Johann Walther; both were composers who probably would use an older style of notation). These five signs, said to occur in "artistic sonatas of other authors," were 24/32, 10/8, 12/6, 4/3, and 9/6. "Betreffend die erst *Species,* ist zwar gewiss/ dass es/ wie aus obigen *numero* 24 zu sehen/ ein Tripel sey/ worinnen Vierund Zwanzig dreymahl gestrichene/ oder *Chromata Triplicata* aufm Tact gehen" (Concerning the first kind, it is certain from the upper number, 24, that it is a triple in which twenty-four three-flagged notes or *chromata triplicata* go to one tact).[37] The other four signs were inverted "proportions."

> Die übrigen 5. *Species* aber *referir*en sich allzeit auf etwas vorhergehendes/ das ist entweder auf einen vorhergehenden *Ordinar-Tact,* oder auf einen vorhergehenden Tripel/ oder ja auf den *Ordinar-Tact absolutè,* obschon solcher nicht vorangangen ist. . . . Setze allhier *pro Exemplo* wiederum den drey viertel-*Tripel.* Dieser drey viertel-Tripel wird in dem *Ordinar-Tact* versetzet durch 4/3, oder 8/6, oder 16/12, &c. Dann weil dieser Tripel bestehet aus drey viertel oder Sechs-Actel/ oder Zwölf *Semifusen* &c. Als wird der fünfftige *Tact* [4/3] bestehen aus vier drey-Theille/ das ist viertel/ oder aus acht Sechs-theile/ das ist Achtel/ oder aus Sechszehen zwölf-Theile/ das ist *Semifusen,* zweymahl gestrichen &c. welches nichts anders ist/ als der *formale Ordinar-Tact.* Mehrers Nachdencken hierüber/ überlasse den erfahrnen *Musicis.*[38]

The aforementioned five kinds refer always to something that has preceded them, either common time, or a triple measure, or even the "absolute common time"; whether or not it has actually been put down before. . . . Let us take the three-quarter triple for an example again. This three-quarter is put back in common time through 4/3, or 8/6, or 16/12, etc., for because this triple consists of three quarters or six eighths or twelve sixteenths, through [4/3] it would consist of four third-parts or quarters, or of eight sixth-parts or eighths, or of sixteen twelfth-parts or sixteenths, which is nothing but the usual common time. As experienced musicians think more about this, it is given up.

Inverted signatures intended to restore common time, as well as explanations of them, disappear in the later eighteenth century. Sperling continues:

> Zwischen den ersten und andern machen etliche einen Unterschied/ sagend: Das Erste bedeutet einen langsamen/ das andere aber einen geschwinden *Tact;* Solcher Unterschied aber wird von vielen *componist*en nicht *observir*et/ sondern des *Tactus* geschwind- und Langsamkeit mit absonderlichen *terminis* bemercket/ als da sind: *tardo, presto, alla breve* &c. Das dritte bedeutet zwar einen *Ordinar-Tact,* welcher 4. Viertel in sich hat: Es wird aber solcher *Tact* sehr geschwind *tractir*et/

also/ dass zwey dergleichen *Tacte* fast nur so lange dauren als sonsten einer: Diese
3*te* Manier oder *Species* des *Tacts* ist von denen Frantzosen zu uns kommen/ als
welche sich derselben gebrauchen in denen *Ouvertur*en, *Bouré*en, &c.[39]

Between the first (C) and second (₵), many make this difference, the first
means a slow measure and the second a fast measure. Such a difference is not observed by many composers, but the quickness or slowness of the measure is indicated by particular terms such as *tardo, presto, alla breve,* etc. The third (2) indicates common time with four quarters to a measure, but it is beaten so quickly
that two of such measures are nearly of the same length as one. This third kind
of measure comes to us from the French and is used by them in overtures and
bourées, etc.

The classification of time signatures to distinguish between duple and
triple was used by most early eighteenth-century German writers, including
Fuhrmann[40] and Johann Gottfried Walter.[41] Both explained the signatures according to the definitions of Penna and Bononcini.

Brossard's *Dictionaire,* already discussed in its English translation by
James Grassineau, influenced Walther's *Lexicon* of 1732. The same terms were
used—"tempo" for the duple meters and "triple" for the three-part meters, each
under its separate heading. Walther also cited Fuhrmann, Bononcini, Carissimi
(from his German translation), and Praetorius as his sources of information for
the various articles on triple.[42] Walther included 6/4, 6/8, and 12/8 under
triples but called them "spondaic triples" and equated them with the *triple
binaire* of Brossard and the *sextupla* of Praetorius.

Walther cited Johann Mattheson in amplifying his discussion of the difference between the "spondaic triples" (6/8 and 6/4) and those that were completely triple:

> Die Mensur ist ja nicht ungerade, eben so wenig als die Theilung; dann
> ob sich 6 gleich sonst in drey Theile schneiden lassen, so geschiehet doch solches
> nimmer in obigen Tact-Arten, da *partes aequales* vorhanden sind, und der Nieder-
> Schlag so wohl als der Auffschlag drey *membra* haben muss. Wer in *proportione
> sesqualtera* 3/2, sechs Viertel betrachtet, und mercket, was die 4 im Niederschlage,
> und die 2 im Auffschlage für ein *mouvement* enthalten, der wird den Unterscheid
> zwischen Tripel und *aequal* Tächten mit Händen greiffen konnen.[43]

> The measure is not triple and its subdivision is just as little triple, for should
> six equal notes be divided into three parts, the measure could never be written in
> the meter signature above (6/4), which is for equal parts, in which the downstroke
> as well as the upstroke must have three pulses. Whoever sees six quarters in *pro-
> portione sesqualtera* 3/2, and knows that four are contained in the downbeat and
> two in the upbeat of one complete conducting gesture, understands the difference
> between triple and equal beating of the hand.

Although there was general agreement in classifying time signatures, it
was not total. Johann Mattheson's system of classification was derived from
even and uneven *tactus* beats and it divided all meters into duple and triple.[44]

The duple meters included 2, 2/4, C, 6/4, 6/8, 12/4, 12/8, 12/16, and "12/24." This last meter sign may have been a slip of Mattheson's pen, but it was retained by later theorists until it was finally denounced by Leopold Mozart in 1756. The triples included three subdivisions: simple, composed, and mixed. The simples were 3/1, 3/2, 3/4, and 3/8, and the composed were 9/8 and 9/16. Several duple meters, 12/4, 12/8, 12/16, and 24/16, were assigned to the category of mixed triples.

Mattheson emphasized the distinction between tempo (which he usually called *le mouvement*) and meter (*Mensuram*). He considered tempo "spiritual," as more expressive of feeling and emotion, and meter "physical."[45] His interpretation of the sign 12/8 offers a particular example of the separation of tempo and meter that points to the changing function of time signatures in the early eighteenth century:

> 12/8 Ist nur/ als Zwölfachtheil/ kleinerer *proportion*, sonst *in numero* und *membris* wie in Theilen/ eben als der vorige *Tact* [12/4], das ist/ sie *differiren* nur in *qualitate* nicht aber *in quantitate*. Dieser ist sehr geschickt vor die Sachen *à la moderne*, weil darinnen/ obgleich die Glieder mit dem 6/8 in gleicher Geltung sind das verlängte *Mouvement* und die doppelte Anzahl eine gewisse Ernsthafftigkeit/ mit der/ den achteln sonst abhängenden/ hurtigkeit/ dermassen verbindet/ dass man die sonst hüpffende *Mensur* zu den aller *tendre*sten und beweglichsten Sachen gar wol/ es sey in Kirchen/ oder *Theatral-vocal-Music* wie auch in *Cantaten* &c. zu gebrauchen weitz. Vorzeiten hat man nach dieser *Mensur* nichts anders/ als gar geschwinde Sachen/ wie es denn noch gewisser massen geschiecht/ gesetzet/ als nemlich in *Giquen* und dergleichen; heutiges Tages aber dienet dieselbe vielmehr traurige und *touchante Affecten* denn lustige zu *exprimi*ren.[46]

> 12/8 is in a smaller proportion than 12/4, but in number and parts as well as beats it is the same. That is, it differs only in quality, not in quantity. It is much used for pieces *à la moderne* because in it, although the notes are of the same value as in 6/8, the slower tempo and doubled number add a certain gravity to the quickness attached to the note value. The otherwise hopping meter is widened in use to include all tender and changeable pieces, whether in church or theater vocal music and also in cantatas. Formerly this was used only for fast pieces such as gigues and the like. Nowadays it is used to express sad and touching passions as well as merry ones.

In a later chapter on note values, Mattheson mentions the tempo of 12/8 again, as an example of a general notational trend.

> Es ist zwar oben bey Gelegenheit des zwölfachtel *Tactes* erinnert worden/ dass die langsame *Music* es bey itziger Zeit der geschwinden abgewinne; dem ungeachtet aber hat man nicht vor nöthig gehalten/ auch die langen grossen und *choquanten Noten* wieder hervor zu suchen/ sondern man hat die kleinern *Proportiones* behalten/ und ihnen nur ein langsahmeres Mouvement gegeben. Wobey der wichtige/ aber wenigen recht bekandte unterschied zwischen *Tact* und *Mouvement*, welches die meisten vor einerley nehmen/ oder doch nicht recht kennen/ beyläuffig angemercket und *in praxi* untersuchet werden mag.[47]

In discussing the 12/8 measure above, we observed that nowadays slow music is prevailing over fast, despite the fact that long, big, and disagreeable notes are no longer used; but quick proportions are used, although they are given a slower tempo. In connection with this, the important but little-understood difference between measure and tempo which is taken to be the same by many, or not correctly understood, can be recognized and examined in practice.

12/8 may have an "affective" tempo or a fast tempo, yet the measure is the same. This is possible with other measures, and the performer needs to gauge the important, yet delicate, distinction according to his judgment and taste.

Despite such important variations, Mattheson suggests a standard tempo for each of the fifteen time signatures in general use, based on the genre of composition or its *affekt,* and on the size of the notes in each measure. Time signatures with 16 as denominator (12/16, 24/16, and 9/16) are all faster versions of time signatures with 8 as denominator (12/8, 6/8, 9/8). Likewise 8 as the denominator suggests a faster tempo than 4. Signatures are neither proportions nor tempo indications: note values indicate an absolute speed, which, however, can be modified by the genre of the piece or by a tempo word.

Joseph F. B. L. Maier classified many time signatures according to whether they were even (duple) or uneven (triple). The duple meters were 2, 2/4, C, 6/4, 6/8, 12/4, and 12/8, and the triple meters were 3/1, 3/2, 3/4, 3/8, and 9/8.[48] Maichelbeck,[49] Eisel,[50] Münster,[51] and Adlung[52] followed this classification system. Adlung paraphrased Mattheson and faithfully copied out the errant time signature 12/24 but added a footnote to the effect that he did not really understand it, and included it only because Mattheson had.

Quantz[53] and Leopold Mozart[54] retained duple-triple categories for meter signs. C is called *viervierteiltact* rather than *schlechter* or *ordinarii* (common) time. Leopold Mozart exhorted:

> Let not our friends the critics be startled if I omit the times 4/8, 12/8, 9/8, 9/16, 12/16, 12/24, and 12/4. In my eyes they are worthless stuff. One finds them seldom or not at all in the newer pieces; and there really are enough variations of times for expressing everything, to be able to do without these last. He who likes them, let him grasp them with might and main. Yea I would even generously present him with the 3/1 time, were it not that it still gazes defiantly at me out of a few old church pieces.[55]

In the same year, Marpurg subdivided the classification of duple-triple into simple and compound duple and triple.[56] Hiller[57] and Kalkbrenner[58] classified measures as: "Duple two-part, thus 2/2, 4/2, 2/4, 4/4; duple three-part, thus 6/4, 6/8, 12/8; triple two-part, thus 3/2, 3/4, 3/8, [two-part in the sense of two pulses of the *tactus inaequalis*], and triple three-part, thus 9/4, 9/8."

Kirnberger's classification was more complicated because he distinguished two-part from four-part even meters, as well as separated triple from duple:

Simple even measures of two times:
1) 2/1 measure (Ⴔ) — tripled is 6/2 measure.
2) 2/2   "   (Ⴔ) —   "   " 6/4   "
3) 2/4   "   —   "   " 6/8   "
4) 2/8   "   —   "   " 6/16   "
Simple even measures of four times:
1) 4/2 measure (O) — tripled is 12/4 measure.
2) 4/4   "   (C) —   "   " 12/8   "
3) 4/8   "   —   "   " 12/16 "
Simple uneven measures of three times:
1) 3/1 measure (3) — tripled is 9/2 measure.
2) 3/2   "   —   "   " 9/4   "
3) 3/4   "   —   "   " 9/8   "
4) 3/8   "   —   "   " 9/16   "
5) 3/16   "   —   "   " 9/32   ".59

Kirnberger summarizes the significance of meters in German compositions of the eighteenth century, particularly for the music of J. S. Bach, his idol and teacher. For Kirnberger, note values had a definite tempo significance, just as described by Mattheson in 1713, and they also implied articulation or a style of performance. Large note values were described as "weighty and emphatic" (*schwere und nachdrückliche*) in 2/1, 6/2, 4/2, 3/1, and 9/2. Small note values were "light and quick" (*leicht und lebhaft*) and allowed no stress on the first notes of beats in 6/16, 24/16, 12/16, 9/16, and 3/16. Violinists were to play these quick notes of light meters with the point of the bow, but weightier meters required a longer stroke and more bow pressure.

One of the most important points made by Kirnberger is that there is a *tempo giusto*, or "natural tempo," for every meter. He stated that these would best be learned by studying all kinds of dance pieces, their meter signatures, and the note values used. Tempo words such as "*largo, adagio, andante, allegro, presto,* and their modifications *larghetto, andantino, allegretto,* and *prestissimo,* modify this natural tempo, rather than set absolute tempos determined by the words alone."60 The kind of dance or the genre of the piece also determines the tempo; for example, a sarabande in 3/4 is slower than a minuet in 3/4.

Kirnberger implies that individual time signatures can be grouped into categories of tempos, although he does not give any absolute indications of their speed. He states that those in the slowest category (2/1, 6/2, 4/2, 12/4, 3/1, and 9/2) are seldom used, and that their tempos are designated by signs in the next faster category, to which the word *Grave* is added. All imply "weighty tempos and emphatic performance."

The signs in the next faster category are Ⴔ, ⅔, 6/4, 3/2, and 9/4. In these the shortest note values commonly used are eighth notes. Ⴔ is "twice as fast as the note values indicate," apparently a reflection of the ancient proportional significance of this sign. Generally these are "serious and emphatic," with 3/2 being "ponderous," and 6/4 "more moderate."

C, 12/8, 3/4, and 9/8 are in the middle category of tempos. C and 12/8 indicate a more lively tempo and execution than ¢, and may include sixteenth notes. 3/4 is lighter than 3/2; it includes mainly eighths but allows occasional sixteenths. The *tempo giusto* of 3/4 is that of the minuet, and therefore it is rather fast, but it can be modified by *allegro, adagio,* etc. 9/8 has the same tempo as 3/4.

The next faster signatures are 2/4 (which has the same tempo as alla breve but is lighter and more playful) and 3/8 (having the *tempo giusto* of the passepied). Quicker yet are 2/8 and 4/8, with "fast tempos and light execution."

The fastest tempos of all are indicated by 6/16, 24/16, 12/16, 9/16, and 2/16. All of these are "extremely light and quick" and are not frequently used, to Kirnberger's regret. He says that they are usually replaced by their next slower equivalents, with the addition of the word *presto,* which adequately indicates the tempo but not the required lightness of articulation.

Some additional fine distinctions are made clear by Kirnberger, such as the difference between 3/4 with eighth-note triplets and 9/8, which have the same tempo. In 3/4, the triplets are to be performed very lightly without the slightest pressure on the last of the three, but in 9/8 the eighths are heavier with some weight on the last eighth note. This allows a change of harmony on the last eighth note in 9/8, but not on the third triplet in 3/4. Triplets in 3/4 cannot be subdivided into arpeggiated sixteenth notes, but eighths in 9/8 can be. If these special qualities are not observed, 6/8 gigues might as well be written in 2/4, and 12/8 written in C.[61]

Kirnberger's classification of meters, although logical and suited to the use of eighteenth-century composers, did not serve as a model for other theorists, even Heinrich Christoph Koch, who was otherwise strongly influenced by Kirnberger's discussion of meter. Koch and other writers divided meter into simple: 2, 2/4, C; simple triple: 3/2, 3/4, 3/8; mixed measures, such as a duple 2/4 that made use of triplets; and compound measures, divided in turn into compound duple and compound triple.[62] This is almost the classification adopted by Scheibe, which is frequently accepted as the norm today: (1) simple even meters (duple or quadruple), (2) simple triple meters, (3) compound even meters, and (4) compound triple meters.[63]

Notational Reforms

Many theorists suggested reforms of metrical notation in the eighteenth century. According to Jean-Philippe Rameau, the impulse for reform arose from the desire for simplicity:

> Il faut supposer d'abord, que puisque la mesure ne se distingue qu'en 2, 3, ou 4, tems, nous n'avons pas besoin d'autres chiffres pour la marquer, & rien ne seroit plus propre à nous faire distinguer sa lenteur & sa vitesse, que la valeur des Nottes

dont chaque mesure peut être remplie; car sçachant que le mouvement de la Ronde
est plus lent que celui de la Blanche, & ainsi de la Blanche à la Noire, de la Noire
à la Croche, & de la Croche à la double-Croche; qui est-ce qui ne comprendra pas
sur le champ, qu'une mesure où la Ronde ne vaudra qu'un tems, sera plus lente que
celle où la Blanche vaudra un temps.[64]

We must first say that since the measure has only 2, 3, or 4 beats, we have no
need of other signs to indicate this, and nothing will be more appropriate to distinguish slowness or quickness than the value of the notes which make up each measure. As we know that the speed of the whole note is slower than that of the half
note, and the half note slower than the quarter, and the quarter slower than the
eighth, who would not understand immediately that a measure in which the whole
note is worth one beat will be slower than one in which the half note is worth
one beat.

Rameau demonstrated how the various kinds of measures would be equal
to different Italian tempo terms, presumably by definition first and later by
practice. Expressive terms would still be needed, such as *tendrement, détaché,*
and *louré,* but the note values themselves would replace the terms *allegro* and
andante.

Le chiffre mis à la tête d'une Piece nous marquant la quantité des temps de
chaque mesure; & ne s'agissant plus que de sçavoir distinguer la valeur de la Notte
qui doit remplir chaque temps, l'Auteur pourra (pour l'intelligence des Concer-
tans) mettre immédiatement avant la Clef, la Notte qui conviendra pour lors, pour
épargner la peine de calculer une certaine quantité de Nottes, dont chaque temps
peut être composé, & dont la valeur doit égaler celle des Nottes qui valent pour
lors un temps; l'on peut mettre de plus cette Notte sur la ligne du Ton dans lequel
la Piéce est composé comme pour l'observons dans les Examples suivans.

Il sera inutile de mettre ces mots *lentment, vif,* &c. parce que cela est désigné
par la lenteur ou par la vitesse naturelle aux Nottes placées à la tête de chaque
Piéce; mais le triste & le lugubre étant naturels aux movemens lents, le tendre & le
lugubre aux mouvemens lents & gais; le furieux aux mouvemens trés-vifs & c. l'on
peut y ajoûter ces mots, quand l'expression le demande.[65]

The signature marked at the beginning of the piece would indicate the number
of beats in each measure; it is not intended to do more than to indicate the note
value that is equal to one beat. The composer could put the appropriate note just
before the clef. This would be for the information of the performers, to save them
the trouble of calculating the beat-note, that is, the quantity of notes that make up
each beat. Further, the note could be placed on the line of the key note of the piece,
as can be seen in the following examples [Ex. 2.1].

It would be needless to add the words *lentement, vif,* etc. because this is indicated by the natural speed of the note at the beginning of each piece, but sadness
and lugubriousness are suitable in slow tempos, tenderness and graciousness in
moderate and gay ones, and fury in very fast tempos; these words may be added
when needed in order to indicate the proper affect.

EX. 2.1

Rameau, therefore, confirms Mattheson's and Kirnberger's use of note values as the primary indication of tempo, although he retains descriptive terms to convey the emotional quality of a piece of music.

Rameau provided a separate signature for *temps inégaux* (the *tactus inaequalis*) by placing two note values before the clef, such as a half note and a quarter note; the first of these was the value of the downbeat, the second the value of the upbeat. *Mouvements à temps inégaux* are distinguished from measures of three equal notes.

> L'habitude où l'on est de marquer des mêmes chiffres ces mouvements à temps inégaux; & ceux où l'on fait passer trois Nottes d'égale valeur pour chaque temps, nous ôte la facilité de les distinguer, & fait qu'on les confond souvent; d'où il arrive que l'on ne donne pas toûjours à un Air le mouvement qui luy convient; car les temps inégaux obligent d'appuyer un peu sur le second, le quatriéme, & le sixiéme temps, en introduisant je ne sçai quoi de gracieux dans les premier, troisiéme, & cinquiéme temps, dont l'effet est bien different de celui que produiroient ces mêmes mouvemens battus à temps égaux.[66]

> The custom we have of marking measures with unequal beats the same as those with three equal notes on each beat robs us of the faculty of distinguishing them and causes them to be often confused. From this it happens that an air is not always given the animation that suits it. Unequal beats cause [the performer] to lean a little on the second, fourth, and sixth notes, while giving a certain gracious *je-ne-sçai-quoi* to the first, third and fifth notes. This is entirely different from the effect produced by the same tempo given with equal beats.

Rameau provides examples of the notation of equal and unequal beats (Ex. 2.2).

The examples of beats *à deux temps inégaux* with the signature 2 are equivalent to the *tactus inaequalis,* but those with the signatures 4 and 6 are more complicated.

EX. 2.2

La mesure à six temps inégaux n'est pas fort en usage, par la difficulté qu'il y a à la battre: Ceux qui voudront cependent s'en servir (car il est certain qu'elle convient à des expressions particulières) pourront frapper le premier temps, baisser la main au deuxiéme par un mouvement du poignet, & la baisser encore plus au troisiéme par un mouvement du bras, en le levant ensuite pour les autres temps, comme dans la mesure à quatre temps.[67]

The measure of six unequal beats is not much used because it is difficult to beat. For those who nevertheless want to use it (as it certainly is suitable to some affects), give a downbeat on the first beat, lower the hand by a movement of the wrist on the second, lower it again by a movement of the arm on the third, and then raise it after that for the other beats as in the four-beat measure.

This method of beating suggests a slow tempo. The assignment of a *je-ne-sçai-quoi de gracieux* to the unequal beats, while charming, is not precise enough to help the performer. It is not easy to describe the subtleties of measure organization.

In an expanded version of his *Nouvelle Méthode,* Montéclair described another reform of notation: "Tous les musiciens conviennent que toutes les mesures se raportent à deux et à trois temps. Pourquoi donc employent-t-ils jusqu'à 19 signes pour marquer ces deux mesures? La mesure à quatre tems n'est autre chose que la mesure de deux temps doubles" (All musicians agree that all measures are of two or three beats. Why then do we use up to 19 signatures to indicate these two measures? The measure of four beats is nothing but a two-beat measure doubled).[68]

Montéclair did not wish to rely exclusively on note values as tempo indications. Although in general, larger note values indicated a slower tempo than smaller ones, the genre of the piece of music also conveyed a sense of tempo. For instance, the passepied and passacaille were both marked 3, but the first was fast and the second was slow. Montéclair advocated replacing the tempo significance of time signatures with the terms *grave, lent, aisement, modéré, gay, leger,* and *vîte.* This is intended to prevent any confusion about the speed of the piece.

In Montéclair's system, meter signs became a simple 2 for duple, or 3 for triple measures when there was a duple subdivision of the principal beat, and $\frac{2}{4}$ or $\frac{3}{4}$ when there was a triple subdivision of the principal beat. The measure of four beats was abandoned, and with it the whole note or semibreve. Example 2.3 is a diagram of the system. No provision was made for the subdivision of eighth notes, either duple or triple. Montéclair supports his system by a quasi-historical account of seventeenth-century changes in mensural notation.

EX. 2.3

Another reform of notation was offered by Jean-Jacques Rousseau, who made this his first endeavor on arriving in Paris from the provinces in 1742. Rousseau began by describing the needless difficulties of musical notation and then proposed to substitute seven arabic numerals for the notes of the scale and to change time signatures to just 2 for duple and 3 for triple.

Rousseau flatly contradicted Rameau on the subject of note values as desirable tempo indicators:

> Un défaut considérable dans la musique est de représenter, comme valeurs absolues, des notes qui n'en ont que de relatives, ou du moins d'en mal appliquer les relations: car il est sûr que la durée des rondes, des blanches, noires, croches, etc., est déterminée, non par la qualité de la note, mais par celle de la mesure où elle se trouve: de là vient qu'une noire, dans une certaine mesure, passera beaucoup plus vite qu'une croche dans une autre; laquelle croche ne vaut cependant que la moitié de cette noire, et de là vient encore que les musiciens de province, trompés par ces faux rapports, donneront aux airs des mouvements tout différents de ce qu'ils doivent être, en s'attachant scrupluleusement à la valeur absolue des notes, tandis qu'il faudra quelquefois passer une mesure à trois temps simples beaucoup plus vite qu'une autre à trois huit, ce qui dépend du caprice du compositeur, et de quoi les opéra présentent des exemples à chaque instant.[69]

> It is a considerable fault in music to represent notes as having an absolute value when their value is only relative, and to make wrong applications of their relations; as it is certain that the duration of whole notes, half notes, quarters, and eighths is determined not by the quality of the notes but by the measures in which they are found. It follows from this that a quarter note in one measure may be made faster than an eighth in another; that eighth note, nevertheless, is worth only half of the quarter. Misled by these false relationships, provincial musicians give some airs quite different tempos than they should by adhering closely to the absolute duration of the notes, whereas it is sometimes necessary to play a measure of

trois temps simples (3/4) much faster than another of 3/8, as this depends on the caprice of the composer. Many examples of this can be found in operas.

Rousseau objected to the insufficiency of notation to indicate the subdivisions of triple in duple meters without extra signs, and also to the lack of a sign to divide each beat from every other. His system proposed that a straight line be drawn over or under the number of notes—whether two, three, or four— that combine to form one beat. Each beat would be set off by a comma.[70]

Rousseau also provided rests (indicated by a zero) and prolonged notes or tied notes (indicated by a dot to signify undetermined duration). Rousseau's system was best suited to single-line melodic notation and posed significant problems to anyone reading music for harmonic relationships. By abandoning conventional notes and the staff, Rousseau made it much more difficult for musicians to adopt his system than it would be to adopt the comparatively mild reforms of Rameau and Montéclair. Rousseau repeated his proposed reform and gave more examples in his *Dissertation sur la musique moderne* (Paris, 1743), but the *Dictionnaire de musique,* which included his music essays for the *Encyclopédie,* restricted itself to conventional notation and added only a paragraph of criticism of the many signs of meter.

Rousseau was probably aware of Montéclair's *Principes,* published six years earlier, and their systems were similar in some respects. The idea of reforming musical notation was evidently in the air in eighteenth-century France; still another reform was proposed by the Abbé Joseph de Lacassagne in 1776.

Lacassagne gave a thorough explanation of conventional meter signs, and divided them into *mesures simples* and *mesures composées.* The *mesures simples* were 2 or ¢, 2/4, or 4/8 (*à deux temps*); C or ¢ (*à quatre temps*); 3/2, 3/4 or 3, 3/8 (*à trois temps*). *Mesures composées* were 6/4, 6/8 (*à deux temps*); 12/4, 12/8 (*à quatre temps*); 9/4, 9/8 (*à trois temps*) (Ex. 2.4).[71]

He continued:

> Les chiffres qu'on place au commencement d'un Air pour indiquer l'espèce de Mesure qui en fait le caractère, pouroient se réduire à un 2. un 3. et 2/3. Cette réduction suffiroit pour exprimer tous les Movements possibles. Le 2. Signifieroient la Mesure partagée en Deux Temps égaux. Le 3., en Trois-Temps aussi égaux. Le 2/3 signifieroient la Mesure à Deux-Temps inégaux, et on l'écriroit comme s'il n'y avoit qu'un 3. La différence qu'on trouveroit dans cette inégalité, seroit la même que celle de 2 à 1, c'est-à-dire que si trois Notes de la même espèce composaient la valeur d'une mesure, on en mettroit deux pour le premier Temps; et une pour le second.[72]

The signatures put at the beginning of an air to indicate the kind of measure and determine its character can be reduced to 2, 3, and 2/3. This reduction will suffice to express all possible tempos. The 2 will signify the measure divided into two equal beats, the 3, the measure of three equal beats. The 2/3 will signify the measure of two unequal beats, which will be written as if it had the signature 3. The difference found in this inequality is that of 2 : 1, that is to say that if three notes of the same kind make up the value of a measure, two would be on the first beat and one on the second.

Lacassagne agreed with Rousseau that note values should have no tempo significance, so he advocated the use of the conventional Italian and French tempo words.

> Si je n'ai pas le mérite d'être le premier à proposer cette Réforme utile, j'ai du moins celui de démontrer par des principes et des Exemples sensibles, celle que je crois la plus practicable; et d'adopter sans restriction les vues des grands maîtres (Mrs. Rameau, Rousseau et Montéclair) qui ont traité le même sujet.[73]

> Although I do not have the merit of being the first to propose this useful reform, at least I am the first to show by principles and understandable examples that part which is, I believe, the most practical, and to adopt without restriction the views of the great masters (Messrs. Rameau, Rousseau and Montéclair) who have considered this subject.

Lacassagne entirely rejected compound measures, so that only the simple duple, simple triple, and his equivalent of the *tactus inaequalis* remained. It is

EX. 2.4

Exemple des mesures simples à deux et à quatre temps qu'on reduit au seul signe d'un **2**

Exemple des mesures composées à deux temps qu'on peut diviser, en désignant par les chiffres ⅔

Exemple des mesures composées à quatre temps qu'on peut diviser en les chiffres ⅔

difficult to understand why the distinction between a simple triple and an uneven two-beat measure was necessary, unless it was for clarification in beating the measure.

Lacassagne proposed a different system later in the same book. This second proposal reduced the measures to two formulas that were not fully explained but seem to have been invented in order to include compound measures. He stated that it would not matter which system was adopted—either would be a boon to students—and he suggested an "Académie de Musique" to consider reforms and decide on one that would be adopted all over France as the "indispensable rule for all musicians who write new music." Lacassagne's proposals and those of other reformers were ridiculed in Boyer's letter to Diderot.[74]

Jean-Benjamin de Laborde, a violinist-composer who was court chamberlain to Louis XV, accused Lacassagne of not perceiving "the essential constituent differences between certain measures." This criticism is found in his four-volume *Essai sur la musique ancienne et moderne*,[75] which in turn was severely criticized by Fétis as "a masterpiece of ignorance, disorder, and carelessness."[76] However, the raillery to which Laborde subjected the proposed "Académie de Musique" was not wholly undeserved. Laborde had the misfortune to be guillotined in 1794, the result of a more serious controversy than the one with Lacassagne.

However, the spirit of musical reform remained alive, for in 1801 another attempt was made, this time by Frédéric Thiémé, who reduced all time signatures to either 2, 3, or 6/8.[77] The quarter note was to be used as the common denominator of music. He thought that Italian tempo indications, which were imprecise, should be replaced by a system of numbers, beginning with 1 for *largo* and continuing to 5 for *presto*. Intermediate speeds could be indicated by adding the word *vif* to the numbers, as in 1 *vif*, 2 *vif*, etc.

Reformers' projects are more likely to be taken seriously when there are only a few of them. The very number of these systems of reform in eighteenth-century France was an indication of their lack of practical success.

The proposed reforms of notation differ on the subject of whether or not note values in themselves indicate tempo. The view that they do follows a practice of notation established in the mensural system that was continued in the eighteenth century. Mattheson and Kirnberger agree with this view, as does the practice of J. S. Bach. However, there were enough uncertainties about the tempos indicated by notation that the necessity for tempo words remained. The more forward-looking reforms emphasized notation that showed metrical order divorced from tempo significance.

Additional Meanings of Time Signatures

The following summary shows some of the special associations of the most frequently used time signatures of the eighteenth century, as gleaned from the comments of theorists.

DUPLE METER SIGNS

The first signature mentioned in many theory books was C; it was derived from the mensuration sign "imperfect of the less" and indicated a duple meter. In the seventeenth century, diminution signs often indicated a change in the speed of the *tactus* instead of a change in the speed of notes in relation to the *tactus*. Consequently the precise meaning of C, ₵, Ɔ, and ₵ varied depending on the signs' relations to one another. In come cases ₵, in contrast to C, meant a 2 : 1 change of tempo, in others, merely a faster tempo not necessarily in the ratio of 2 : 1.

In the eighteenth century most theorists agreed that ₵ indicated a speed "somewhat faster" than C. Among those who advocated "somewhat faster" were Malcolm,[78] Turner,[79] Prelleur,[80] Maier,[81] David,[82] and Rameau in his English translation.[83] Grassineau quoted Malcolm on this subject, but did not acknowledge the quotation.[84] Kirnberger said that "allabreve" (₵, 2̸, or 2/2) was suitable for "church pieces, fugues, and elaborate choruses." It was considered "serious and emphatic, yet performed twice as fast as its note values indicate, unless *grave*, or *adagio* is added."[85]

Another interpretation of the difference between these signs—an interpretation that did not specify a time relationship—was that ₵ indicated a two-beat measure and C a four-beat measure. French writers made this distinction, among them Borin,[86] Démotz de la Salle,[87] and Corrette.[88]

Some writers maintained the 2 : 1 diminution ratio, among them Tans'ur,[89] John Stickney,[90] Brossard,[91] and Quantz.[92] The retorted C (Ɔ) was considered to double the tempo of C.

2

The meter sign 2 was regarded as an alternate to ₵ by the French and by Quantz.[93] David[94] considered ₵, 2, and 2/2 to be identical. Corrette said 2 was used in rigaudons, bransles, bourées, gaillardes, villageoises, cotillions, and gavottes, etc.;[95] Mattheson[96] and Maier[97] said that it was commonly used in the first part of overtures, gavottes, rigaudons, and entrées.

2/4

2/4 was sometimes considered to be the equivalent of ₵, and sometimes of retorted ₵; it was regarded as quicker than the other signs of duple meter.

Mattheson wrote that "it produces singing pieces almost by itself."[98] Corrette said that it was often used for the "reprise of overtures and it is much used by Italians in pieces marked Vivace, Allegro, Presto, and in ariettes. Composers presently use it for Andante and Adagio."[99] Lacassagne said that it was used in the rigaudon, bourée, gavotte, and tambourin, with a tempo range from *modéré* to *très vif*.[100] Quantz, who related his tempos to the pulse, said that in Allegro 2/4 or quick 6/8 time, there was one pulsation for every bar.[101] Kirnberger said that 2/4 has the same tempo as ¢ but is more playful and is performed much more lightly.[102]

Triple Meter Signs

Triple meter signs indicated definite tempos to some and vague ones to others. Tans'ur interpreted 3/2 as a proportion sign, which meant that three half notes should be equivalent to two of common time.[103] Triple meter signs that included the mensural C with the numerical fraction were sometimes still interpreted as proportion signs. On the other hand, Turner described "the *moods* in *Triple-time* [as] not at all denoting now, (though formerly they did) what is to be sung *slow* or *Fast*, as they do in *Common Time*."[104]

3/2

Mattheson wrote, "It is found in many pieces, particularly sad arias, in sonatas, adagios, sarabandes, and pieces which depend on the composer's fantasy, but it is not frequently used today."[105] Corrette said that this signature was seldom used by the French but frequently used by Italian composers for Sarabands and Adagios.[106] Tans'ur said that it was used mostly in church music and performed slower than the rule.[107] Kirnberger agreed that it was suitable for church pieces because of its ponderous and slow quality when the fastest notes are eighth notes. In the chamber style, sixteenth notes may be used in 3/2.[108]

3

Turner[109] objected to the use of this signature, but Grassineau[110] called it the same as C3/4 or 3/4. Démotz said it indicated "a measure of three beats (*Tems*) more or less fast. . . . each beat is a quarter note or its value."[111] Corrette said that it was used in "menuets, sarabandes, courantes, passacailles, chaconnes, and in the folies d'Espagne."[112] Grassineau said it was usually played *affectuoso* or *allegro*.[113]

3/4

Mattheson writes, "It is the most frequently used of all the triples and is applied to many pieces, mostly merry ones, of which menuets are the greater part."[114] Maier states: "The three quarter measure is the most used and it consists of three quarter notes which make up a whole measure. It is used especially in happy pieces." [115] Corrette said that it was used in the courantes of sonatas, [116] and Tans'ur said it was used mostly in anthems, menuets, etc. [117] Grassineau wrote: "When the character 3/4 is used, the air is to be played in a tender affecting manner, of a moderate movement, neither quick nor slow." [118] Kirnberger says that the *tempo giusto* of 3/4 is that of the menuet, and that its execution is much lighter than 3/2. It is therefore not much used in the church style but very often used in the chamber and theatrical styles. It can assume all degrees of tempo, from indications of *allegro* to that of *adagio*. It is "gentle and noble, particularly when containing mostly quarter notes." [119]

3/8

Mattheson wrote, "*Par affectation* (played more slowly and emotionally) this often takes the place of the preceding (3/4), and has become so favored that it is used in arias, with the addition of *adagio* or the like, even though it is properly used in the passepied, canarie and other hopping dances." [120] This statement is echoed by Maier. [121] Grassineau said, "This kind of triple is usually gay or animating," [122] but Tans'ur said, "This sort is mostly used for Minuets but is *Gently slow*." [123] Corrette wrote that it is "used in French music in passepieds and sometimes in the reprise of overtures. Italians use it in allegros, adagios, affectuosos, vivaces and ariettes. Look in the Italian operas of Handel, Bononcini, Pepusch, Scarlatti, Porpora and all the sonatas composed by our illustrious Frenchmen, where this meter is found. It is song-like and tasteful in sentimental pieces (*les Affetuoso*)." [124] Kirnberger wrote that it indicates the lively tempo of a passepied, performed in a light but not entirely playful manner. It is widely used in the chamber and theatrical styles. [125]

6/4

Mattheson said, "this is used for serious pieces, in particular the slow gigue that is called the loure," [126] a statement echoed by Maier. [127] According to Corrette, "French music uses this for loures, forlanes, and sometimes in the reprise of overtures; it is found very little in Italian music." [128] Lacassagne amplified this: "The loure is an *air grave* marked 6/4. It begins usually with a short eighth note that is the middle of the second beat. . . . The forlane is an *air modéré* marked with 6/4." [129] Grassineau said, "This movement is very proper for moving, tender expressions, though some use it in very hasty motions." [130] Tans'ur wrote, "The 6/4 has no meaning for Jiggs, unless for very slow ones." [131]

6/8

"6/8 is proper for gay, lively, animating strains," said Grassineau. [132] Mattheson wrote, "it is used most beautifully by composers today and is suitable for flowing melodic pieces as well as fresh and quick pieces." [133] Corrette adds:

"French music uses this for canaries, gigues and sometimes for the reprises of overtures. It is often found in sonatas and concertos."[134] According to Lacassagne, "The Gigue is an air more or less long, marked by 6/8, its tempo is very quick."[135] The 6/8 was "for moderate lively menuets or Dancing casts, of equal down and up, being both lively gentle Sicilian movements," according to Tans'ur.[136]

9/8

According to Corrette: "This is found very little in French music, but often enough in Italian music, such as gigues, allegros, prestos, and sometimes in adagios; see Vivaldi, etc."[137] Grassineau commented, "This is proper for brisk and gay pieces."[138] Tans'ur said that "9/8 and 12/8 are only for very brisk jiggs."[139] Kirnberger wrote that 9/8 meter is derived from and has the same tempo as 3/4, but the eighth notes are performed more lightly than in 3/4.[140]

12/8

"This is fit for gay and brisk movements. Sometimes the words *affetuoso* and *adagio* are placed to direct what the movement is to be; for itself 'tis naturally quick," said Grassineau.[141] Turner said this was appropriate in "very swift Movements, as jiggs, etc., but why it should be made use of in slow (sometimes very slow) movements I cannot conceive."[142] Mattheson commented at length on the use of this fast meter for slow pieces, in that it gave a feeling of gravity despite the usual quickness of eighth notes. He felt that using 12/8 for slow music, marked *grave* or *adagio,* was a sign of the general preference for slow music.[143]

By the end of the eighteenth century, time signatures in the form of numerical fractions replaced almost all mensural signs, even though C still held its place against the 4/4 sign that rationally should have replaced it. The more conservative notation of the eighteenth century retained the concept that notes had tempo significance in themselves. Tempo words were regarded as subsidiary indications of the speed of the music, and as modifiers of a "natural" tempo. Tempo words also suggested a composition's proper expressive quality. In more modern notation, tempo words gained an almost absolute significance. As this trend continued, time signatures indicated only metrical structure.

Some writers discussed conducting or time-beating patterns that depicted the measure as a single beat or a group of beats. As tempo influenced a musician's perception of the beat and indicated whether beats were simple or compound, it was essential to know the tempo in order to determine the metrical structure. The time signature alone, therefore, was often inadequate, and the additional information provided by a conducting pattern became critically important.

The fact that there were various classifications of time signatures does not indicate fundamental differences in notation. By the end of the eighteenth century, time signatures were defined in very nearly their present-day significance. In the nineteenth century, note values seem to have lost even more of their power to indicate tempos, and tempo words seem to have gained more importance. Until the creation of notation devised for partially improvised styles in the twentieth century, the time signatures and tempo words of the late eighteenth century continued to serve as the standard for musical notation.

III

⊘⤙⤚⊘

Rhythmopoeia: Quantitative Meters
in Poetry and Music

ANOTHER PERSPECTIVE on metrical organization is provided by *rhythmopoeia,* a study that translates quantitative poetic meters into their equivalents in music. *Rhythmopoeia* defined metrical units, unlike the *tactus,* which regulated the flow of music without regard for metrical groups. The "musical feet" of *rhythmopoeia,* equivalent to poetic feet, were symmetrical or asymmetrical and could be simply repeated or constantly varied to form a phrase.

Rhythmopoeia illustrated the effect of the quantitative meters of Greek and Latin to young scholars, but it was used also by theorists as a model of word-music relationship in modern languages. The differences between modern accentual language and ancient quantitative language made *rhythmopoeia* rather pedantic and impractical. However, the steps and metrical structures of dance rhythms could be compared to the metrical units of *rhythmopoeia.* The importance of *rhythmopoeia* waned when the musical measure became associated exclusively with accent in the second half of the eighteenth century.

"Musical Humanism" in the Sixteenth Century

C. F. Abdy Williams discusses Aristoxenus's definitions (ca. 330 B.C.) of three basic terms in Greek rhythmic theory: *rhythm, rhythmizomenon,* and *rhythmopoeia.*

> "We must imagine" he says, "two different natures, that of *rhythm* and that of the *rhythmizomenon,* having the same relations to one another as a plan has to the object that is planned." The *rhythmizomenon* is the raw material which is sub-

jected to rhythm; and there are three kinds of *rhythmizomenon,* namely, music, poetry, and dancing. Melody alone consists of a succession of intervals, without meaning. Only when it is subjected to *rhythm* does it take shape and form. Ordinary speech consists of a succession of accented and unaccented syllables in no definite order; when, however, these are subjected to *rhythm,* the speech becomes poetry. The steps of a person walking or running are continuous, but if they become ordered in some recognizable arrangement by rhythm, the dance arises. Intervals, speeds and steps are the three *rhythmizomena,* the respective materials to which rhythm is applied.

Rhythmopoeia is the art of applying *rhythm* to the *rhythmizomenon.* This art was carefully studied, and more attention was given to it in theory than is the case with us. It has to do, not only with the construction of the phrases, but of the measures themselves. . . . Aristoxenus calls the *rhythmopoeia* of the complete phrase, as opposed to that of the single measures, "continuous *rhythmopoeia.*" [1]

Medieval theorists used the words *rhythmopoeia* and *melopoeia* to indicate, in a general way, the rhythmic and melodic-harmonic elements of music. [2] Thus *rhythmopoeia* was a term that represented ancient scholarship in music theory. However, due to a growing consciousness of meter and its notation during the seventeenth century, the concept of *rhythmopoeia* was of renewed practical importance.

D. P. Walker uses the term "musical humanism" to refer to artistic experiments in the late sixteenth and early seventeenth centuries that were intended to re-create ancient musical theory and practice. [3] In 1507 Petrus Tritonius (Peter Treybenreif) set the *Odes* of Horace to music. Gustave Reese describes his setting as "in four parts, moving in block chords, the note values of the chords faithfully reflecting the longs and shorts of the text meters." [4] The settings were inspired by the humanist poet Konrad Celtes and were intended to help students learn the nineteen meters used in the Horatian odes and epodes. Similar settings of the same odes were later composed by Hofhaimer and Senfl. [5] In 1556, Statius Olthof set metrical Latin psalm paraphrases to music that faithfully reflected the longs and shorts of Horatian meters. [6]

The didactic nature of German musical humanism is well illustrated by these many settings. They were inspired by and became a part of the Latin dramas performed in German schools throughout the sixteenth century and into the seventeenth century. [7] Athanasius Kircher may have depended upon this tradition for his compendium of musical equivalents of Greek and Latin poetic feet published in the *Musurgia Universalis* of 1650. [8] However, it seems that the development of *rhythmopoeia* as a theory of meter organization in the seventeenth century was not German but French.

According to D. P. Walker's studies of *musique mesurée à l'antique,* most humanistically inspired music of the sixteenth century attempted to unite the arts of poetry and music. To this impulse we owe the invention of opera by the Florentine Camerata as well as the *chansons mesurée à l'antique* of Claude le Jeune, Maudit, and du Caurroy. Italian writers such as Doni and Galilei were

interested in the humanist experiments that led to opera but were not interested
in the metrical theories of *rhythmopoeia*. It was in France that the development
of *rhythmopoeia* took on its later form, as a consequence of the particular
rhythmic theories of poets, musicians, and writers involved with *musique
mesurée*. Marin Mersenne was the chief theorist of *musique mesurée,* even
though his *Harmonie Universelle* was published long after the height of crea-
tive activity by poets and musicians.[9]

"The desire to resuscitate the ethical quality of music is the driving force
behind the theory and practice of the more enthusiastic class of humanist."[10]
Walker cites Mersenne's early work as typical of this group, although some
cooling of enthusiasm can be observed in his later work.[11] A belief in a musical
ethos led to the dominance of the text over the music, the "reintroduction of
the practical use of the chromatic and enharmonic genera, . . . generally reforming intonation, and . . . reviving the proper use of the modes."[12]

Humanist composers subordinated music to the text in order to achieve
"the vivid expression of the sense of the text; the preservation of its rhythm;
and the preservation of its audibility."[13] Walker comments on the second of
these objectives: "Quite apart from anything to do with the effects, this would
have been part of any musical humanist's beliefs, since his classical authorities,
with however some important exceptions, unmistakably implied that musical
and poetic rhythm were one and the same thing."[14] Walker shows that although there was agreement as to the importance of preserving the rhythm of
the text, there was disagreement on how this was to be done. Two theories,
both based on classical authority, were expressed, one by Galilei and Tyard, the
other by Salinas and Mersenne.[15] The Galilei-Tyard method used only two note
values, long and short, in a 2 : 1 proportion. Mersenne, however, is quoted as
stating:

> [Compositeurs] Ne sont pas obliges de faire toutes les syllables longues d'une
> mesme longeur, car ils peuuent donner le temps d'vne crochue aux syllables longues,
> pouruue que dans une mesme mesure ou diction, ils vsent des notes d'vn moindre
> temps pour les syllables briefues.[16]

> [Composers] are not obliged to make all long syllables the same length, as
> they can give even as little as the duration of an eighth note to long syllables pro-
> vided that in the same meter or speech they use notes of smaller length for short
> syllables.

Baif and de Courville, who began to write *vers et musique mesurées à
l'antique* about 1567, attempted to modify Greek and Latin meters to suit the
French language. "Their meter was meant to be quantitative, but owing to the
nature of the French language this was impossible. They did, however, come
near to achieving an accentual version of the metrical patterns of Greek and
Latin verse."[17] The discrepancy between the accentual languages of the seven-

teenth century and the quantitative language of the ancients lent a quality of artificiality to all subsequent attempts to create a union of poetry and music through *rhythmopoeia*.

Seventeenth- and Eighteenth-Century Discussions of Rhythmopoeia

The long and short syllables of quantitative Greek and Latin poetic feet were translated more or less directly into music by either the Galilei-Tyard method or by the less strict principles of Mersenne and Salinas. Lists of these translations were made in the seventeenth century, as in Kircher's *Musurgia Universalis,* and every conceivable poetic foot was illustrated by a word and its musical equivalent. Quantitative poetic meters could then be translated easily into their precise musical form by using these catalogs of "musical feet."

Rhythmopoeia was applied to instrumental music not to insure fidelity of music to poetic meter but to stimulate composers to greater variety as well as to organize metrical units in categories. Mersenne took the view that "musical feet" were already found in common musical practice and only needed to be recognized by musicians:

> Encore que les mouuemens qui seruent aux Airs et aux dances, appartiennent à la Rhythmique dont nous n'auons pas encore parlé, neantmoins il a esté necessaire d'en traiter icy, afin de faire comprendre les differentes especes des Airs et des chants dont vsent les François: mais il est si aysé d'entendre tout ce qui concerne ces mouuemens, qu'il n'est pas necessaire d'en faire vn liure particulier, puis que les plus excellens pieds metriques, qui ont donné le nom & la naissance à la Rhythmique des Grecs, sont pratiquez dans les airs de Balet, dans les chansons à dancer et dans toutes les autres actions qui servent aux recréations publiques ou particuliers, comme l'on aduoüera quand on aura reduit les pieds qui suiuent aux airs que l'on récite, ou que l'on ioüe sur les Violons, sur le Luth, sur la Guiterre et sur les autres instrumens.
>
> Or ces pieds, peuuent estre appellez mouuemens afin de s'accommoder à la maniere de parler de nos Practiciens, & compositeurs d'airs; c'est pourquoy ie me seruirez désormais de ce terme, pour ioindre la Théorie a la Pratique.[18]

Since the rhythms that make up airs and dances belong to the theory of rhythm of which we have not yet spoken, it was necessary to deal with them here in order to teach the different kinds of airs and melodies used by the French. But it is so easy to understand everything concerning rhythms, that it isn't necessary to write a separate book about them here. The most excellent metrical feet, which have given the name and birth to Greek theory of rhythm, are already in use in the *airs de Balets,* dance melodies, and all other occasions which serve as private or public amusements. This will be seen by an analysis of the feet that are used in airs that are sung or that are played on violins, the lute, guitar, and other instruments.

Consequently these feet may be called rhythms in order to accommodate ourselves to the manner of speech of performers and composers of airs. This is why I use this term from now on, in order to join theory with practice.

He went on to advocate the use of *rhythmopoeia* by "composers of bransles":

> Mais s'ils prennent la peine de mettre deuant eux les pieds ou mouuemens tant simples que diminuez les Grecs et des Latins, que nous auons expliquez cy-deuant, afin de choisir ceux qui leur agreeront dauantage pour les employer à leurs compositions, ils les enrichiront beaucoup plus aisément, & en feront vne plus grande multitude qu'à l'ordinaire, sans se troubler en nulle maniére.[19]

> If they would take the trouble to set before themselves the very simple feet and rhythms that the Greeks and Latins varied and ornamented, explained above, in order to choose those most useful to them in their compositions, they would enrich their work much more easily, and use a greater number of rhythms than ordinarily is done, all without the least trouble at all.

Mersenne delighted in the investigation of rational possibilities, and his discussion of *rhythmopoeia* was an attempt to widen the horizons of the composers of his day, not to reduce music to narrow rules of practice. There are many poetic feet that may be introduced in duple and triple measures (a long syllable is indicated by -, a short syllable by v):

> Il faut seulement remarquer que la *mesure binaire,* composée de deux temps égaux, se rapporte aux Pyrriches [v v], aux spondées [- -], aux dactyles [- v v], & aux Anapestes [v v -], &c. qui sont composez de 2 ou de 4 temps, comme la mesure ternaire au Tribrache [v v v], à l'Iambe [v -], au Trochée [- v], & à tous les autres pieds composez de 3, 6 ou de 12 temps. Mais les autres pieds contiennent plusieurs autres sortes de mesures, qu'il est aisé de mettre en pratique, par exemple, le Bacchien [v - -] contient 5 temps, & s'exprime auec 5 notes noires, lors qu'il est dissous, ou auec deux notes minimes, & vne noire: le Paeon [- v v v] a semblablement 5 temps, car il est composée d'vn Iambe et d'vn Trochée, comme le Choriambe [- v v -]. Quant aux Epitrites [v - - -], ils sont composez de 7. temps, de sorte qu'ils peuuent se rapporter aux termes de la raison sesquitierce, que fait le Diatessaron parce qu'il faut chanter 4 notes en frappant & 3. en leuant, ou au contraire, 3. en frappant & 4. en leuant: comme les Paeons ressemblent en quelque façon au Diapente, parce qu'il faut chanter trois notes en baissant, & deux en leuant, ou au contraire: c'est ce que l'on doit proprement appeler mouuement & mesure *sesquialtère* ou *hemiole:* car quant aux trochées & ïambes, ils forment plustost vne mesure double semblable a l'Octave qu'vne mesure ternaire, puis que 2. bat contre vn: comme le spondée forme vne mesure égale, plustost que binaire, afin qu'elle se raporte à l'vnisson.[20]

> It is only necessary to note that the two-part measure composed of two equal beats agrees with pyrrhic [v v], spondaic [- -], dactylic [- v v], and anapestic [v v -] feet, etc. which are composed of two or four beats. The three-part measure agrees with tribrachic [v v v], iambic [v -], trochaic [- v] feet, and all others composed of three, six or twelve beats. But other feet contain many other kinds of meters that are easy to put into practice. For example the bacchic [v - -] foot has five beats, and is expressed by five quarter notes when it is broken up, or with two half notes and one quarter. The paeon [- v v v] also has five beats as it is made up of one iambic and one trochaic foot, like the choriambic foot [- v v -]. As for the epitritic feet

[v - - -], they are composed of seven beats so that they agree with the sesquitertia proportion, which makes the diatessaron or [interval of the] fourth, because four notes are sung on the downstroke and three on the up. In this way the paeons are like the [interval of the] fifth, because three notes are sung on the downstroke and two on the upstroke, or vice versa. It is properly called the measure and rhythm of sesquialtera, or hemiolia. As for trochaic and iambic feet, they often make a ternary measure in 2:1 proportion, comparable to the octave because the beats are as 2 to 1. The spondaic foot makes an equal measure rather than a binary measure, because it is comparable to the unison.

Mersenne gives a number of examples of metrical feet and their musical equivalents (Ex. 3.1).[21]

EX. 3.1

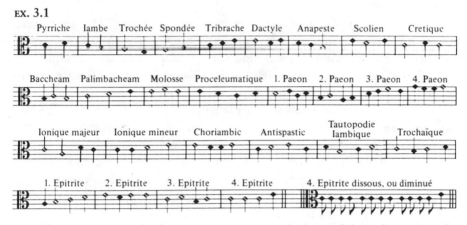

The concept of *rhythmopoeia* was particularly useful in discussing the meter of dance music because of its consistent metrical structure. For Mersenne, *rhythmopoeia* provided a convenient organizational system that clarified measure-like patterns in mensural notation. A *bransle gay* in *Harmonie Universelle* consisted of repetitions of the "ionic minor" foot, v v - - (Ex. 3.2).[22]

EX. 3.2

The short and long elements of each musical foot seem to represent the pulses on which the dancers place their feet, and therefore they mark the underlying metrical structure of the dance music. The melody is sufficiently decorated that the dance meter may not be evident without the clarification of *rhythmopoeia*.

Wolfgang Caspar Printz uses dances by Lully and D. C. Horn to illustrate musical feet. Johann Mattheson attempts to prove "with clear, comprehensible, and applicable examples that it is possible by means of mere sound-feet and their variation . . . to make dances from church songs and to make chorales from dances."[23] Example 3.3 is a small portion of one of Mattheson's examples.

EX. 3.3

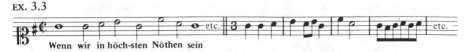

Wenn wir in höch-sten Nöthen sein

Illustrating the continued association of *rhythmopoeia* and dance rhythm later in the century, Joseph Riepel entitles a book about the composition of dance forms *Anfangsgrunde zur musikalischen Setz-kunst . . . De Rhythmopoeia oder von der Tactordnung* (Frankfurt, 1752), even though he does not discuss musical equivalents of ancient meters.

Jean Gerard Lustig discusses *rhythmopoeia* and gives a list of thirty different feet with musical examples. His list is similar to Mattheson's but differs in a few minor points.[24]

The most thorough discussions of *rhythmopoeia* after Mersenne were written by Johann Mattheson and Wolfgang Caspar Printz. Mattheson began his discussion of rhythmic organization with *rhythmopoeia* and identifies the "sound-foot" as the elementary musical unit to be found at the base of any hierarchy of metrical relationships.[25]

He distinguishes between the "arithmetic content," which is the sound-foot (*rhythmi*) derived from the poetic meter, and the "geometric content," the succession of sound-feet, either repeated or in combination with other sound-feet. In describing the menuet each measure is considered to be an individual sound-foot. The geometric content of the menuet is four, that is, four sound-feet are grouped in a phrase, matching the choreographic structure of the dance. Different sound-feet may be mixed together in a phrase.[26]

Mattheson gives examples of twenty-six feet in his chapter on *rhythmopoeia,* which are illustrated in the appendix. His musical equivalents of poetic feet use relatively longer notes for long syllables (-) and shorter ones for the short syllables (v). Mattheson does not attempt to cover all possibilities or all possible variants:

> Es können alle diese Rhythmi noch auf verschiedene andre Arten ausgedruckt werden; so dass unsre beygefügte Noten die Sache bey wietem nicht erschöpffen: denn die Länge und Kürze des Klanges hat viel Stuffen in der Ton-Kunst, davon die Dicht-Kunst nichts weiss, zu welchen noch mehr Veränderung kommt, von der mannigfältigen Tact-Arten, &c.[27]

> All these sound-feet can be expressed in different ways, so that our musical examples have not by any means exhausted the possibilities. The length and shortness of sounds has many degrees in music, of which poetry knows nothing, and more variety yet comes from the many time signatures.

Rhythmopoeia requires some relaxation of the rules of melody given elsewhere in Mattheson's theoretical discussions. According to the "fifth rule of clarity in the melody," [28] the *caesura,* or small pause at the end of a phrase, could occur only on the (half-note) upbeat or (half-note) downbeat in duple meter, never on the second or fourth quarter of the bar. In triple meter this division could fall only on the downbeat pulse, or first quarter note, not on the second or third quarter notes. All of these caesura points are "intrinsically long" notes, and for this purpose "short" or "bad" notes will not serve. However:

> Eine kleine Ausnahm ist hiebey zu machen nöthig, dass nehmlich in einegen choraischen und melismatischen Dingen auch bisweilen, bey ungeraden Täcten, das letze Gleid gewisser maassen zum Abschnitt dienen muss: wenn eine sonderliche Gleichförmigkeit darin gesucht und durchgehends so fortgeführet wird. Solches geschiehet aber mit Fleiss, und nicht von ungefehr, oder aus Unwissenheit der Regel [Ex. 3.4].[29]

> A small exception must be made here in choraic [Trochaic - v] or melismatic [rhythms broken up by ornamental smaller notes] pieces. Sometimes the last quarter in 3/4 must be used for the pause, when a particular uniformity is sought with that which has occured before. This happens on purpose and not by accident or through ignorance of the rule [Ex. 3.4].

EX. 3.4

In looking through Mattheson's own compilation of *rhythmi*, one finds a number of other examples of sound-feet that seem to have caused a similar relaxation of the rule.

There is another difficulty for Mattheson in reconciling *rhythmopoeia* to measure organization. "Das Haupt-Wesen des Tacts kömmt einmahl für allemahl darauf an, dass eine jede Mensur, ein jeder Abschnitt der Zeit-Maasse nur zween Theile und nicht mehr habe" (The principal requirement of the *tactus,* once and for all, is that each measure, each segment of time measurement, has only two parts, no more).[30] These parts are the upbeat and downbeat, or *arsis* and *thesis*.[31] *Arsis* and *thesis* are of equal duration in duple measures and unequal (2:1) duration in triple measures. Some metrical feet (*rhythmi*) include both *arsis* and *thesis,* some only *arsis* or *thesis,* and some more than one of each. Mattheson never thoroughly explains how measures are to be adjusted to *rhythmopoeia;* his examples in the chapter on *rhythmopoeia* seem to ignore measure organization, but elsewhere in *Der vollkommene Capellmeister* his examples abide by *arsis-thesis* organization.

Wolfgang Caspar Printz's Latin-studded phrases project a more antiquarian outlook than Mattheson's, but in several important respects his treatment of *rhythmopoeia* is more forward-looking. The relationship of *rhythmopoeia* to the measure is resolved in Printz's discussion of sound-feet, by reconciling long and short quantity with "intrinsically long" and "intrinsically short" notes, a topic that will be fully discussed in chapter four.[32]

Printz restricts the number of feet to six; all other patterns are considered variants or ornamentations of these. These six, the iamb (v -), trochee (- v), enantius (v - - or v - v), spondee (- - -), and the "syncopaticus," are expressed by notes of longer or shorter duration and also by notes of the same duration that are considered to be "intrinsically long" or "intrinsically short," as determined by the place of the note within the measure.

Mattheson's musical equivalent of the iambic foot (v -) is a measure of ³⁄₄ ♩♩ |♩♩ |♩♩. One is to consider the duration of the notes regardless of their position in the measure. According to Printz, the first quarter note of a 3/4 measure, coinciding with the *thesis,* is intrinsically long, despite being shorter in actual duration than the half note on beats two and three, on the *arsis.* Therefore Printz's musical equivalent of the iambic foot places the short syllable of the iamb on the *arsis,* which is intrinsically short, and the long syllable of the iamb on the *thesis,* which is intrinsically long. Provided the relationship of the notes to the metrical structure is right, notes of either equal or unequal duration will express the iambic foot (Ex. 3.5).

EX. 3.5

Printz suggested seven techniques by which the six basic sound-feet are varied and ornamented. These are: *incitati* (the addition of a dot to long notes), *dilatario* (delay), *contractio* (abridgment), *commutatio* (alteration), *decurtatio* (shortening, by leaving out a note or part of a note), *prolongatio* (increasing the duration of a note), and *expletio* (adding a note).[33]

In vocal music, practice should always be guided by the requirements of setting texts, but in instrumental music, Printz warns that care must be taken not to vary the musical foot to the point that the original is unrecognizable.

The various sound-feet are single units of meter, but metrical succession combines them by repetition or by mixing several different feet together. Here is Printz's example of the *dichroni contrario-dactylici:* the *contrarius* or *enantius* is v - or v - v, and dactyl is - v v. "Dichronum" is the *numerum sectionalis,* signifying that the measures are grouped two by two. Example 3.6 is a sarabande by Lully.

EX. 3.6

Although this is Printz's own example, it should be noted that the v - or v - v rhythm is incorrectly realized according to his own rules of *quantitas intrinseca.* The first notes of the first, third, and fifth bars are short according to *rhythmopoeia,* but in the 3/4 measure these beats are long, according to *quantitas intrinseca.* Apparently the irrational nature of *rhythmopoeia* could not be

entirely adjusted to the rationality of *quantitas intrinseca,* even by such a
learned theorist.

Johann Adolf Scheibe followed Printz's example in restricting the number
of sound-feet, but he reduced the number to three—iambic, trochaic, and dactylic.[34] These were interpreted in relation to an appropriate consideration of
quantitas intrinseca. He and C. G. Schröter,[35] a follower of Mattheson, en-
gaged in a vituperative quarrel over theories of *rhythmopoeia.* It is difficult to
account for the heat of the argument except that, then as now, scholars took
such matters very much to heart.

Writers after Printz and Mattheson became much less interested in *rhythmopoeia.* Scheibe's short account is mainly concerned with using the ideas of
rhythmopoeia in setting German verses to music.

Rhythmopoeia *and Emotion*

It was a humanist belief that *ethos, Affekt,* or emotion (the seventeenth-century
English word for which was "passion") was conveyed by the meters of *rhythmopoeia.* Various attempts were made by many theorists to describe the emotional quality linked with particular metrical feet.

Mersenne advises:

> Le mouuement égal est propre pour les esprits qui ayment la tranquilité & la
> paix, & qui sont amis du repos & de la solitude, si l'on veut induire à cette
> affection, ou si l'on a veut entretenir, il faut vser du mode Dorien des anciens, et de
> leur Hesycastique, auec le mouuement spondaïque, qui admet tous les pieds dont
> le baisser est égal au leuer. . . . Or ce mouuement égal est appellé *mesure binaire*
> par les compositeurs ordinaires, comme i'ai déia remarquez: mais lors que l'on
> veut faire changer cette affection pour entrer dans vne passion plus turbulente, il
> faut vser du mode Phyrgien & d'vn mouuement double, & des pieds, dont le
> baisser ou le *thesis* est double du leuer ou de l'*arsis,* ou au contraire, & particu-
> lierement du mouvement ïambique, dont les Poëtes se seruent dans leurs Tragedies.[36]

> Because equal rhythm is proper to minds that love tranquility and peace and
> those that are friends of repose and solitude, if you wish to induce this affection or
> entertain it, the dorian mode and the hesychastic music[37] of the ancients must be
> employed with the spondaic rhythm (- -), which allows the use of all feet in which
> the downbeat is equal to the upbeat. Consequently equal rhythm is called binary
> measure by most composers, as I have said. When you wish to make this affection
> change in order to enter into a more turbulent passion, the phrygian mode must be
> used with a triple rhythm, with feet in which the downbeat or *thesis* is twice as
> long as the upbeat or *arsis,* or vice versa, particularly with the iambic rhythm (v -)
> that is used by poets in their tragedies.

This statement does not begin to distinguish the emotional power of each
specific foot, and Mersenne admits:

Certes il est difficile de treuuer la raison de ces différents effets des pieds metriques, ou des mouuemens différents, & de déterminer précisément à quoy chaque pied ou vers est propre, attendu particulierement que tous les Poëtes vsent indifférément de toutes sortes de vers pour representer, ou pour exciter toutes sortes de passions & d'affections, encore qu'ils essayent de mettre plusieurs syllables briefues de suite pour exprimer les choses vistes et légères.[38]

It is difficult to find the reason for the different affects of metrical feet or different rhythms and to determine precisely why each foot or verse is characteristic, particularly because poets use all sorts of verse indiscriminately to represent or to excite all sorts of passions and affections, although they try to put many short syllables together to express that which is quick and light.

Isaac Vossius, a Dutch scholar who taught in England, eloquently expresses the emotional power of the various rhythms; he was convinced of their power to move the listener and induce the appropriate affect. He does not give musical examples.

Ut afficiantur animus, necesse est ut sonus aliquid aut indicet aut significet quod mente & intellectu comprehendere possimus. Si enim significationis expers fuerit sonus, jam quoque nullos poterit ciere affectus cum a perceptione procedat voluptas, nec amare aut odisse possimus, id quod quale sit ignoramus. Si itaque essicere velimus, ut non inanis sit sonus, allaborandum imprimis, ut cantus iis animetur motibus, qui figuras & imagines rerum, quas cantu exprimere & imitare velimus, in se contineant, hoc enim se assecuti fuerimus, minime erit difficile ducere affectus quocunque libuerit, & imperium exercere in animos. Ut vero istiumodi figurae cantui insint, reducendi omniuo sunt pedes musici quibis omnium motuum genera ita copiose continentur ut nullus omnino concipi possit affectus, cujus figuram non exhibeant quam exactissime. Ut leves & volubiles explicentur motus, cujusmodi sunt saltus Satyrorum, aptus est pyrrichius & tribrachys. Graves & tardos exprimit spondaeus coque gravior molossus. Quae mollia & tenera sunt exhibebit trochaeus & aliquando amphibrachys, cum & ipse fractum & effiminatum habeat incessum. Vehemens & iracundus est iambus, ejusdemque fere naturae anapestus cum bellicos & concitatos imitetur motus. Si quod hilare & jucundum sit explicare velimus, advocandi sunt dactyli, qui quales tripudiantium esse solent exhibebunt motus. Durum & refractarium si quid sit, opportune succurret antispastus. Si furorum & insaniam inducentibus numeris opus habeamus, praesto erit non anapaestus tantum, sed & illo potentior paeon quartus. [Denique si quotquot vel simplices vel compositi sunt consideremus pedes, omnibus pecculiarem vim & efficaciam inesse. . . .] Haec ratio, hic modus, haec denique antiquae musicae apud Graecos & Romanos forma fuit & figura, caque quamdin florint, tamdin florint etiam virtus illa exitandis & sopiendis apta affectibus.[39]

That the soul may be affected, it is necessary that the Sound should imply, or bring before us, something which we can comprehend. That Sounds, therefore, may have their full Effect, the Melody must be animated by such Movements, as contain in themselves the *Representations* or *Images* of those things which we mean to *express* or *imitate* by Song. And this if we can do, we may be sure to command the Passions of the Soul. But that we may indeed catch and call for these

Images, we must employ that Variety of Musical *Feet,* in which are so fully contained all the several kinds of *Movements,* that no Affection can be conceived, which they do not most exactly express. For the Expression of light and voluble Motions, as of the Dances of *Satyrs,* the *Pyrrhichius* and *Tribrachys* are proper: The *grave* and *slow* are expressed by the *Spondee* and *Molossus:* Whatever is soft and tender, The *Trochee,* and sometimes the *Amphibrachys* will describe; which itself moves with a broken and effeminate pace. The *Iambic* is fierce and *vehement;* and the *Anapest* nearly of the same Nature, as it imitates violent and warlike Motions. If we mean to express what is *cheerful* and *joyous,* we must employ the *Dactyl,* whose Movements are of a correspondent Nature. Whatever is *hard* and *rugged,* the *Antispast* will happily describe. If we require numbers that may express *Fury* and *Madness,* not only the *Anapest* is at Hand, but, what is still more powerful, the *Paeon quartus*—of these various Measures, artificially combined, did the ancient *Greek* and *Roman* Music consist: And while this flourished, so long did Music maintain its Empire over the Passions.

Mattheson refers to Vossius's ideas on the passions and affections of rhythmic patterns, but calls him "Gerhard Johann Voss," which arouses our suspicion that he has not read the book. The emotional affect of musical forms and figures is discussed in *Der vollkommene Capellmeister;*[40] each dance described is assigned a specific affect. Of the twenty-six "sound-feet" that he defines, Mattheson discusses emotional affects for only eleven. Affects are attributed to rhythms by virtue of the authority of classical authors, although in a few instances Mattheson seems to rely on his own imagination. The spondee (- -) and molossus (- - -) are considered to be heavy and serious and expressive of difficulty or weariness; the dactyl "is a very common rhythm which gives music an earnest or joking melody according to how the tempo is regulated." The bacchius (v - -) "takes its name from Bacchus, the wine-god, because this rhythm has something hobbling or staggering in it; the victims of Bacchus themselves tend to use it."[41]

Anecdotes derived from ancient authority characterize some sound-feet, and etymological meanings characterize others. "The anapest takes its name from certain mocking and satyrical poetry . . . in joyous and unusual melodies it is more effective than the dactyl." "The trochee or choraeus (- v) . . . takes its first name from running and its second from dancing and singing. In the melodic sense, it does not express much hardness and sarcasm." "The paeon is derived from παηων, hymnus, because it is dedicated to singing praises. It serves us in overtures and introductions." The pyrrhic foot is derived from the dance of soldiers, the proceleusmaticus (v v v v) indicates the "imperative, encouraging cry of sailors, *clamoren hortatorium nautarum.*" "Amphimacer is named from battles and fights because it has been used with warlike instruments and it is suitable to such instruments (- v -)." "Ionicus is known from the province of Ionia and is a sound-foot suitable for dances."[42] The rest of his *rhythmi* are cited without any description of affect.

The Decline of Rhythmopoeia

The decline of *rhythmopoeia* as a forceful idea can be seen in Jean-Jacques Rousseau's *Dictionnaire de musique* in his article on *rhythms,* where it is treated as something of antiquarian interest. Rousseau sees the discrepancy between quantitative Greek and Latin meters and accentual modern French, but instead of seeking a way to reconcile these differences, as everyone else concerned with *rhythmopoeia* had done, he is content to point out their existence.[43]

Rousseau's explanation of *rhythmopoeia* is clear, and he agrees with Printz about the need to restrict the number of feet, but he includes the more unusual feet that were advocated by Mersenne. However, Rousseau's view of *rhythmopoeia* is more impractical and less useful than other accounts, despite being more reasonable. He does not speculate about the emotional associations of metric patterns.

> Il se divisoit, ainsi qu'eux, en deux temps, l'un frappé, l'autre levé; l'on en comptoit trois genres, même quatre, et plus, selon les divers rapports de ces temps; ces genres étoient l'*égal,* qu'ils appeloient aussi dactylique, où le *rhythme* étoit divisé en deux temps égaux; *double,* trochaïque ou ïambique, dans lequel la durée de l'un des deux temps étoit double de celle de l'autre; le *sesqui-altère,* qu'ils appeloient aussi *péonique,* dont la durée de l'un des deux temps étoit à celle de l'autre en rapport de 3 à 2; et enfin l'*épitrite,* moins usité, où le rapport des deux temps étoit de 3 a 4.[44]

> They [the feet] were divided, as with us, in two parts; one downstroke the other upstroke, and there were three varieties, perhaps even four or more, according to the different combinations of these pulses. These varieties were the duple which they called dactylic and in which the rhythm was divided in two equal parts; the triple, trochaic, or iambic, in which the duration of one of the two parts was double that of the other; the *sesquialtera* which they also called peonic, in which the duration of the two parts was in the proportion of 3 to 2; and finally the *epitrite,* less used, in which the proportion of the two parts was 3 to 4.

The combination of various feet could be of three different sorts:

> Le *rhythme* pouvoit être toujours uniforme, c'est-a-dire se battre à deux temps toujours égaux, comme dans les vers hexamètres, pentamètres, adoniens anapestiques, etc.; ou toujours inégaux, comme dans les vers purs ïambiques, ou diversifié, c'est-a-dire mêlé de pieds égaux et d'inégaux, comme dans les scazons, les choraïmbiques, etc.[45]

> Rhythm can be always duple, that is, the beat can be given always by two equal strokes, as in hexameters, pentameters, adonians, anapests, etc.; or it can be always triple, as in purely iambic verse; or be diversified, that is, mixed together duple and triple feet as with scazons, choriambs, etc.

Rousseau quotes Vossius's opinions:

Vossius, dans son livre *de poëmatum Cantu, et Viribus rhythmi*, relève beaucoup le *rhythme* ancien; et il lui attribue toute la force de l'ancienne musique: il dit qu'un *rhythme* détaché comme le nôtre, qui ne représente aucune image des choses, ne peut avoir aucun effet, et que anciens nombres poétiques n'avoit été inventés que pour cette fin que nous négligeons; il ajoute que la langage et la poésie modernes sont peu propres pour la musique, et que nous n'aurons jamais de bonne musique vocale jusqu'à ce que nous réformions notre langage, et que nous lui donnions, à l'exemple des anciens, la quantité et les pieds mesurés, en proscrivant pour jamais l'invention barbare de la rime.[46]

Vossius reconsiders ancient rhythm in his *de poëmatum Cantu, et Viribus rhythmi;* he attributes to it the entire power of ancient music. He says that rhythm that is detached as ours is, that represents no image of anything, can have no meaning. The variety of ancient poetic meters was invented only for this goal which we neglect. He adds that modern language and poetry are little suited to music and that we will never have good vocal music until we reform our language, on the example of the ancients, and give it quantitative poetic feet while forever proscribing the barbarous invention of rhyme.

Rhythmopoeia was often considered only in relation to vocal music by writers in the latter part of the eighteenth century, and it lost much of its interest as a theory of meter. It became instead a method of prosody.

Associations of emotional affect with the sound-feet of *rhythmopoeia* had been based on respect for classical authority. In Rousseau's writing, respect for authority diminished considerably and individual intuition became the guide.

Mais d'où vient l'impression que font sur nous la mesure et la cadence? Quel est le principe par lequel ces retours, tantôt égaux et tantôt variés affectent nos âmes, et peuvent y porter le sentiment des passions? Demandez-le au métaphysicien: tout ce que nous pouvons dire ici est que, comme la mélodie tire son caractère des accents de la langue, le *rhythme* tire le sien du charactère de la prosodie, et alors il agit comme image de la parole: à quoi nous ajouterons que certaines passions ont dans la nature un caractère *rhythmique* aussi-bien qu'un caractère melodieux, absolu, et indépendant de la langue; comme la tristesse, qui marche par temps égaux et lents, de même que par tons remises et bas; la joie par temps sautillants et vites, de même que par tons aigües et intenses; d'où je présume qu'on pourroit observer dans toutes les autres passions un caractère propre, mais plus difficile à saisir, à cause que la plupart de ces autres passions étant composées, participent plus ou moins tant des précédentes que l'une de l'autre.[47]

But what causes the impression that is made on us by meter and cadences? What is the principle by which those repetitions, sometimes unchanged, sometimes varied, affect our souls and carry the passions? Ask the metaphysicians; all we can say here is that as melody draws its character from language accents, rhythm draws its essence from the nature of prosody and then acts as an image of the word. To this we may add that certain passions have a rhythmic as well as a melodious character that is absolute and independent of the language. Sadness, for example, moves in equal slow beats, with hesitant low notes. Joy moves with jumping quick beats, with high intense notes. From this I presume that one should be able to observe an individual character in all of the other passions, though this is difficult to do, because most of the others, being compounds, have more or less in common with the preceding passions as well as with one another.

From Descartes's *Les passions de l'âme,* French aestheticians of the eighteenth century inherited the belief that every emotion had an observable character and that it could be expressed in an artistic work. The conventions based on this belief seem to have been well established. Humanist artists and scholars employed different conventions but shared the belief that emotional character could be conveyed by artistic devices.

In subsequent writings, this rational approach based on observation rather than authority produced only passing mention of *rhythmopoeia,* or no mention at all.[48] Metrical feet, or the terms "spondaic" and "iambic," were used, but without conviction. *Rhythmopoeia* was reduced to the following account by the early nineteenth-century English writer, John Callcott:

> A small portion of Melody, with one principal Accent, including the value of a Measure, is termed in this work a *Musical Foot.*
> The knowledge of this Rhythmic subdivision of Melody is of great importance in practical music; as the Singer must not take breath, not the Performer on Keyed Instruments separate the Notes, in the Middle of a Foot.
> It has been usual with some Authors (Printz, Sat. Comp. P. III, p. 100; Mattheson, Vollkom. Capel. Meister, p. 164.) to apply the names of the ancient poetical Feet to corresponding musical passages; but the difference between ancient and modern Quantity and Accent, leaves a doubt concerning the propriety of using the terms of Grecian Rhythm.[49]

Callcott then went on to illustrate the setting of English metrical feet. A few pages later he wrote: "As a Musical Foot is equal in value to a Measure, although it differs in Accent, on account of the place of the Bar; so in the compound Measures the Feet are double, and may be resolved into two by dividing the Measure."[50]

"Accent" superseded all of the subtle distinctions of *rhythmopoeia.* Needless to say, no hint of the "doctrine of affections" is found in Dr. Callcott's book.

Dr. Burney wrote what might be regarded as the epitaph of *rhythmopoeia:*

> As to simplicity in music, there are degrees of it, which border upon dryness, rusticity, and vulgarity; and these, it is the business of every composer to avoid. However, some who call themselves lovers of simplicity, would reduce music to the same metrical laws as poetry, and make long and short syllables determine melody; which would be neither suffering more than one sound to be given to one syllable, nor a longer or shorter duration to that sound, than the poetical rhythmus requires; but in this case, what would vocal music be but a mere *Recitative* with which every one is tired and disgusted! Mankind will certainly judge of their own pleasures; and it is natural to suppose, that when a new style of composition or

performance *generally* prevails among the refined part of them, that it has something more captivating in it than that which they quitted. However, caprice, vanity and a fondness for singularity, on one side, and obstinacy, pride, and prejudice, on the other, will always make it difficult to reconcile different sects, or to draw a line between truth and falsehood.[51]

The chief problem in theories of *rhythmopoeia* was the relationship of measures, with their time signatures and regular bar lines, to the various and changing phrases made up of "musical feet." In Mattheson's theory, the measure and time signature were secondary to and supplementary to *rhythmopoeia*. Bar lines were ignored when they conflicted with "musical feet." Printz's theories of *rhythmopoeia* and the measure attempted to reconcile the two ideas by restricting the former. The inconsistencies in his explanation and his examples show, perhaps, that the two concepts cannot be reconciled, in relation either to accentual language or to musical practice.

Rhythmopoeia was a curious and rather irrational topic to explore in the Age of Reason. There were conflicting explanations regarding its nature, and we cannot gauge its influence on musical composition. However, it is a concept of meter that unites poetry and music without depending on accentuation. The flexible rhythmic units of "musical feet" could be applied to instrumental as well as vocal music, and the primary usefulness of *rhythmopoeia* may have been in providing a model for the meter of dance music.

IV

❧

Quantitas Intrinseca:
The Perception of Meter

TIME SIGNATURES EVOLVED in order to specify what note value was to be equated with the beat and how many beats were to be included in a measure. But what is it that enables us to distinguish the beat, or groups of beats, in a measure? This question arose when the measure of the *tactus* no longer coincided with the beat.

Theorists described meter using words nearly as elusive as the perception of meter itself. Although meter is clear to our senses, it is difficult to describe. This may be as much a factor of the mysterious way our minds work as it is of musical organization.

John Holden says that notes that come on the beat are notes to which we give a "superior regard." German theorists call them "intrinsically long" notes, Italian theorists call them "good" notes, and notation places these "good" notes after bar lines and on odd-numbered beats of the measure. It is not necessary to perform these notes in any special manner in order to associate them with the beat, although musicians may articulate them in such a way as to enhance this perception.

To clarify this point, John Holden asks the reader to consider the steady, equal, unstressed sounds of a watch:

> We find them proceeding by pairs . . . which is owing to the pulses being alternately a little stronger and weaker: 1 2, 1 2, 1 2; each single pulse . . . may repre-

sent the time of a semiquaver. We can also . . . place our regard on the alternate stronger pulses and disregard the weaker ones, so as to apply the same way of counting 1 ; 2 : 1 ; 2 : in a slower manner to the successive pairs . . . considering each pair as constituting one pulse . . . answering the time of a quaver.

This perception of pairs, and of the coupling of pairs together, is a model of the meter of **C**, or common time, according to Holden.

He continues,

> In the performance of music, there is a certain emphasis or accent laid on the beginning of every measure, which plainly distinguishes one species of time from another; so that a hearer is naturally led to distribute a tune into its proper measure, though he should take no notice of the manner of beating time; nay though he should know nothing at all of the rules. . . . The emphasis always falls upon the number 1, in the method of counting a watch . . . and accompanies the putting down of the hand, or toe, in beating time.
>
> There is no occasion to make the beginning or emphatic part, of the measure always stronger, or louder than the rest, though it is sometimes best to do so; for it is not so much the superior loudness of the sound, as the superior regard which a hearer is led to bestow upon it that distinguishes one part of the measure from another. This is a truth of great importance as will hereafter appear, and deserves to be well fixed in mind, before we proceed.[1]

Holden's interpretation of accent or emphasis as distinct from the perception of rhythmic order is indeed a "truth of great importance."

Joshua Steele's definition of measure organization attempts to explain speech rhythms in terms borrowed from music.

> As all speech, prose as well as poetry, falls naturally under emphatical divisions, which I will call cadences: let the thesis or pulsation, which points out those divisions, be marked by bars, as in ordinary music. Modern musicians, very improperly, use the words *accented* and *unaccented* in the place of thesis and arsis. . . . Of modes of time there are only two genera; the one, where the whole time of a bar or cadence, is divided by 2, and its sub-duples or sub-triples; the other, where the whole time of a bar or cadence is divided by three, and its sub-duples or sub-triples. But here let it be observed, that this emphasis of *cadence* and the *expression* of loudness, are not to be considered as equivalent terms or affections of the same kind; for the arsis or *remiss*, may be loud, or forte; and the thesis, or *emphatic*, *piano* or soft occasionally. The thesis and arsis being periodically alternate, whether expressed or supposed: whereas the application of the *forte* and *piano* are *ad libitum* or *apropos*. . . .
>
> Here then are the two general modes or measures of time. The first, wherein each step makes a cadence, and is divided equally by the even number 2, and the pace, or double cadence, by 4; and is in music called common time, andante, or the measure of a march. The second, where the whole pace, making only one cadence, may be equally divided by the number 6, as the double of 3; and is called triple time or the measure of the *menuet* and *jigs*.
>
> The affections of *heavy* and *light* were always felt in music, though erroneously called by some moderns *accented* and *unaccented;* however the *accented* or

heavy note, was never understood to be *necessarily loud,* and the other *necessarily soft;* because if it were so, there could be no occasion for separate directions, where to apply the forte and piano, in as much as the affections of *heavy* and *light* are continued in every cadence of every air, . . . whereas the *forte* and the *piano* are often applied directly contrary to *heavy* and *light.*[2]

John Holden's "superior regard" and Steele's "pulsation and remission" indicate a perception of the essence of metrical order. This concept was also defined, although with less precision, in the discussions of *quantitas intrinseca,* or of "good" and "bad" notes that were offered by German, Italian, and French writers in the seventeenth and eighteenth centuries.

Quantitas intrinseca is discussed in the *Satyrischer Componist* of Wolfgang Caspar Printz:

> Ferner ist zu wissen/ dass die Zahl eine sonderbare Krafft und Tugend habe/ welche verursacht/ dass unter etlichen/ der Zeit nach/ gleich-langen Noten oder Klängen/ etliche länger/ etliche kürzer zu seyn scheinen: Welches sonderlich wohl zu mercken/ so wohl wegen des Textes/ als auch wegen der *Consonantien* und *Dissonantien.*
>
> Diese unterschiedliche Länge etlicher/ der Zeit oder Währung nach/ gleich-lange Noten/ wird genennet *Quantitas Temporalis Intrinseca,* die innerliche Zeit-Länge.
>
> Dass dieses seinen Grund *in re ipsâ,* in der That selbst habe/ kan ein jeder leicht sehen und hören/ wenn er einen Text unter gleich Noten setzet. Als zum Exempel [Ex. 4.1].
>
> In diesem Wort ist die erste und dritte Sylbe lang/ die andere und vierdte kurz. Wird nun solches Wort mit denen *Sonis* ABCD gesungen/ so wird es fein ins Gehöre kommen/ und jede Sylbe seine rechte Länge haben. Verwechsele ich aber die Zahl der Noten/ ob ich schon die Noten selbst behalte [Ex. 4.2].
>
> So wird es gar unanmuthig und Wiederwärtig ins Gehöre fallen/ weil die langen Sylben *chri* und *a* mit kurzen *Sonis* E & G hergegen die kurzen Sylben *sti* & *nus* mit langen *Sonis* F & H hervor gebracht und gesungen werden: Welches nicht seyn könte/ wenn die *Soni* EFGH keinen Unterschied an innerlicher Zeitlänge hätten.
>
> Diese *Quantität* recht zu erkennen/ muss man wissen/ dass jede Note entweder in zwey oder drey gleiche Theile getheilet werde.
>
> Ist der Theiler der Noten die zweyte Zahl/ so seyn alle Noten/ so mit einer ungeraden Zahl/ als 1, 3, 5, 7, &c. gezehlet werden/ lang; Hergegen/ die mit einer geraden Zahl, als 2, 4, 6, 8, &c. gezehlet werden/ kurz.
>
> Hieraus erhellet/ dass eine jede *Semibrevis* oder ganzer Tact auch der innerlichen *Quantität* nach/ lang sey/ weil sie mit einer ungeraden Zahl, Nehmlich 1 gezahlet wird: Sintemahl allezeit, im Niederschlagen des Tactes, das Zehlen sich anfangen muss.
>
> Ingleichen seyn alle und jede *syncopirte* Noten lang/ weil in denselben die gerade und ungerade Zahl zusammen kommen und sich vereinbaren.
>
> Ist die dritte Zahl der Theiler/ so ist die erste lang/ die andere und dritte kurz. Wenn aber die erste schweiget/ so ist die andere lang die dritte kurz.[3]

Further, the position in the measure has a peculiar power and virtue which cause notes equal to one another, according to the time signature, to seem longer or shorter. This should be especially noted as much because of the text as because of consonance and dissonance.

The apparent different length of notes that are equal according to their time or value, is called *Quantitas Temporalis Intrinseca,* or the inner duration. It can easily be seen that this has its basis in the notes themselves when a text is set to notes of like duration [Ex. 4.1].

EX. 4.1

Chri - sti - a - nus

In these words, the first and third syllables are long and the second and fourth are short. If they are sung to notes ABCD above, they sound right to the ear and each syllable is the correct length.

If the position of the notes in the measure is changed, whether or not the notes themselves are changed [Ex. 4.2], the phrase falls disagreeably and contrarily on the ear because the long syllables *Chri* and *a* are used and sung with the short sounds E and G, and the short syllables *sti* and *nus* are used and sung with the long sounds F and H. This would not occur if the sounds EFGH were not different in their inner duration.

EX. 4.2

Chri - sti - a - nus

To know these quantities correctly, one must know that every note is divided into either two or three like parts.

If the subdivisions of notes are duple, all odd numbered notes 1, 3, 5, 7, etc. are considered long and all even numbered notes 2, 4, 6, 8, etc. are short. . . .

I explain here that every semibrevis or entire *Tactus,* according to the inner quantity, is also long because it is figured with an odd number, one, since this number always begins on the downbeat of a measure.

Also each and every syncopated note is long because the odd and even numbers are mingled together and mixed in it.

If the subdivisions (of a note) are three in number, the first is long and the second and third are short.

When the first part is silent, the second is long and the third is short.

Printz does not advocate lengthening or shortening the duration of notes in the *Satyrischer Componist:* he implies that it is only the listener's perception of their "peculiar power and virtue" that distinguishes long from short.

Heinichen used the terms *notae virtualiter longae* and *notae virtualiter breves* for "long and short" when explaining the harmonic passing tone in figured bass.[4] J. A. Scheibe used *anschlagende* (struck) for "long" and *durchgehende* (passing) for "short."[5] These terms seem to have been applied in relation to harmonic rather than rhythmic considerations.

In Italian treatises beginning with Girolamo Diruta,[6] *nota buona* and *nota cattiva,* "good" and "bad" notes, are used to refer to metrical order. Diruta explained that when a two-note group comes on the beat, the good note is the first and the bad note is the second. His fingering rules for keyboard performance place "good" fingers, the second and fourth, on good notes, and "bad" fingers, the first, third, and fifth, on bad notes.[7] Lorenzo Penna[8] and subsequently other writers, both German and Italian,[9] used these terms in broader contexts than that of determining fingerings for the keyboard.

"Good" and "bad" notes and their musical consequences are carefully explained by Georg Muffat in Latin, German, Italian, and French in the preface to *Florilegium secundum* (1698). Muffat was trained in both the Italian and French styles of composition and performance; he studied in Paris from 1663 to 1669, and with Pasquini in Rome in 1681–82, where he became acquainted with Corelli's music.[10] According to him, bar lines precede good notes and mark recurring patterns of organization, most of which reflect dance steps. Good and bad notes are identified by their position in the measure.

> Of all the notes found in any composition to be played, there are those that are good (*nobiliores; edle; buone e principali; bonne, noble ou principales*), and others that are bad (*ignobiliores, seu viliores; schlechte; cattive, ò vili; chetives ou viles*). Good notes are those that seem naturally to give the ear a little repose. Such notes are longer, those that come on the beat or essential subdivisions of measures, those that have a dot after them, and (among equal small notes) those that are odd-numbered and are ordinarily played down-bow. The bad notes are all the others, which like passing notes, do not satisfy the ear so well, and leave after them a desire to go on.[11]

Muffat uses the Italian idea of good and bad notes to clarify his presentation of French performance directions to German musicians, a truly international undertaking. Walther's *Lexikon* defines all these terms, German as well as Italian, as befits a dictionary:

> *Quantitas Notarum extrinseca, & intrinseca* [lat.] die äusserliche und innerliche Geltung der Noten; nach jener art ist jede note mit ihres gleichen in der *execution* von gleicher; nach dieser aber, von ungleicher länge: da nemlich der ungerade Tact-Theil lang, und der gerade Tact-Theil kurz ist.[12]

> *Quantitas notarum extrinseca,* and *intrinseca* [lat.] is the apparent (or outward) and the inner value of the notes. According to the former, every note is performed equal to other notes of the same value, but according to the latter the notes are of unequal length: since, to be specific, the uneven-numbered parts of the beat are long and the even-numbered ones short.

Walther defined good and bad notes, *tempo di buona* and *tempo di cattiva,* as follows:

> *Tempo di buona* [ital.] der gute Tact-Theil, ist in *Tactu aequali,* unter 2 Minimis die erste Minima, oder die erste helffte des Tacts; unter 4 Vierteln, das 1ste und 3te Viertel; unter 8 Achteln, das 1ste, 3te, 5te, und 7te Achtel u.s.w. Weil erwehnte *tempi* oder ungerade Tact-Theile bequem sind, dass auf ihnen eine *Caesur,* eine

Cadenz, eine lange Sylbe, eine *syncopirte Dissonanz,* und vor allen eine *Consonanz* (als von welcher eben der Bey-Nahme: *di buona* entstanden) angebracht werde.

Tempo di buona [ital.] is the good part of the beat. Under the equal *tactus,* the first of two minims, or the first half of the beat is good; also the first and third of four quarter notes, the first, third, fifth and seventh of eight eighth notes and so forth, because these *tempi,* or odd-numbered parts of the beat are suitable for the placement of a caesura, a cadence, a long syllable, a syncopated dissonance, and above all a consonance (from which comes its name—*di buona*).

Tempo di cattiva, oder *di mala* [ital.] der schlimme Tact-Theil, ist in *Tactu aequali,* unter 2 Minimis die zweyte Minima, oder die zweyte Helffte des Tactes; unter 4 Vierteln, das 2te und 4te Viertel; unter 8 Achteln, das 2te, 4te, 6te und 8te Achtel; weil Nurbesagte *tempi* oder gerade Tact-Theile einige von ober-zehlten Stücken Nicht, wohl aber desen *contrarium* leiden.[13]

Tempo di cattiva, or *di mala* [Ital.] Is the bad part of the beat. In the *Tactu aequali* or beat with two equal strokes, the second of two minims or the second half of the beat is bad; also the second and fourth, sixth and eighth of eight eighth notes, because these *tempi* or even-numbered parts of the beat are all different from the above-mentioned parts, and are their opposites.

In the discussions of the terms *quantitas intrinseca,* "good and bad" notes, or Holden's "superior regard," no method of enhancing or articulating these differences is specified.

Hiller's *Anweisung* defines the elusive concept of meter more clearly than any other German treatise of the eighteenth century. Hiller's concept of musical meter follows the tradition of the seventeenth- and earlier eighteenth-century theorists, even though his compositional style reflects his admiration of more modern composers such as Hasse, J. C. Bach, and Quantz, rather than Sebastian Bach. His good sense and pedagogical skill are evident in the clarity of his explanation of meter:

Unter zwo neben einander stehenden, der Gestalt und dem Werthe nach gleichen Noten, ist, bey gleicher oder gerader Abtheilung des Tacts, der innerlichen Quantität nach (Die ausserlich Quantität verändert sowohl die Gestalt als den Werthe der Noten; wir haben es als dann mit ganzen und halben Tactnoten, mit Vierteln, Achteln u.s.f. zu thun . . .) *immer die eine lang, und die andere kurz.* Dieser Umstand hat seinen Grund in dem Natürlichen Gefühle der Menschen, und äussert sich sogar in der Sprache; indem man nicht zwo Sylben nach einander aussprechen kann, dass nicht die eine kürzer scheine, als die andere, die Prosodie mag auch dagegen einwenden, was sie will. Welche nun unter zwo gleichgeltenden Noten lang, und welche kurz sey, das muss die Tactabtheilung bestimmen. Auf dem Papiere geschieht diess vermittelst eines Strichs, welcher durch alle fünf Linien gezogen wird, und daher den Namen eines Tactstrichs (Was zwischen zween solchen Strichen stehet, er mögen nun eine, zwey, drey oder zwanzig Noten seyn, wird ein Tact genennt) fürt, bey der Ausführung eines Stücks aber geschieht es durch das Niederschlagen und Aufheben der Hand. (Ein paar Kuntswörter, die wir den Griechen abgeborgt haben, und welche in diesem Werke sich wohl bisweilen mit eindrängen möchten, so gern ich auch sonst alles deutsch sage, was sich deutsch sagen lässt, mag man sich im voraus bekannt machen. Das Niederschlagen der hand heisst *Thesis*, und das Aufgeben derselben, oder wie man insgemein sagt, der Aufschlag, *Arsis*. In einigen musikalischen Büchern findet man diese beyden Wörter, in der Anwendung auf die Tacttheile, anders verdeutscht und das erste durch guter Tacttheile, das andere durch schlimmer Tacttheile, nach dem italiänischen *nota buona, nota cattiva*, übersetzt. . . . So erlaube man mir immer statt guter Tacttheile; *langer Tacttheile*, und statt schlimmer, *kurzer Tacttheile* zu sagen. Schlimm im Gegensatze von gut, ist so viel als böse; das ist nun wohl von dem armen Tacttheile zu lieblos gesprochen. . . .) Das letze gilt für die kurze, das erste für die lange Note, wenn nicht mehr als zwo Noten in einem Tacte beysammen sind. Der Tactstrich, welcher zugleich den Niederschlag andeutet, steht allemal unmittelbar vor der langen Note.[14]

Between two notes, side by side, of the same kind and value, and in a duple or equal division of the beat, one will always be long and the other short, according to their inner quantity (the outward or apparent quantity deals with the change in the kind and value of notes; we are concerned with whole and half notes, with quarters, eighths, etc.). . . . This fact has its basis in man's natural feelings, and also in speech. Two syllables cannot be spoken together without it appearing that one is shorter than the other, although prosody sometimes wishes to take exception to this. The division of the measure determines which of the two is long and which is short. This is made apparent on paper by means of a line drawn through all five lines, called a bar line (what is included between two bar lines, whether one, two, three or twenty notes is called a measure); and in performance by a down-and-up motion of the hand. (Note: These two technical terms, which we have borrowed from the Greek, must be explained, for although I like to say everything in German that German can say, in this work I will be forced sometimes to use them. The downstroke of the hand is called *thesis* and the upstroke, or as is sometimes said, the upbeat, is called *arsis*. These two words are found in several books to describe the parts of the measure, others translate this to "good part" and "bad part" of the measure, after the Italian words *nota buona, nota cattiva*. . . . Therefore allow me to say "longer part" instead of "good part" and "shorter part" instead of "bad part. . . .") The latter [*Aufheben*] refers to the short, and the former to the long note if there are no more than two notes in a measure. The bar line, which indicates the downbeat, always comes directly before the long note.

According to Hiller, various terms used by earlier writers to describe metrical perceptions are identical; his explanation is easily reconciled with the definitions of Holden and Steele. It seems to be the belief of most seventeenth- and eighteenth-century theorists that musical meter is naturally and adequately perceived by the listener and only secondarily heightened through performance techniques. Most performers today are aware of how crude it is to suggest that the measure is identified by a regular accent or dynamic stress based on bar lines and time signatures. This confidence in the listener's basic metrical perception as defined by *quantitas intrinseca* gives rise to a remarkable variety of subtle articulation techniques that delicately enhance and shape that perception.

V

❧

Articulation of
Quantitative Meter

THE PERCEPTION OF *quantitas intrinseca,* or "good" and "bad" notes, gave essential information to performers about standard articulation patterns. Instead of relying on markings for slurs, staccato marks, sforzandos, and accents, seventeenth- and eighteenth-century performers interpreted their unmarked scores through habits and formulas learned as part of their elementary instruction. No matter how subtle and polished a performer eventually became, articulation determined by the meter of the music was embedded in his or her technique.

Some metrical articulations are immediately audible and define a style of performance as well as the beat, as in the lilting quality of the French practice of *notes inégales.* Other articulations may be less overtly apparent to the listener, but they also persuade the ear to a greater appreciation of metrical structure.

Articulations are sometimes specific to a particular instrument, for instance, minute silences result from keyboard fingering patterns that require some fingers to lift early in order to make way for the placement of others. Tonguings for wind instruments and bowings for stringed instruments use varying degrees of sharpness of attack. Articulations are sometimes explained as a means of producing an instrumental equivalent to pronunciation that can be subtly and infinitely varied to fit different musical circumstances.

When editors attempt to help musicians today to perform seventeenth- and eighteenth-century music by supplying phrasing and articulation marks, they are all too often based on the articulation practices of a later style of performance.

Patterns of articulation that do not depend on accent or dynamic stress are discussed in this chapter.

Notes Inégales

Notes inégales is a performance practice associated with French style in the seventeenth and eighteenth centuries. It imparts a graceful swing to quickly moving melodic notes and enhances meter through lengthening good notes and shortening bad notes.[1] Any degree of inequality, from the slightest (such as 9:7) to the greatest (3:1), is in marked contrast to equal performance. Perception of the beat and also the sense of style are influenced by the degree of inequality.

The practice of performing quick-moving conjunct equal notes unequally can be traced to the sixteenth century, when it was not considered to be specifically French. It was one of a number of liberties exercised by performers in ornamenting and improvising. The first mention of this practice is found in a pamphlet by Loys Bourgeois in 1550. He states that notes performed unequally are restricted to those moving at one-quarter of the speed of the *tactus* and are sung "two by two, staying a bit longer on the first than on the second, as if the first had a dot."[2] Diego Ortiz describes *notes inégales* as among the simplest techniques of ornamentation (Ex. 5.1).[3]

EX. 5.1

Sometimes ornamentation was initially conceived as melodic elaboration in even notes and later complicated by rhythmic alteration. A section from Tomás de Santa Maria's *Libro llamado Arte de tañer fantasia* describes how to enrich the practice of improvising ornamentation by performing notes unequally.[4]

Musicians continued the tradition of metrical freedom and the practice of diminutions in the early seventeenth century, but with a change in attitude that is expressed by Giulio Caccini.[5] According to him, exuberance of decoration ideally is tied to a specific affect or to the articulation of a phrase. Perhaps it was at this time that rhythmic alteration began to be appreciated for its ability to enhance the awareness of metrical organization. From the viewpoint of the twentieth century, however, even the comparatively precise rules of the seventeenth and eighteenth centuries allow performers considerable freedom.

After 1650, unequal performance of notes written as equal became associated primarily with French practice. Although Bacilly,[6] Marais,[7] and Jean Rousseau[8] all discuss inequality, the first thorough account is in Etienne Loulié's *Elemens* of 1696. Loulié's rules governed the practice of French musicians until the demise of *notes inégales* in France, apparently in the second half of the eighteenth century.

The rules for inequality are combined with explanations of time signatures and gestures for beating time. Since the relation of note values to the beat determines which notes are to be performed unequally, this arrangement was a logical one. Here is Loulié's explanation of two-beat meters:

Deux   C Barre   Deux Quatre
2   ¢   2/4

La mesure à deux Temps ne se bat que d'une maniere: Un *Frapper* & un *Lever*. Le 1. et le 3. quart de chaque Temps sont plus longs que le 2. & que le 4. quoy qu'ils soient marquez égaux, dans quelque mesure que ce soit.[9]

The beat of duple meters is given in only one way, one downstroke and one upstroke. The first and third quarters of each beat are longer than the second and fourth quarters, even though they are written as equal, no matter in which measure they occur.

Each *temps* of the *mesure à deux temps* is a beat, within the comfortable physiological and psychological tempo range required, and each beat is divided into two pulses. Unequal notes are eighth notes in 2 and ¢, and sixteenth notes in 2/4.

Loulié continued with a description of triple measures:

3/1, 3/1, 3/4, 3/8, 3/16, & 3

La mesure se bat de trois manieres: 1. 2 frappers & un lever pour les mouvements lents. 2. 1 frapper qui vaut 2 temps & un lever pour les mouvements plus vites. 3. 1 frapper qui vaut trois temps pour les mouvements très vites. Dans quelque Mesure que ce soit, particulierement dans la Mesure à trois Temps, les demi-temps s'excutent de deux manieres differentes, quoy que marquez de la même maniere. 1. On les fait quelque fois égaux. Cette maniere s'appelle *détacher les Nottes,* on s'en sert dans les chants dont les sons se suivent par Degrez interrompus. 2. On fait quelque fois les premiers demy-temps un peu plus longs. Cette maniere s'appelle *Lourer.* On s'en sert dans les chants dont les sons se suivent part Degrez non interrompus. On appelle *Degré interrompu* lorsqu'un son est suivy d'un autre son que est au 3. ou 4. degré & plus du 1. soit en montant, soit en descendant, comme ré, la, fa. Il y a une troisiéme maniere, ou l'on fait le premier demi-temps beaucoup plus long que le deuxiéme. Mais le premier demi-temps doit avoir un point. On appelle cette 3. maniere *Piquer* ou *Pointer.*[10]

The measure is given in three ways: (1) two downstrokes and one upstroke for slow tempos, (2) one downstroke, lasting two times, and one upstroke, for faster tempos, (3) one downstroke, lasting three times, for very fast tempos. In any measure, and particularly in triple measures, the notes equal to a half beat are performed in two different ways, even though they are written the same. (1) They are sometimes played equal, this is called "detached," and it is appropriate when notes succeed one another disjunctly. (2) Sometimes the first part of the half beat is played a little longer, this is called *lourer* and it is used when melodic progression is conjunct. Disjunct signifies that one note is followed by another after an interval of more than one pitch, either ascending or descending. There is a third way; the first half beat is played much longer than the second half beat, but the first must have a dot after it. This is called dotted.

Much later in the book, Loulié added another explanation:

> On avoit oublié de dire dans la 2. partie en parlant des signes de mesures de trois temps, que les premiers demi-temps s'excutent encore d'une quatriéme maniere, sçavoir en faisant le 1. plus que le 2. ainsi [Ex. 5.2].[11]

> I forgot to mention in the second part, speaking of time signatures of three beats, that the first half beats are played in a fourth way; with the first shorter than the second, thus [Ex. 5.2].

EX. 5.2

Loulié and many other French writers demonstrate that *lourer,* or *notes inégales,* became an accepted custom in the performance of all French music and remained so until late in the eighteenth century. The rules of *notes inégales* were restated with further refinements and particulars by subsequent theorists.

The question of whether *notes inégales* was a performance practice of musicians outside of France is difficult to answer conclusively. By far the greater number of treatises discussing it are French, yet it is defined and discussed in a number of German instruction books. The practice of *notes inégales* would have been spread by French musicians who had careers outside France, for example, in the famous orchestra at Dresden that had many French performers: J. B. Volumier was the leader of the violins, Pierre Gabriel Buffardin the flutist, and François LaRiche the oboist. At least a dozen French oboists were employed in Germany in various cities, and Bach's bassoonist at Cöthen was J. C. Torlée.[12] French musicians were active in London; the names of Jacques Paisible, P. J. Bressan, J. B. Loeillet, and Charles Dieupart come readily to mind.

Georg Muffat lived in Paris from 1663 to 1669, from age ten to sixteen, and studied with Lully. His preface to *Florilegium secundum* (1698) describes the customs of the "Lullists" to his German contemporaries and offers one of the most thorough descriptions of French performance available from this period. Muffat's directions (in Latin, German, Italian, and French) cover many details of performance—bowings, ornamentation, descriptions of dances—and include the following discussion of *notes inégales:*

> 3. Les notes diminuantes du premier ordre, telles que sont les doubles crochuës sous la mesure à quatre tems; les crochuës sous celle à Deux, ou alla breve; celles qui vont de la moitié plus vîte qu'une partie essentielle de la mesure aux triples un peu gays, & aux proportions, étant mises de suittes ne se jouënt pas les unes égales aux autres, comme elles sont marquées; car cela auroit quelque chose d'endormy, de rude, & de plat; mais se changent à la Francoise en adjoutant à

chacune de celles qui tombent au nombre non pair comme la valeur d'un point par le quel devenant plus longue, elle rend la suivante d'autant plus courte.[13]

The small notes of the first class, which are sixteenths in C, the measure of four beats; eighths in 2 or allabreve, the measure of two beats; those notes that are twice as fast as essential parts of the beat in the faster triples and proportions (provided these notes are conjunct)—all these are not played equal to each other as they are written. This would be sleepy, inelegant, and flat. Rather, the odd numbered notes are played as if they were altered by the addition of a dot in the French style, and by becoming longer they cause the following notes to become shorter.

In Walther's *Lexikon, notes inégales,* under the name of *lourer,* is similarly defined and noted as French in origin.[14] The next, and the best-known, German description of *notes inégales* is that of J. J. Quantz, a flute student of Buffardin's. Quantz did not identify *notes inégales* as French or refer to it as a foreign practice, but at the French-speaking court of Frederick the Great, where Quantz spent most of his life, perhaps French performance practice was not considered foreign.

Ich muss hierbey eine nothwendige Anmerkung machen, welche die Zeit, wie lange jede Note gehalten werden muss, betrifft. Man muss unter den *Hauptnoten,* welche man auch: *anschlagende,* oder nach Art der Italiäner, *gute* Noten zu nennen pfleget, und unter den *durchgehenden,* welche bey einigen Ausländern *schlimme* heissen, einen Unterscheid im Vortage zu machen wissen. Die Hauptnoten müssen allezeit, wo es sich thun lässt, mehr erhoben werden, als die durchgehenden.[15]

I must in this connection make a necessary remark concerning the length of time that each note must be held. A distinction in performance must be made between principal notes, also called "struck" or "good" notes, after the Italian custom; and passing notes, which are called "bad" notes by some foreigners. Wherever possible, the principal notes must be brought out more than the passing notes.

This was not just a general introduction to the remarks that followed. The terms—"struck notes" and "good notes"—are those used to define *quantitas intrinseca.* These notes were to be "brought out" (*mehr erhoben*). However, "struck" or "good" notes are not the same as *notes inégales:*

Dieser Regel zu Folge müssen die geschwindesten Noten, in einem jeden Stücke von *mässigem Tempo,* oder auch im *Adagio,* ungeachtet sie dem Gesichte nach einerly Geltung haben, dennoch ein wenig ungleich gespielet werden; so dass man die anschlagenden Noten einer jeden Figur, nämlich die erste, dritte, fünfte, und siebente, etwas länger anhält, als die durchgehenden, nämlich, die zweyte, vierte, sechste und achte: doch muss dieses Anhalten nicht so viel ausmachen, als wenn Puncte dabey stünden. Unter diesen geschwindesten Noten verstehe ich: die Viertheile im Dreyzweitheiltacte; die Achtheile im Dreyviertheil- und die Sechszehntheile im Dreyachttheiltacte; die Achtheile im Allabreve; die Sechszehntheile oder Zwey und dreissigtheile im Zweyviertheil- oder im gemeinen geraden Tacte: doch nur so lange, als keine Figuren von noch geschwindern oder noch einmal so kurzen Noten, in jeder Tactart mit untermischet sind; denn alsdenn müssten diese letztern auf die oben beschriebene Art vorgetragen werden. Z. E. Wollte man Tab IX Fig. 1. die acht Sechzehntheile unter den Buchstaben (K) (M) (N) langsam in einerley Geltung speilen [Ex. 5.3]; so würden sie nicht so gefällig klingen, als wenn man von vieren die erste und dritte etwas länger und stärker im Tone, als die zweyte und vierte, hören lässt. Von dieser Regel aber werden ausgenommen: erstlich die geschwinden Passagien in einem sehr geschwinden Zeitmaasse, bey denen die Zeit nicht erlaubet sie ungleich vorzutragen, und wo man also die Länge und Stärke nur bey der ersten von vieren anbringen muss. Ferner werden ausgenommen: alle geschwinden Passagien welche die Singstimme zu machen hat, wenn sie anders nicht geschleifet werden sollen: denn weil jede Note von dieser Art der Singpassagien, durch einen gelinden Stoss der Luft aus der Brust, deutlich gemachet und markiret werden muss; so findet die Ungleichheit dabey keine Statt. Weiter werden ausgenommen: die Noten über welchen Striche oder Puncte stehen, oder von welchen etliche nach einander auf einem Tone vorkommen; ferner wenn über mehr, als zwo Noten, nämlich, über vieren, sechsen, oder achten ein Bogen steht; und endlich die Achttheile in Giguen. Alle diese Noten müssen egal, das ist, eine so lang, als die andere, vorgetragen werden.[16]

In accordance with this rule, the quickest notes in every piece of moderate tempo, or in the *adagio,* though they seem to have the same value, must be played a little unequally, so that the struck notes of each group, namely the first, third, fifth and seventh notes are held somewhat longer than the passing notes, which are the second, fourth, sixth and eighth, although this lengthening must not be as much as it would be if the notes were dotted. Among the quickest notes I include the quarters in the three-two measure, the eighths in the three-four measure and sixteenths in the three-eight measure; the eighths in allabreve; and sixteenths or thirty seconds in two-four or common time; but this is true only so long as no figures of still more rapid notes or doubly quick ones are mixed in, in whatever time signature, for then these last named have to be performed in the manner described above. For example, if one were to play the eight sixteenth-notes under letters (K) (M) and (N) slowly and evenly [Ex. 5.3], they will not sound as pleasing as if the first and third were held somewhat longer and played somewhat louder than the second and fourth. This rule has the following exceptions: fast passages in a very fast tempo, when there is not enough time for them to be performed unevenly and therefore only the first of each group of four notes can be given (extra) length and force. Also excepted are all fast passages for the voice, when they are not to be slurred, for every note in this type of vocal passage must be marked and made clear by a gentle expulsion of air from the chest, and thus unevenness has no place in such passages. Further exceptions are: when notes have dashes or dots over them, or when there are several successive notes of the same pitch; also when there is a slur over more than two notes—that is over four, six or eight; and finally eighth notes in gigues. All of these notes must be played even, that is, one as long as the other.

EX. 5.3

Quantz's instructions are more detailed than those of Loulié, as they combine a consideration of *notes inégales* with that of "good" and "bad" notes, or *quantitas intrinseca.* This description remained in both later editions of the *Versuch* (1780 and 1798). *Notes inégales* is mentioned in the *Klavierschule* of Daniel Gottlob Türk [17] as one of several techniques for varying ornamentation, somewhat the same as in Ortiz's treatise of 1553.

Explanations of the practice of *notes inégales* were less frequent in the second half of the eighteenth century. In France the theorists were no longer in agreement: An unknown musician of the Comédie-Italien wrote a *Noveau manual musical contenant les elements de la musique, des agrements, du chant,* cited and dated as 1781 by Jane Arger,[18] that does not mention *notes inégales.* French writers had long recognized that the practice of *notes inégales* was not appropriate to the performance of Italian music, which was written according to the true values of the notes.[19]

Italian style invaded France in the early eighteenth century through the sonata and the cantata. Italian opera gained a resounding success with Pergolesi's *La serva padrona,* Italian musicians came to France, and Italian style became familiar to French musicians. The practice of *notes inégales* may have lost favor as musical taste changed. Pierre Marcou wrote in 1782 that there was no general agreement on *notes inégales* and that its practice was better left to the individual performer.[20] Although it was a particularly French style of performance, it seems to have been known wherever French music and musicians were popular.

Keyboard Fingering

The study of keyboard fingering technique shows that the performer's choice of fingers depended on the position of notes in the measure. Performers usually began their study of the instrument with simple pieces in which there was a close connection between the choice of fingers and the meter of the music. Explanations of fingering patterns in keyboard music were often illustrated by scales or scale passages derived from division-style ornamentation. This basic technique was adapted by accomplished performers when they met the demands of different styles in more difficult music. Fingering that enhanced the perception of notes grouped by twos or fours, through crossing the middle finger over either the index or ring finger, often remained a part of advanced technique.

A somewhat detached articulation of all notes is specified by a number of writers from Tomas de Sancta Maria in 1565 to Friedrich W. Marpurg in 1755. Marpurg wrote:

> Sowohl dem Schleifen als Abstossen ist das ordentliche Fortgehen entgegen gesetzet, welches darinnen besteht, dass man ganz hurtig kurz vorher, ehe man die folgende Note berühret, den Finger von der vorhergehenden Taste aufhebet. Dieses ordentlich Fortgehen wird, weil es allezeit voraus gesetzet wird, niemahls angezeiget.[21]

The usual way is contrasted both to legato and staccato, and consists of lifting the finger from the preceding key just before you touch the following note. This usual way is not indicated by sign, since it is always presupposed.

Thus, a style neither legato nor exaggeratedly detached was considered usual in keyboard performance. This practice is confirmed and amplified in Türk's *Klavierschule*, where clear distinctions are made between "playing in the customary fashion, neither detached nor slurred," and articulation that is indicated by slurs or dots. In the "customary fashion," the finger is "lifted a little earlier from the key than is required by the duration of the note," and for slurred notes, "the finger should be allowed to remain on the key until the duration of the given note is completely past, so that not the slightest separation results." [22]

Exceptions to this partially detached style were marked with slurs or dots, although such indications were rare until the mid-eighteenth century. The range of articulation also included super-legato fingerings, advocated by François Couperin and Jean-Philippe Rameau. This technique was done by holding one key down until after the next one was depressed, and only then releasing it. [23] Articulations for a finished performance must necessarily have encompassed a wide range of touch, from super-legato to highly detached.

Raising the finger before depressing the next key produces a minute silence between notes. Elementary fingering techniques that require the fingers (but not the thumb) to cross over one another in extended scale passages also result in silences. Such fingerings provide silences of articulation involuntarily and allow the performer to place his awareness on the fingering patterns rather than on the articulation that will result. Novice keyboard players from the sixteenth through the eighteenth centuries were taught such crossover fingerings by matching their fingers to metrically significant notes; the thumb or the fifth finger was used only at the beginning or at the end of scale passages.

Girolamo Diruta associated notes that were metrically good or bad with good or bad fingers. The good fingers were to be used on the first of paired notes and on dotted notes, and the bad fingers used on the second of paired notes and the notes following dotted notes. When a keyboard player had established these patterns of fingering, they would be the ones he would be most likely to employ in the performance of compositions that included scale patterns (Ex. 5.4). [24]

EX. 5.4. *B* indicates *buona* (good) and *C* indicates *cattiva* (bad).

The toccatas in *Il transilvano* are filled with scale passages for which the repeated use of 3 and 4 on pairs of ascending notes and 2 and 3 on pairs of descending notes suggests metrical groups of two; the bad notes are connected to the good against the beat. Example 5.5 is from the *intonazione nono tono* by Giovanni Gabrieli.[25]

EX. 5.5

Music suitable to novice players, such as the "Brande Champanje" in the Susanne van Soldt manuscript, sometimes specified fingering patterns that identified good and bad fingers differently than Diruta did. Articulation silences between notes bear a different relationship to the beat than in Diruta's music. In Ex. 5.6, connections are made from good to bad notes, with silences coming just before the beat.[26]

EX. 5.6

Harald Vogel comments on this passage:

At the beginning of the seventeenth century, the fingerings in use incorporated three different concepts. These are illustrated in the original fingerings at the beginning of the first composition in the Susanne van Soldt manuscript, the "Brande Champanje." In the first two measures of the piece, fingerings from around 1600 are written in. In the first half of measure one, the third finger is the "good" finger, and is used consistently on the "good" notes. The second half of the same measure shows the second possibility: the playing of as many notes as possible from a single hand position, regardless of which fingers play which "good" notes. In the second measure, we find the third possibility: a combination of the first two. Most of the time the "good" third finger is placed on the "good" note, but when it is possible to play a long passage without a shift in hand position, this is done, even if it means using the fifth finger on the highest note of the passage. Thus, in order to better understand the discussion of fingerings, it is necessary that the application of "good" finger to "good" note is only part of the story. The other principle that was also considered very important was the idea of playing a figuration in *one* hand if possible.[27]

Julane Rodgers comments on sixteenth-century Spanish practice:

Scale fingerings found in the Spanish sources are of two types. The first type uses two fingers in alternation: in the right hand 3 4 3 4 ascending, 3 2 3 2 descending; in the left hand 2 1 2 1 ascending, 3 4 3 4 descending. This type of fingering seems to be the basic scale fingering and is the one more commonly used. It is perhaps older than the fingerings which use the thumb. The second type of fingering involves the use of three or four fingers consecutively, repeated as many times as necessary, such as 1 2 3 4   1 2 3 4. Some fingerings mix the two kinds, for instance the right hand ascending fingering, 1 2 3 4   3 4 3 4, which begins with four fingers consecutively, then continues alternating two fingers to the end of the passage.[28]

Groups of either two or four notes would be followed by articulation silences, however slight, that would mark metrical groups. The selection of the fingering pattern is determined by the metrical position of the notes in relation to the *tactus* or to the bar line.

Robert Parkins shows that these fingerings continued to be taught in the Spanish treatises of the later seventeenth and early eighteenth centuries. In contrast to the Spanish sources, English, Italian, and Dutch treatises prefer the two-finger groups recommended by Diruta.[29]

English scale fingerings in the early seventeenth century show a preference for 3 4 3 4 in the right hand ascending, and 3 2 3 2 descending. Left hand ascending uses 1 2 1 2, and descending 3 4 3 4.[30]

The German keyboard performance tradition included scale fingerings that suggest grouping by pairs or by fours.

> C. P. E. Bach deals with the octave scales of all twenty-four keys in the first chapter of his *Versuch* and thus shows signs of the pedagogic movement that was to result in the practising of multi-octave scales by all learners of keyboard instruments over at least the last century and a half. Thus it is reasonable to assume that when he gives three different fingerings for C major they should produce a similar effect, i.e. one of even touch modified by neither phrasing nor expression [Ex. 5.7]. But concerning the situation in 1715, three things in particular are still very uncertain: that scales as such were ever practiced, that the evenness required of them in later periods was already desired at that period, and that such evenness (though it may have been easier in some keys) was characteristic of all keys. If the 1 2 3 4 3 4 3 4 fingering was meant to produce an even line by means of controlled fingers, one can imagine this as a characteristic of scales as scales, not of music. If such a scale-like pattern occurred as a contrapuntal motif—as in the *Orgelbüchlein* chorale BWV 644—it could well be that 3 4 3 4 fingering resulted in a degree of pairing.[31]

EX. 5.7

Practicing scales and scale exercises as a path toward virtuosic keyboard technique is not found in pedagogy until the late eighteenth and nineteenth centuries. However, since fingerings for scale patterns are indicative of elementary training in keyboard technique in the seventeenth and eighteenth centuries, we may assume that metrical groupings were embedded in every player's fingers. This evidence says nothing about accentuation (although the clavichord could give an accent), and it does not prove rhythmic inequality, although these fingering patterns are compatible with *notes inégales*. These elementary techniques of fingering can be mastered so thoroughly that a player achieves remarkable smoothness, evenness, velocity, and flexibility through their use. Metrical groups may well have been apparent, but perhaps they were perceived almost subliminally by both player and audience.

The use of elementary fingerings in the performance of a large-scale composition is illustrated in Alessandro Scarlatti's *Toccata prima*. This work offers a diversity of passages with fingerings; supposedly these are for the instruction of Scarlatti's pupils, including his son, Domenico. Scale passages are in paired or four-note groupings, and many other passages are fingered so that an effect of metrical units of two or four would be difficult to avoid. It seems that the performance of this piece was intended to demonstrate a clear metrical structure resulting from the motions of the fingers. Rhetorical or lyric phrasing seems not to have been planned through fingering, but may well have been the goal of performance after the finger patterns were thoroughly mastered.[32]

Fingering patterns in a polished performance depend on much more than the elements learned through metrical fingering of scales. C. P. E. Bach stresses that every musical figure has its own proper fingering, and that new ideas in music therefore introduce new fingerings.[33] Fingerings for rhetorical passages such as quick runs leading up to high notes or down to low notes sometimes alternate the hands. This facilitates a smooth sweep of notes leading to the climax, and any kind of metrical subdivision within the run itself is ignored, as we can see in Ex. 5.8, an excerpt from Azzolino Della Ciaja's Sonata op. IV, no. 2.[34]

EX. 5.8. Bars 101–102 of Azzolino Della Ciaja's Sonata op. IV, no. 2, from *Sonate per cembalo, opera quarta* (Rome, 1727).

Notable changes in fingering took place in the eighteenth century, many of them associated with the performance of J. S. Bach, who placed much greater demands on the technique of keyboard players than did his contemporaries. Peter Williams discusses what is known of Bach's fingering technique, and the difficulty of interpreting his technique through his students' writings and fingerings, most of which were published long after Bach's death. The legends that Bach was the inventor of modern fingering and that he was the first performer fully to use the thumb have gained popular currency; however, these are falsifications or, at the least, exaggerations.[35]

Comments and instructions that illustrate Bach's keyboard technique are important for what they suggest, but they are open to question and interpretation on many levels. Fingerings, stemming either from Bach or from student copyists, illuminate specific passages rather than a basic technique. Metrical fingerings (which imply groups of two or four notes in scale-wise passages) as well as "modern" fingerings and two-hand alternations (which imply smooth unbroken passages) can all be justified in appropriate places. The musical style itself holds the essential clues on which a performer must base his interpretation, in that he must select those techniques appropriate to the nature of the music.

Daniel Gottlob Türk, organist of the Halle *Frauenkirche* from 1787 to the end of his life in 1813, bases the instructions in his *Klavierschule* on the clavichord. In this he follows a long tradition of organists who learned and practiced on that instrument. In Türk's instructions, metrical patterns are marked by accents, not by silences of articulation. He outlines a style of fingering that makes considerable use of crossing the thumb under the longer fingers as well as crossing 3 over 4 ascending, or 3 over 2 descending in the right hand.

> Putting the thumb under, and crossing over, both of which are most useful in fingering, must be practiced until they can be skilfully done without twisting the fingers and hands. Above all, even in skips, there should not be the slightest perceptible break in the legato, the keys should not be struck harder, etc. In short, one should not hear when and where the player makes use of these two devices.

Evidently, any articulation or metrical enhancement is done quite independently of fingering patterns, even though the notes were expected to be somewhat detached when not marked legato.[36]

The treatises and music of the late eighteenth and early nineteenth centuries indicate a change of technique due to a different use of scales as technical exercises, as seen in the quotation from C. P. E. Bach cited by Peter Williams above. Czerny reported that Beethoven thought that the playing of Mozart's time was "gehackte und kurz abgestossene" [37] (choppy and cut-off short), tempting us to believe that detached articulation was still a part of Mozart's, and perhaps other late eighteenth-century keyboard players', techniques. Czerny comments on the legato style of performance he learned from Beethoven's approach to fingering.

Clementi advocated a legato style in articulation in 1801, perhaps influenced by Beethoven's performance, and in contrast with the "normal" articulation advocated for keyboard performance throughout the seventeenth and eighteenth centuries. He describes the new style:

The best general rule, is to keep down the keys of the instrument the FULL LENGTH of every note. . . . When the composer leaves the LEGATO and STACCATO to the performer's taste, the best rule is to adhere chiefly to the LEGATO; reserving the STACCATO to give SPIRIT occasionally to certain passages, and to set off the HIGHER BEAUTIES of the LEGATO.[38]

Although an elementary keyboard technique that had endured for well over two centuries was losing favor, new ways emerged to make metrical structure evident to the listener. Both aesthetic sensibility that favored a different musical style and keyboard technique that suited the sensational new piano forte may have been involved in a change of fingerings and articulation in the late eighteenth century.

Wind-Instrument Tonguing Patterns

Tonguing patterns for wind instruments are also used to heighten the listener's perception of musical meter. Tonguing patterns, like rhythmic inequality of equal notes, can first be found in sixteenth-century performance instructions for diminutions. The rhythmic and melodic formulas of diminutions were taught to performers in method books much like Hanon's exercises for the piano, except that the Renaissance exercises trained both fingers and memory with formulas that were intended to be the basis for improvisation. The use of tonguing patterns was important, since every note of the diminution was expected to be articulated.

When these patterns were applied to ornamentation formulas, they fully supplied phrasings and articulations. To the modern performer, this "unmarked" music seems to require either slurring or a mixture of slurring and tonguing; however, this is a great deal of unnecessary interpretation. Richard Erig has presented a thorough summary of the wind-instrument articulations of the sixteenth and early seventeenth centuries, from which the later seventeenth- and eighteenth-century wind articulations developed:

> All long notes, which in vocal pieces are also those which carry the text, are spoken with "single tonguing," with the syllables te or de; each t or d creates a small accent, and thus a separation from the previous note, thereby setting off the notes from one another.
> For the fast notes there were three types of "tonguings," each of which joins two notes together: lere, tere, and teche (and variants thereof).
> The most important of these tonguings, because of its particular gentleness, was the "lingua riversa" (lere); it is described as "dolce." For Dalla Casa and Rognoni, who point out its similarity to the "gorgia," the virtuosic throat technique used in singing, it was the "prima lingua." Rognoni writes that it is preferred by the "boni Sonatori" and does not mention the other two types.[39]

All three fast tonguings mentioned above group notes by twos and yet give each note a separate impulse. Rognoni's illustrations are melodies in which tonguings are mixed, for example, sixteenth notes repeated on the same pitch are tongued *te te te te,* but ascending or descending sixteenths are tongued *te re le re*. Fantini's trumpet tonguings even include words and sentences, for example, "da tondella butta sella," which corresponds to a trumpeter's battle calls.

The consonants used in the tonguing syllables undergo relatively small changes in the wind-instrument instruction books of the late seventeenth and eighteenth centuries, but the vowels *e* and *a* of earlier players are changed to *ü* and *i* in the method books of Freillon Poncein, Hotteterre, and Quantz. Erig suggests that the palatal *r* becomes an *l* in Romance languages and a *d* in German. For example, Quantz uses *did'll* instead of *der ler*.[40]

The oboist Jean Pierre Freillon Poncein described the following varieties of tonguings:

> Des coups de langue. & de la manière dont il faut les marquer. Il faut remarquer que generalement dans toutes les mesures où il y a trois, quatre noires ou croches, il faut marquer *tu* sur la premiere, *re* sur la seconde, & *tu* sur les autres, en passant la derniere un peu plus vîte que les autres, apres avoir demeuré sur la précédente sur tout lors qu'elle est blanche ou d'égale valeur [Ex. 5.9].
>
> Lorsque c'est à trois temps, il faut faire la blanche longue & la marquer *tu* & passer la seconde legèrement en la marquant *ru* [Ex. 5.10].
>
> Aux mesures de 4 & 6, de 8 & 6, de 3 & 9, de 8 & 9, de 4 & 12, de 8 & 12, on marquera la seconde de chaque tems *ru* & les autres *tu* [Ex. 5.11].
>
> Aux blanches, aux noires & aux croches, pointées de toutes sortes de mesures, il faut en user autrement car aprés fait *tu* sur la premiere & sur la croche qui la suit il faut faire *ru* sur la troisiéme & *tu* sur la quatriéme [Ex. 5.12].
>
> Les croches simples, doubles & triples lorsque le nombre est pair, c'est à dire lors qu'il n'y a point de noires pointées, ou de demy soûpir auparavant, on doit les marquer *tu, tu, ru, tu, ru* jusqu'à la fin; & quand le nombre est impair; *tu, ru, tu, ru* & continuer de même, & que celle où l'on finira soit marquée *ru* quand même elle seroit blanche [Ex. 5.13].
>
> Les doubles des mesures du 2, du ₵ barré, du 4/8, 3/8, & les croches & doubles croches du 6/4 & 6/8, comme elles se passent vîte lors qu'il y en a 8, au plus on les doit marquer *tu, ru, tu, ru,* jusqu'à la fin, comme on le peut voir aux Ex. F [Ex. 5.14] & de même à l'égard des autres mesures qui doivent aller vîte pour avoir plus de liberté de la langue & pour les passer plus legerement.[41]

> Tonguing and how it is done: Generally in all meters containing three or four quarters or eighths, the first is played *tu,* the second *ru,* and *tu* on the others. The last is played a little faster than the others after having rested a little longer on the note preceding it, especially when it is a half note or a note of equal duration [Ex. 5.9].

tu   ru   tu   ru tu   tu ru tu tu   tu   ru   tu   ru tu   tu ru tu tu

In a meter of three beats, play the half note long, say *tu* and play the second quickly saying *ru* [Ex. 5.10].

EX. 5.10

In 6/4, 6/8, 9/3, 12/4, 12/8 measures the second (note) of each beat is marked *ru* and the others *tu* [Ex. 5.11].

EX. 5.11

For dotted half notes, dotted quarters and dotted eighths in all measures, tonguings are used differently. After using *tu* on the first and on the eighth that follows it, *ru* must be used on the third and *tu* on the fourth [Ex. 5.12].

EX. 5.12

When there are even numbers of eighths, sixteenths, and thirty-second notes, that is, when there are no dotted quarters or eighth rests before them, the tonguings should be *tu tu ru tu, ru* [beginning the next group], to the end; and when there are uneven numbers of them; *tu ru tu, ru* [beginning the next group] and continuing the same, even though the last note would be tongued *ru* if it were a half note [Ex. 5.13].

EX. 5.13

If they are played quickly and if there are as many as eight of them, the six-teenths in the measures of 2, ¢, 4/8, 3/8, and the eighths and sixteenths in 6/4 and 6/8, use *tu ru tu ru,* until the end, as is shown in example F [Ex. 5.14].

EX. 5.14

The same should be followed in other measures played fast to have more liberty for the tongue and to be able to play more quickly.

Modern performers use a "double tonguing," *te ke* (equivalent to *tu ru*), in fast passages when it is not possible to tongue *te* repeatedly and quickly. In present-day performance the ideal is to pronounce *te* and *ke* in such a way that no difference can be detected by the listener. However, there is no reason to suppose that eighteenth-century performers tried to eliminate the pronunciation difference between *tu* and *ru*.

Freillon Poncein's tonguings provide for a differentiation between notes through articulation in addition to facilitating the performance of fast passages. *Tu* causes the reed of the oboe to be articulated by the tip of the tongue and *ru* causes the column of air to be stopped by the middle of the tongue. Most modern oboists cannot articulate notes except by touching the tip of the tongue to the reed, and therefore can use only *tu*. Both tongue strokes can be done on the flute and recorder, with good effect. *Tu* is precise, although it can be done very softly and gently, and *ru* may be strong but not as precise in its initial impact as *tu*. By accepting the difference between *tu* and *ru,* or even heightening it, Freillon Poncein's tonguings reinforce metric grouping.

Hotteterre also advocates *tu* and *ru* tonguings, although he frequently uses them differently than Freillon Poncein. Hotteterre's method is primarily for the flute, and Freillon Poncein's for the oboe. The important point is that there is a difference between *tu* and *ru,* not that they are used in the same patterns.

> Pour rendre le jeu plus agréable, & pour éviter trop d'uniformité dans les coups de Langue, on les varie en plusieurs manieres; Par exemple on se sert de deux articulations principales; Sçavoir, *tu* & *ru*. Le *tu* est le plus en usage, & l'on s'en sert presque par tout; comme sur les Rondes, les Blanches, les Noires, & sur la plus grande partie des Croches; car lorsque ces dernieres sont sur la même ligne, ou qu'elles sautent, on prononce *tu*. Lorsqu'elles montent ou descendent par degrez conjoints, on se sert aussi du *tu*, mais on l'entremêle toûjours avec le *ru*, comme l'on peut voir dans les Exemples cy-après [Ex. 5.15], où ces deux articulations se succedent l'une à l'autre.
>
> On doit remarquer qu le *tu, ru,* se reglent par le nombre des Croches. Quand le nombre est impair on prononce *tu ru,* tout de suite, comme l'on voit au premier Exemple. Quand il est pair on prononce *tu,* sur les deux premiéres Croches, ensuite *ru* alternativement, comme l'on voit dans le deuxiéme Exemple. On fera bien d'observer que l'on ne doit pas toûjours passer les Croches également & qu'on doit dans certains Mesures, en faire une longue & une breve; ce qui se regle aussi par le nombre. Quand il est pair on fait le premiére longue, la second breve, & ainsi des autres. Quand il est impair on fait tout le contraire; cela s'appelle pointer. Les Mesures dans lesquelles cela se pratique le plus ordinairement, sont celles à Deux-temps, celle du triple simple, & celle de six pour quatre. On doit prononcer *ru,* sur la note qui suit la Croche quand elle monte ou descend par degrez conjoints [Ex. 5.16].[42]

> In order to make the performance more agreeable and to avoid too much uniformity in tonguings, they are varied in several ways. For example, there are two principal articulations used: *tu* and *ru*. *Tu* is most frequently used and everywhere, on whole notes, halves, quarters, and on the greater number of eighths, as when these last are [repeated] on the same line or when they move disjunctly. When they

rise or descend conjunctly *tu* is also used, but it is mixed with *ru,* as can be seen in the example following [Ex. 5.15], where these two articulations come one after the other.

EX. 5.15

It must be noted that *tu, ru* is governed by the number of eighths. When the number is odd, *tu ru* is pronounced immediately, as in the first example. When it is even, *tu* is pronounced on the first two eighths, then alternatively with *ru,* as in the second example. It is well to observe that the eighths should not always be played as equal, in certain measures one must be long and the other short; this also is determined by the number. When it is even, the first is long, the second short, and so on with the others. When it is odd, they are done entirely the opposite, this is called *pointer.* The measures in which this is most usually done are the *Deux-temps* (2) the *triple simple* (3 or 3/4) and the 6/4. *Ru* must be pronounced on the note that follows the eighth, when it rises or descends by conjunct motion [Ex. 5.16].

EX. 5.16

Directions for playing *notes inégales* were interspersed with those for various articulations. This proximity heightens the impression that they were considered useful in much the same way, even though no specific comment to this effect was made.

Hotteterre's articulation of the 3x2 measure, marked 3/2, should be considered in contrast to the 2x3 measure illustrated in Ex. 5.16, marked 6/4:

> Dans la Mesure du Triple double, on prononce *tu, ru,* entre les Noires, & *ru,* sur la Blanche qui est precedee d'une Noire, en montant ou en descendent, par degrez conjoints [Ex. 5.17].[43]

In the *triple double* [3/2] measure, *tu, ru* is pronounced on the quarter notes, and *ru* on the half note that is preceded by a quarter note that rises or descends conjunctly [Ex. 5.17].

EX. 5.17

This example provides a means of differentiating between these two measures that supplements the articulations mentioned by Butler, Malcolm, and Rousseau.

Quantz's *Versuch* discussed many different tonguing patterns, including *ti, di, di ri, ti ri,* and *did'll.* Quantz specifically associated *ti ri* with the passages that "are played with some inequality," and *ti* is said on the shorter, *ri* on the longer note. "Bey diesem Wörtchen *tiri* fäll der Accent auf die letzte Sylbe" (the accent in the word *tiri* falls on the last syllable), so that *ri* is said on the good note and *ti* on the bad. The resulting grouping is against the beat, from *arsis* to *thesis. Did'll* has the opposite accentuation, with the accent falling on the first syllable. Most oboists cannot use *did'll* because a relatively stiff oboe reed requires that the tongue come in contact with it in order to articulate sounds.[44]

Quantz is one of the first to discuss extensively the subject of slurs or ties in woodwind performance. Only the first of a group of slurred notes is tongued, using *di* rather than *ti.* If a *strich* or staccato mark is used on the note preceding a slur, the syllable *ti* is used on both that note and the first of the slurred notes. If passage-work must be played more quickly than *tiri* can be tongued, then either the first two notes or the last two notes of groups of four should be slurred together and the other two tongued.[45]

The most extensive use of slurs in Quantz's musical examples occurs in the musical illustration for chapter XIV, "Of the manner of playing the adagio." Slurs are used to link groups of notes in his Italianate, division-style, florid ornamentation and seem to be included as an illustration of how to perform the written-out melismas. The unornamented version of the adagio melody has conspicuously few slurs.[46]

Articulation patterns that tongue every note in a passage were taught to performers throughout the eighteenth century by many later editions of Hotteterre's *Principes*[47] and Quantz's *Versuch.*[48] However, a number of flute method books beginning about 1735 taught other tonguings and different patterns of articulation.

Corrette's flute method (ca. 1735) disdained the use of the syllables taught by Hotteterre and suggested that flutists imitate the articulation of violin bow strokes. Indications of phrasing originally used for violin bowings were adapted for the flute, such as a dot over the note indicating staccato. The dot over notes had been used in French music to indicate that the notes were not played unequally, but now it came to mean a short articulation. Delusse (ca. 1761) described an imitation of the violinist's "slurred staccato" as the "pearl stroke"; every note was to be articulated with the individuality and perfection of a pearl on a string. Delusse also advocated articulation by impulses of the breath alone, which he indicated by "hu, hu" beneath the notes. On repeated notes, this articulation was notated by a combination of dots over the notes with a slur connecting them all together.[49]

Devienne (1795) recommends an alternation of two notes slurred and two notes tongued in fast passages when articulation is not specified, a practice that was first mentioned by Quantz for fast passages. It seems to have become popular with performers in the late eighteenth century and continues to be used extensively today.[50]

From this brief survey of woodwind articulations, it is evident that wind players applied many patterns of articulation to the apparently unphrased music that we see in original notation. The variety of both patterns and tongue strokes provided many different shadings of articulation. The early eighteenth-century manuals teach articulations in order to group notes and define measure organization, rather than to heighten particular melodic ideas or introduce a dramatic effect, as modern articulations often do. The various systems of tonguing patterns differ in specific details but testify to the importance attached to distinguishing between notes according to their relative position in the measure.

Stringed-Instrument Bowings

Wonderfully rich and varied possibilities for shaping and inflecting sound are available to the players of bowed stringed instruments. These include shadings of tone quality, a wide dynamic range, and control over intonation as well as techniques of articulation to clarify metrical structure.

The most basic and elementary distinction made in using the bow is whether it is drawn up or down. On the violin, this entails moving the weight of the arm, hand, and bow by or against the force of gravity, and on the viola da gamba, moving the bow toward or away from the body.

The basic rules for guiding the choice of up- or down-bow strokes depend on the metrical position of notes in the measure. The down-bow stroke on the violin is stronger, more precise and definite in effect, and the up-bow stroke is lighter and more delicate. "Up-bow" on the viola da gamba, actually a stroke from right to left, toward the body, is the equivalent of down-bow on the violin, and "down-bow," from left to right, is equivalent to up-bow on the violin. This is obvious to players, of course, and was mentioned by Marin Mersenne as a clear distinction in technique between the instruments.[51]

Rules for choosing up- or down-bow on the viola da gamba are given by Jean Rousseau[52] and summarized and discussed by Hans Bol.[53] Rousseau's rules were not new at the time but are a summary of bowing practices that can be seen in the examples of Ganassi in the sixteenth century[54] and in the descriptions of Mersenne,[55] Simpson,[56] and Danoville.[57] These are remarkably similar to the rules for choosing violin bowings given by Georg Muffat, derived from the practice of Lully's performers, except for the opposite direction of drawing the bow.

The differences between the advanced techniques of the viola da gamba and the violin are many and subtle and deserve careful delineation beyond the scope of this chapter. Let us consider elementary bowing technique in relation to the violins in the later part of the seventeenth century.

Violin technique was discussed in the writings of J. A. Herbst[58] and Gasparo Zannetti,[59] and by Georg Muffat late in the seventeenth century.[60]

Violinists distinguished between a great variety of possible bowings, although the effect of the down-bow or up-bow was the most basic. The "Rule of Down-Bow" was best defined in detail by Georg Muffat in the preface to *Florilegium secundum:*

However it is well known that the Lullists, whom the French, the English, those from the Low Countries, and many others follow, all observe an identical way of bowing, even if a thousand of them play together. They all observe the same way of playing the principal notes in the measure, above all those that begin the measure, those that define the cadence, and those that most clearly emphasize the dance rhythm. . . .

1. The first note in each measure, when there is no rest or pause, should be played down-bow, regardless of its value. This is the principal and almost indispensable rule of the Lullists, on which almost the entire secret of bowing depends and which differentiates them from the others. All subsequent rules depend on this rule. In order to know how the other notes fall into place and are to be played, one must attend to the following rules.

2. In common time, which the theorists call "tempus imperfectum," the measure is divided into equal parts. Odd-numbered notes (1, 3, 5, etc.) are played down-bow, and even-numbered notes (2, 4, 6, etc.) should be played up-bow [Ex. 5.18]. This rule applies also in triple meter, or any meter when the beats are diminished equally by half. I call diminutions all those notes that are faster than those values indicated in the time signature [Ex. 5.19]. This way of counting equal divisions of beats is similarly observed if rests of the same value appear instead of notes [Ex. 5.20]. All the finest masters agree readily with the French on this second rule.

EX. 5.18

EX. 5.19

EX. 5.20

3. Since, according to the first rule, the first note in the measure is down-bow, the second of three equal notes (which comprise a complete measure in triple time) is always up-bow, and the third is once again down-bow, at least when one plays rather slowly; therefore in beginning the measure following, one must play down-bow for the second time in succession [Ex. 5.21]. More often, however, the second and third notes are played in the same up-bow stroke, divided distinctly in two. This is called *craquer*. It allows the measure to go a little faster with greater ease [Ex. 5.22].

EX. 5.21

EX. 5.22

4. In *Proportione Sextupla,* the measure is divided into two basic parts [Ex. 5.23]. In *Proportione Nonupla* the measure is divided into three parts [Ex. 5.24]. In *Proportione Duodecupla* the measure is divided into four parts [Ex. 5.25]. In these distributions, each part contains three of those values indicated in the time signature. The first of the three equal notes is almost always played down-bow, for a clearer sound, even if the group does not begin the measure, and the two others are played in an up-bow stroke, divided in two. If there is a rest instead of the first note, the following note should unquestionably be played down-bow in triple measures (a) and other proportions (b) [Ex. 5.26].

EX. 5.23

EX. 5.24

EX. 5.25

EX. 5.26

5. When several notes, each of one measure duration, appear in succession, each should be down-bow [Ex. 5.27]. In six, or in twelve, several successive notes of equal value should be played alternately down-bow and up-bow according to whether they fall on an odd or even note, as explained in the second rule [Ex. 5.28]; but in nine they follow the first aspect of the third rule (triple meter) [Ex. 5.29].

EX. 5.27

EX. 5.28

EX. 5.29

6. Several equal successive syncopated notes usually require down-bow and up-bow alternately. This is all concerning notes of like value [Ex. 5.30].

EX. 5.30

7. As far as mixed note-values are concerned, the first of the smaller values following longer values should be counted the odd number, so that it can be played down-bow, if it should come out that way [Ex. 5.31], or divided up-bow, if it should occur this way [Ex. 5.32]. The first two beats of smaller value are played with divided up-bows [Ex. 5.33]. If other smaller values follow after that, they are played up-bow and down-bow alternately. As far as pauses and rests are concerned, they can be counted as notes [Ex. 5.34].

EX. 5.31

EX. 5.32

EX. 5.33

EX. 5.34

8. When subdivisions of the measure consist of three notes, and the first has a dot after it, it is ordinarily down-bow [Ex. 5.35].

EX. 5.35

9. Several successive notes, each completing the measure (or subdivision) after a pause or rest, should be down-bow and up-bow alternately, regardless of the said rest or pause [Ex. 5.36].

EX. 5.36

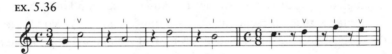

10. The little note by itself before the beginning of the measure (20a) as well as the one that passes quickly after a dot or after a short rest (20b) and likewise the smaller note that follows a larger syncopated one, (20c) should always be up-bow [Ex. 5.37]. If the longer syncopated note is also up-bow, it will be necessary to divide the up-bow stroke in half, thereby adding the following note to it (indicated by ˙) [Ex. 5.38].[61]

EX. 5.37

EX. 5.38

The use of bowings, therefore, to establish metric relationship among notes was basic to this school of violin playing. This bowing discipline allowed any number of violinists to play in unanimity in orchestral ensembles. It seems likely that the differences between the sound of down-bow and up-bow were subtle, as is the case with wind articulations, so as not to overwhelm the flow of the music. The effect of different bow strokes on an individual instrument is magnified by the unison of an orchestral section.

Corelli's musicians in Rome sometimes numbered as many as one hundred and fifty. Georg Muffat commented that the concerti were "performed with the utmost accuracy by a great number of instrumentalists."[62] Boyden comments that while Muffat's bowing directions are primarily for the performance of dance music, "it is likely that at first the sonata players adopted the same basic principles . . . considering dance bowings carefully before rejecting or amplifying them. We do not know in what respects, if any, the sonata players before 1650 deviated from the basic bowing principles of the dance violinists."[63] As there are no treatises that consider Italian bowing technique in the late seventeenth and early eighteenth centuries, for all we know, the "Rule of Down-Bow" could have been used to produce the unity of Corelli's orchestra as well as of Lully's.

French violinists seem to have retained Muffat's "Rule of Down-Bow." Dupont[64] and Montéclair[65] continue to teach the basic rules but give more examples in which exceptional bowings are explored. Marc Pincherle comments that Corrette (1738), Leopold Mozart (1756), and the Abbé le fils (1772) continue, at least in part, to teach the "Rule of Down-Bow."[66]

Although bowing directions similar to Muffat's are found in Quantz's *Versuch,* he remarks that "present musical writing" requires an equal strength from the up-bow and the down-bow in orchestral violin playing.[67] Perhaps this remark should be taken to mean that before "present musical writing," up-stroke and downstroke were not even; that is, that Muffat's bowings did not give the effect of evenness. Leopold Mozart also comments that upstroke and downstroke must be played alike in order to achieve the results he desires.[68] His bowings are almost identical to those of Muffat.

Referring to scale passages, Geminiani (1751) warns: "There it must be observed, that you are to execute them by drawing the bow up and down, or down and up alternately; taking care not to follow that wretched Rule of drawing the Bow down at the first note of every Bar."[69] Geminiani continues:

> So in playing Divisions, if by your Manner of Bowing, you lay a particular Stress on the Note at the beginning of every Bar, so as to render it predominant over the rest, you alter and spoil the true air of the piece, and except where the composer intended it, and where it is always marked, there are very few Instances in which it is not very disagreeable.[70]

Perhaps the proper assumption is that only an inept violinist would mechanically accent the first note of every bar. Stress or accent was mentioned but not featured in descriptions of measure organization in the first half of the eighteenth century, although many instruments were capable of it. Geminiani's warning against accent seems in accord with the general attitude of the time.

David Boyden summarizes the elementary technique of both violin and viola da gamba bowing in the seventeenth and early eighteenth centuries as the "Rule of Down-Bow,"[71] although for the viola da gamba it should be called the "Rule of Up-Bow." He equates both the down-bow stroke and good notes with accent or stress, despite the care used by writers in the earlier sources not to use the words "accent" or "stress." In order to facilitate his explanation, Boyden has adopted the usual twentieth-century idea that meter is identical with stress. Unfortunately, this interpretation distorts the effect and intent of bowing technique in the seventeenth and eighteenth centuries.

The variety of individual bow strokes discussed in late eighteenth-century treatises is much greater than those mentioned in the seventeenth-century treatises of Zannetti, Herbst, and Muffat. If the discipline of the "Rule of Down-Bow" was preserved in the late eighteenth century, it was interpreted with a new richness in variety of sounds, colors, and nuance. Robin Stowell describes three strokes: the staccato stroke (called *détaché* in French treatises), the "bounding" stroke (called *sautillé*, spiccato, or "flying staccato") for bravura passages, and the legato bowing strokes that imitate the voice. Many kinds of slurred bowings were used as well as special strokes such as *bariolage* (playing the same note alternately on two strings) and *ondegglando* (moving the bow back and forth across two or more adjacent strings).[72] All of these techniques were described and used on the bows preceding the introduction of the more rigid and powerful Tourte bow in 1761.

The viola da gamba bow stroke, whether up or down, was capable of much subtlety, and John Hsu has distinguished six different bow strokes that were mentioned by Hubert Le Blanc[73] and described in some detail by Etienne Loulié.[74] The basic stroke is divided into three parts, the *première impression* (which gives almost the effect of plucking the string), a prolongation of the sound, and the release of the tension of the bow on the string, which results in the sound's fading. Loulié's other bow strokes expand the volume of sound after the *première impression*, sustain the sound at the same level, stop the sound after the *première impression*, go quickly into the preparation for the next note, or articulate more than one note while moving the bow in the same direction.[75]

The employment of such a repertory of articulations, based on the practice of Marin Marais and Antoine Forqueray, gave great variety and subtlety to the performance of the French school of viola da gamba players in the late seventeenth and early eighteenth centuries.

Elementary bowing practices agree fundamentally on the importance of enhancing the metrical structure of music in performance. The "Rule of Down-Bow" is clearly identified with musical meter, and varieties of bowings are tied to various time signatures. The results from even the most meticulous recreation of performance based on the "Rule of Down-Bow" are dependent on many kinds of up- or down-bow strokes, many ways of continuing the sound after the initial moment, and different ways of terminating the sound. Almost all pedagogical or theoretical discussions of musical performance are only sketches; imagination must infuse them with the subtlety of a finished performance.

Engramelle's La tonotechnie

The effect of bowings, fingerings, and tonguings is difficult to specify, since it probably varied from performer to performer and certainly varied according to the style of the music. However, there is one source of information about performance that is uniquely precise about the effect of metrical articulation. Directions for making a mechanical organ in Father Marie-Dominique-Joseph Engramelle's *La tonotechnie* (1775) give such accurate information about performance that it has been possible to make a recording of the melodies he describes.[76] The mechanical organ cylinder illustrates two aspects of quantitative articulation with absolute clarity: longer and shorter durations of equal notes, and *notes inégales.* Perhaps Engramelle's directions can illuminate some of the less precise instructions of other musicians.

Engramelle goes into more detail than the usual descriptions of performance technique because such specificity is required in order to record music for a mechanical organ, where pins, or bridges linking pins, are embedded in a rotating cylinder to trip the keys. In the middle of plate 6 there is a drawing of the cylinder, below which are various sizes of pins and bridges and a gauge for measuring them. Plate 7 shows the cylinder in place with a handle to turn it, the gears that engage with the cylinder, and a dial that measures the space on the cylinder. The *noteur* arranged the pins by measuring the space between notes according to divisions of the dial.[77] Plate 8 is the frontispiece from *La tonotechnie,* which shows two craftsmen, one working on a *serinette* (canaryorgan), the other working on a larger cylinder. The room is filled with mechanical musical instruments, including a mechanical harpsichord, Vaucanson's mechanical flute player, a mechanical organ (over the doorway), and a musical clock.

Forty turns of the *serinette*'s handle make one complete revolution of the cylinder, and each turn of the handle may be divided into as many parts as necessary to mark each note and the subdivisions required for silences of articulation and for ornaments. Each subdivision of the dial, a *module,* is equivalent to the smallest note value or silence in the music, usually the length of one of the *battements* in an ornament. The length of the piece, its tempo, and its character or expression determine what number of divisions of the dial is most suitable.

Engramelle uses the singing voice as his primary model for articulation in *notage* by simulating silences in pronunciation before hard consonants, the articulation of a syllable without a tongue-stroke, and pauses to take breath. These are mixed with articulations that are purely instrumental in concept, such as the separation of notes from one another required by raising the finger from one key in order to strike the next:

> Si, par exemple, il se rencontroit deux noires de suite, dont la seconde dût être frappée d'un coup de langue, la première de ces deux noirs n'étant *tenue* qu'à

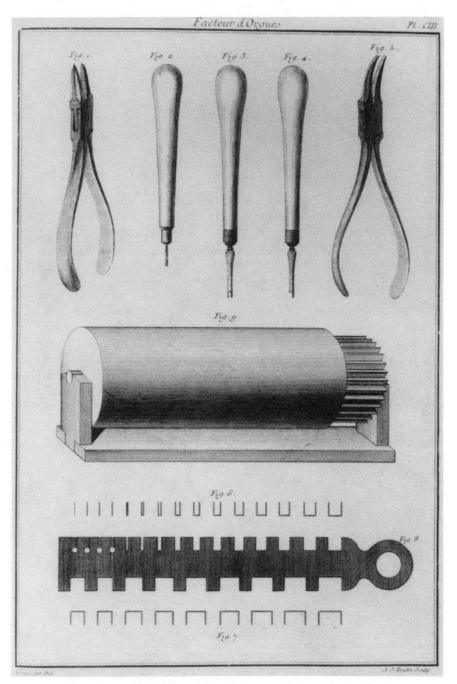

PLATE 6. *Serinette* cylinder and tools. (Plate CIV from *L'Art du facteur d'orgues* by Dom Bédos de Celles.)

PLATE 7. *Serinette*. (Plate CIII from *L'Art du facteur d'orgues* by Dom Bédos de Celles.)

PLATE 8. Frontispiece of Engramelle's *La tonotechnie*.

demi, ou ne parlant que pendant la première moitié de sa valeur, l'autre moitié restant en silence, seroit un détaché qui équivaudroit à un coup de langue sur la seconde de ces deux noires; & plus on augmenteroit le *silence* de la première, plus le coup de langue sur la seconde seroit ressenti & détaché.

Si au lieu de deux noires, il se rencontroient deux croches, dont la seconde dût être marquée par un coup de langue, en ne faisant qu'une *tactée* de la première, le *silence* qui resteroit à la suite produiront sur la seconde l'effet d'un coup de langue.

Aux notes *tenues,* qui ne doivent pas fournir des coups de langue sur leurs suivantes, leur *silence* doit être plus court pour ne faire qu'un simple détaché, afin qu'elles ne se confondent pas avec celles qui les suivent immédiatement; ce *silence* de détaché doit être de la valeur d'une double croche, à moins que ces notes ne soient marquées liées; pour lors leur *silence* ne seroit que d'une triple croche ou environ.

Pour les reprises d'haleine, les *silences* sont ordinairement d'une noire pointée, même quelquefois de la valeur d'une blanche, suivant l'espace qui se trouvera depuis le commencement d'une note à l'autre, ce qui ne se peut déterminer que conséquemment au genre d'expression qui convient à la piéce de musique qu'on veut exécuter.[78]

If, for example, the second of two successive quarter notes is to have the effect of a tonque-stroke, the first of the two should be held only half of its value with the other half silent, this makes the second detached in a manner equivalent to having a tongue-stroke. The greater the silence after the first note, the more the tongue-stroke is perceived as detaching the first note from the second.

If, in place of two quarter notes we have two eighths, of which the second is to be marked by a tongue-stroke, by making the first *tactée,* the following silence produces the effect of a tongue-stroke on the second.

For held notes not preceding tongue-strokes, the silence should be shorter to give the effect of a simple detached note that does not merge with the following note. This silence of detachment should be the value of a sixteenth note, at least if the notes are not marked slurred. If they are slurred the silence is no more than a thirty-second note, or thereabout.

For taking a breath, silences are ordinarily a dotted quarter note or sometimes a half note, according to the space found between the beginning of one note and the next. This can be determined only as a consequence of the kind of expression suitable to the piece of music one wishes to perform.

Without exception, says Engramelle, every note is partly sustained and partly silent, but notes may be identified as either *tenues* or *tactées* by the duration of the sustained part. A *tactée* is barely "touched"; only the very first part of the note is sounded and the remainder is silent. A *tenue,* on the other hand, sounds through half or more of the length of the note, followed by a short silence. In the ordinary performance of a succession of eighth notes, and sometimes quarters or sixteenths, *tenues* and *tactées* alternate in order for two-note groups to be discerned as though they were separate syllables.

In Engramelle's musical examples, reproduced in plates 9, 10, and 11, marks are added above the notes to illustrate these principles to the *noteur.*

PLATE 9. Music examples 1–4 from Engramelle's *La tonotechnie*.

Tenues are symbolized by a horizontal line and *tactées* by a vertical stroke. Longer pauses are indicated by dots over the *tenue* lines. In the *Menuet de Zelindor* (see plate 9), each dot is equivalent to a sixteenth-note triplet. The first of two tied notes is followed by only a thirty-second note silence, and the second note is *tactée*. All of the eighth notes are performed as equal.

Ornaments are indicated by abbreviated versions of common French signs for *agréments*. With one important exception, the melodic shape of Engramelle's ornaments agrees with French *agréments* in use from the time of D'Anglebert. The exception is an ornament that begins and ends on the main note and alternates with the upper neighbor note, called a *tremoletto* by the Italians in the seventeenth and eighteenth centuries, and sometimes called an "inverted mordent" today. Engramelle calls it a *martellement*.

It is interchangeable with an ornament that alternates between the main

PLATE 10. Music examples 5–8 from Engramelle's *La tonotechnie.*

note and its lower neighbor, a familiar pattern in the French music of the early eighteenth century. In his description of Mr. Balbastre's *Romance,* in *L'art du facteur d'orgues,* Engramelle remarks on this ornament: "La premiere note de la seconde mesure est une blanche sur le *la,* martelée avec le *si;* on pourroit aussi la *marteler* avec le *sol dieze;* on choisira, elle seroit également un bon effet" (The first note of the second measure is a half-note *a,* ornamented with a *b.* It could also be ornamented with a *g♯,* the choice is open, and it would sound as well).[79]

Each note in the quick alternations of *agréments* is ordinarily equal to one division on Engramelle's dial, or one *module.* In the *Menuet de Zelindor,* each *module* is equal to a single sixteenth-note triplet. Usually the number of *battements* in the ornament allows sufficient time for the main note to sound, followed by the necessary silence before the next note. However, cadential trills

PLATE 11. Music examples 9–12 from Engramelle's *La tonotechnie.*

sometimes require more *battements* than there are modular divisions in the note. The usual method of noting these is temporarily to decrease the space on the cylinder for each *module,* so that they will fit into the available time.

An alternate method of accommodating florid ornaments gives each module of trills a full division of the dial. This results in a ritardando, which Engramelle employs for occasional final cadences, for instance, the cadential trill of the second part of the *Menuet de Zelindor,* where two or three sixteenth-note triplets are added to the duration of the penultimate measure. If a ritardando is used, the spaces on the cylinder cease to correspond to the numbers on the dial, and the exact meter of the piece is disturbed. Engramelle omits the numbers of the dial below the music at such points, as in *La Marche du Roy, Menuet de Zelindor,* and the *Romance.* You may wish to hear the recording of *Le Menuet de Zelindor* at this point.

Engramelle describes his analytical method for determining the silences of instrumental articulation:

Pour se convaincre de la nécessité de ces *silences* à la fin de chaque note, qu'on exécute sur un orgue, un clavessin, épinette, ou toute autre instrument à clavier que ce soit tel air qu'on voudra, & qu'on l'exécutant on fasse plutôt attention à l'exécution qu'à la manière dont on le note sur le papier, on s'appercevra qu'un doigt qui vient de finir un note, est souvent levé long-tems auparavant que de poser le doigt pour le note suivante, & cet intervalle est nécessairement un *silence,* et si l'on y prend bien garde, il se trouvera entre toutes les notes de ces intervalles plus ou moins longs, sans lesquels l'exécution seroit mauvaise: il n'est même pas de modules de cadences qui ne soient séparés par des très-petits intervalles très courts entre la levée & la pose de doigts sur les touches: ce sont tous ces intervalles plus ou moins longs, que j'appelle les *silences d'articulation* dans la Musique, dont aucune note n'est exempte, pas plus que la prononciation articulée des consonnes dans la parole, sans lesquelles toutes les syllabes n'auroient d'autre distinction que le son inarticulé des voyelles.

Un peu d'attention dans la prononciation sur l'articulation des syllabes sera appercevoir aisément que, pour produire l'effet de presque toutes les consonnes, le son des voyelles se trouve suspendu & intercepté, soit en rapprochant les levres l'une contre l'autre, ou en rapprochant la langue contre le palais, les dents, &c. toutes ces suspensions ou interceptions du son des voyelles sont autant de petits *silences* qui détachent les syllabes les unes des autres pour former l'articulation de la Musique, à la différence près que le son d'un instrument étant partout le même, & ne pouvant, pour ainsi dire, produire qu'une seule voyelle, il faut que les *silences d'articulation* soient plus variés que dans la parole, si l'on veut qu'elle produise une espéce d'articulation intelligible & intéressante.[80]

In order to be convinced of the need for these silences at the end of each note, play whatever you wish on an organ, harpsichord, spinet, or any other keyboard instrument, and while playing, pay more attention to the performance than to the way it is noted on the page. It will be seen that after playing a note, a finger is often lifted a long time before it is placed for the following note. This interval is necessarily a silence, and if you notice it, you will find it between all notes in smaller or greater measure. Without these the performance is bad; even the notes of trills are separated by very short intervals between raising and lowering the fingers on the keys. These are the longer or shorter intervals that I call "silences of articulation" in music. No note is exempt from this rule, any more than is the pronunciation of consonants. Without these, all syllables would be no more distinct than the inarticulate sounds of vowels.

With a little attention to the articulation of syllables it is easily seen that in order to give the effect of almost all consonants, the sound of vowels is suspended and interrupted either by the lips coming together or by pressing the tongue against the palate or the teeth, etc. All these suspensions or interruptions are silences separating syllables from one another in order to articulate a word. It is the same in the articulation of music, with the difference being that the sound of an instrument is always the same, so to speak, and not able to produce more than one vowel. It is necessary that silences of articulation be more varied than in speech if they are to be intelligible and interesting.

Engramelle minutely considers how *notes inégales* are performed. He distinguishes between *firsts,* the initial note of a pair, and *seconds,* in successive eighth notes. *Firsts* are *tenue* and *seconds* are *tactée,* so that there is the effect of a tongue-stroke on all *firsts.* In addition, he advises *noteurs:*

Il est une observation essentielle à faire sur les croches qui s'exécutent souvent inégalement de deux en deux. Les papiers notés ne nous indique pas quelle est la valeur de cette différence; si elle est de la moitié du tiers ou de quart: il seroit cependant essential de la fixer; car si l'on suivoit exactement dans le notage la valeur des croches comme elles sont indiquées sur les papiers de Musique, elles seroient toutes égales en *durée,* en *tenue* & en *silence,* & c'est ce qui arrive rarement dans l'exécution, laquelle doit être la régle invariable du Noteur des cylindres: ainsi lorsque cette inégalité entre les croches doit avoir lieu dans l'exécution, pour soutenir le genre d'expression qui convient à l'air, il faut que le Noteur puisse l'apprécier pour la rendre comme il faut, ce qu'il ne peut faire que par l'exécution elle-même.

Ces croches inégales se marquent de deux en deux, c'est-à-dire, de noire en noire; les deux ensemble faisant la valeur d'une noire entière, dont la *première* qui fait la première partie de la noire, est plus longue, & la *seconde* qui fait l'autre partie de la noire, est plus courte: mais quelle est cette différence de la plus longue à la plus courte? Voilà la difficulté qui arrête le plus communément les Noteurs de cylindres.

Il est des cas où cette différence est de la moitié, ensorte qu'il faut exécuter les *premières* comme si elles étoient croches pointées, & les *secondes* doubles croches: d'autres où la différence est d'un tiers, comme si la *première* valoit deux tiers de noire, & la *seconde* l'autre tiers, d'autres enfin où cette différence, moins sensible, doit être comme de 3 à 2; ensorte que la *première* vaudra 3 cinquièmes de noire & la seconde 2 cinquièmes. On trouvera dans le chapitre XXV, en parlant du détail des airs, plusieurs observations sur la différence des *premières* & des *secondes* croches, qui suffiront en saisissant bien le mouvement nécessaire au genre d'expression qui se fait sentir dans l'exécution des piéces, pour apprécier au juste la différence dont je parle, laquelle est souvent dans le cas de varier dans le même air, si l'on veut exprimer certains passages d'une manière plus intéressante.[81]

There is an essential observation to make about eighth notes, which are often performed unequally, two by two. Notated music does not tell us what the value of this difference is, whether it is of half, one third, or one fourth. It is necessary, however, to determine this value because if in *notage* one follows the value of eighths exactly according to the musical score, they would all be entirely equal in duration, sound, and silence. This happens rarely in performance, and it should be the invariable rule of *noteurs* that when inequality between eighth notes occurs in performance, in order to maintain the kind of expression suitable to the air, they must appraise it correctly in order to include what is done in the actual performance itself.

These unequal eighths are evident two by two, that is from quarter to quarter, the two eighths together make up the value of a quarter note. The first, which occupies the first part of the quarter note, is longer, and the second, which occupies the other part, is shorter. But what is this difference between the long and the short? This is the problem that usually stops most *noteurs* of cylinders.

Sometimes this difference is half, so that the *firsts* must be performed as though they were dotted eighths and the *seconds* sixteenths. Other times the difference is a third, as though the *first* were two-thirds of the quarter and the *second* one-third; and finally other times when the difference is less perceptible, it should be as 3:2, so that the *first* equals three-fifths of the quarter and the *second* two-fifths. In speaking of the details of airs in Chap. XXV, there are many observations on the differences between *first* and *second* eighth notes. These are sufficient to allow one to find the rhythm necessary to the proper expression of each piece, and to perceive the differences of which I speak. These often vary in the same air when one wishes to perform some passages in a more interesting way.

This information is considerably more exact than that in any other source. Engramelle's directions for the *notage* of the twelve examples at the end of *La tonotechnie* are even more precise. The "least perceptible" inequality mentioned above, the ratio of 3:2, is given as 7:5 in Menuet no. 6 and in *Le Bûcheron* no. 7. The ratio of 9:7 is discussed for the inequality of eighth notes in *La Barcelonette,* a tune Engramelle gives as an example in *L'Art du facteur d'orgues* (Quatrième Partie, planche CXIV). It is instructive to hear inequality in the precise ratio of 7:5, as in the eighth notes of the second recorded example, Menuet no. 6, with first eighth notes *tenue* and second eighths *tactée.*

Engramelle's comment that the degree of inequality may vary in a performance is the only written indication of this known to me, although such variation might well occur subconsciously as well as through a performer's intent. It is possible that changing the degree of inequality was thought by most writers to be too obvious to mention.

Since many French writers state that inequality is confined to stepwise motion in equal eighths,[82] perhaps arpeggiated passages, such as those in Menuet no. 6, should be performed as equal. While this approach is not a variation in the degree of inequality, mixing equal with unequal eighth notes produces an interesting contrast in the performance of these notes. The third recorded example is of Menuet no. 6, with the arpeggiated passages performed as equal.

One might suppose that inequality would become more pronounced approaching a cadence or an important point of a phrase. The ratios in measures 4, 7, 12, and 20 of Menuet no. 6 in the fourth recorded example change by pairs of eighths from 7:5 to 3:2 to 2:1. The arpeggiated eighths remain equal.

Engramelle states that the degree of inequality depends on the piece:

> J'ai observé en notant des cylindres, qu'il est nombre de marches, entr'autres celle du Roi de Prusse, où la différence des *premières* aux *secondes* croches est de la moitié, comme 3 est à 1, c'est-à-dire, que les premières croches valent des croches pointées, & les secondes croches des doubles croches. Dans certains menuets, entr'autres le *petit menuet Trompette,* la différence est du tiers, comme 2 est à 1; ensorte que les *premières croches* valent 2 tiers de noire, & les *secondes* l'autre tiers; & enfin le différence la moins marquée, comme dans beaucoup de menuets,

est comme de 3 à 2, de 7 à 5, &c. Il faut donc que le Noteur ait assez de goût pour
apprécier ces différences au juste, & qu'il supplée en cela aux principes de musique
qui ne les indiquent pas.[83]

I have observed in notating cylinders that there are a number of marches,
among them that of the *Roi de Prusse,* in which the difference of the *firsts* to *seconds* is one half, as 3:1, that is, the *first* eighth equals a dotted eighth and the
second equals a sixteenth note. In some menuets, as the *petit menuet Trompette,*
the difference is one third, as 2:1, so that the *first* eighth equals two-thirds of a
quarter note and the *second* the other third. Finally the least marked difference, as
in many menuets, is that of 3:2 or 7:5, etc. It is necessary that the *noteur* have
sufficient taste to understand these differences precisely, and that he supply the musical requirements when these are not indicated.

Although Engramelle mentions the ratio of 3:1, he does not use it in any of
the examples in *La tonotechnie. La marche du Roy* uses 3:2 for the first version, and 2:1 for the second. In the Marche no. 10 the degree of inequality is
not specified, although the five divisions of the dial for each quarter note suggest the ratio of 3:2.

Engramelle specifies that eighth notes are performed as equal in *La badine
d'Alarius* and *Les portraits à la mode.* The *Romance* uses the ratio of 5:3, *Le
Bûcheron,* 7:5, and *La Fontaine de Jouvance* uses sixteenths in the ratio of 3:2.
From the number of divisions on the dial, we may assume eighth notes are unequal in the ratio of 3:2 in the Allemande no. 9, and 5:3 in the *Menuet du Roy
de Prusse.*

Engramelle continues:

Il faut cependant observer que tout ce que je dis, dans le détail de tous ces
airs, sur l'inégalité des croches, n'est que pour faire apprécier ces inégalités: c'est
au bon goût seul à apprécier cette variété dans ces inégalités. Quelques petits essais
feront rencontrer le bon & le meilleur, ou pour l'égalité, ou pour les inégalités: l'on
verra qu'on peu plus ou un peu moins d'inégalité dans les croches change considé-
rablement le genre d'expression d'un air.[84]

It is necessary to observe that everything I say about the inequality of eighth
notes, in giving details about these airs, is only to make an estimate of their inequality. Only good taste can correctly determine which variety of inequality to
employ. Some small experience will acquaint you with the satisfactory and the
preferable in equality or inequality. It will be seen that a little more or less inequality in eighth notes changes the expression of the air considerably.

Engramelle's musical examples and ornamentation do not seem to be quite
in the style of the eras of Couperin, Hotteterre, or Rameau, but his instructions
regarding articulation and inequality differ from treatises of the earlier eighteenth century only in that they are much more specific.

Engramelle is not very successful in creating the effect of musical phrasing
through his varied duration and inequality of notes. His *ritardando* of final ca-

dences is so subtle that it fails to have much effect. Performers ordinarily take
great liberty in ritards and in leaving space for taking breath between phrases,
yet they manage to project rhythmic regularity to an audience. If these computer recordings seem overly mechanical, it is largely due to Engramelle's
underestimation of the performer's liberty in taking time to clarify the connections between phrases.

Engramelle's care and subtlety in using the duration of notes to heighten
metrical organization, however, gives vivid results. The precision of his directions for performing equal notes unequally shows remarkable sensitivity to
musical style as well as invention in clarifying meter. The reader may wish to
listen to the remaining recordings of Engramelle's music at this point.

Engramelle's instructions for *notage* of the mechanical cylinder are given
from a completely different point of view than instructions for the technique of
performance on any other instrument. Engramelle tells us something of the
effect that was desired even though the performance on his cylinder organ is
excessively mechanical and limited in scope.

The performance he describes is applicable, with reservations, to keyboard
instruments. Since his *serinette,* the organ, and the harpsichord are incapable
of dynamic stress, they are entirely dependent on note duration as a means of
gaining variety in articulation. However, keyboard technique can use subtle
differences of attack and release to give shape to the beginning and ending of
each note, as well as note duration to mark metrical units. This technique is
beyond the capability of the *serinette.* The amount of separation between notes
that Engramelle specifies for the *serinette* is, quite likely, exaggerated in order
to make up for the lack of any other dimension in articulation. Therefore
Engramelle's examples should be studied rather than imitated, even in keyboard performance.

This survey of seventeenth- and eighteenth-century instructions may give
the impression that meter was articulated with relentless intensity. Every note
was bowed with a separate stroke, or tongued, with part of its duration silent in
order to give clarity to the succeeding note. Such articulation enhances the perception of the beat and its subdivisions and groupings, but the rhythm of
phrases and lyric melodic organization seem neglected. It is easy to envision
that a performance that narrowly adheres to these instructions would be too
rigidly metrical.

A balance between metrical order and larger rhythmic structure must be
found in any successful performance. It is useful to mention some elements of
performance that keep these articulation traditions from being excessively
rigid. The first factor is the absence, or minor role, of the dynamic accent.
Twentieth-century performers are so accustomed to employing dynamic accentuation that it is sometimes difficult for us even to imagine a performance in

which it is not used. The careful avoidance of the word "accent" in a large number of the performance directions examined is not oversight but demonstrates the reliance of eighteenth-century performers on different means of enhancing metrical perception.

Some experimentation with tonguings, bowings, and fingerings as well as an acquaintance with the *serinette* music of Engramelle demonstrates that meter can be adequately clarified without accentuation. Even if a modern performer is intellectually convinced that adding a dynamic accent is unnecessary, he or she may have to retrain fundamental musical instincts in order to avoid this habit in performance.

The effect of tonguings, bowings, and fingerings is greatly variable. Bowing instructions don't tell us how much or how little an articulation was intended to be evident. The degree of separation in tonguings is infinitely variable, and the ear of the listener may hear a nearly smooth legato even when the performer's tongue separates every note. Both woodwind and stringed instruments incorporate a great variety of articulation techniques to vary the beginnings of notes, which may range from explosive to precise, to less definite, to smooth, and even to imprecise and soft. The same variety applies to note endings, although instruction manuals have little directly to say about these. The greatest difference between keyboard instruments and wind and stringed instruments lies in the ability of the latter two to give different sound colors and dynamic variety to notes by swelling and diminishing the sound.

Little is said about meter and singing technique in instruction manuals, except that both *rhythmopoeia* and *quantitas intrinseca* relate poetic meter and word accent to musical meter. A singer's pronunciation is equivalent to the articulation of an instrumentalist and offers an ideal model. The musical instincts of most performers, perhaps then as well as now, are happiest with performance techniques that allow for the widest possible range of expressive possibilities.

VI

❧

Accent as Measure Articulation and as Measure Definition

THE DYNAMIC ACCENT became the predominant means of distinguishing between good and bad notes in the second half of the eighteenth century. The difficult concept of *quantitas intrinseca* and the perception of "superior regard" were more easily explained by describing the beat as having an accent. The measure became associated with a recurring pattern of dynamic stress.

The accent itself was carefully discussed and defined by some theorists, although others gave only simplified definitions. Conservative writers of the late eighteenth century mentioned a variety of articulations, including accent, but even the most thoughtful of them considered accent to be the principal means of defining the measure.

The change from predominantly quantitative to accentual articulation was gradual, of course, but early in the nineteenth century, John Wall Callcott wrote:

> The Bars of Music are not only useful for dividing the Movement into equal Measures, but also for shewing the notes upon which the *Accent* is to be laid.
>
> The Measures of Common Time are divided into four parts; of these, the first and third are accented; the second and fourth unaccented. In the course of this work the accented will be termed *strong* parts and the unaccented *weak* parts of the measure.[1]

Callcott is well informed about eighteenth-century concepts of meter, but he discusses even the quantitative feet of *rhythmopoeia* as accentual groupings: "In the performance of these Rhythms (from poetic feet), the Accent is always shewn by the pressure laid upon the Note which immediately follows the Bar." The measure indicated by the *tactus* beat was described as follows:

> These inferior Accents which belong to the *Times* of the Measure, do not, by any means, destroy that great and predominant Accent that belongs to the first Note which follows the Bar, and which is accompanied by the *Thesis* (The *Niederschlag* of the Germans) or depression of the hand in beating Time. The *Arsis* (The *Aufschlag* of the Germans) or elevation of the hand, always follows on the weak part of the measure.[2]

Callcott's reliance on accent to define meter reflects a change in musical style; dynamic stress, it seems, had become usual in performance. Metrical accent was augmented by an additional articulation, called "emphasis," which occurs "on the weak parts of the Measure, by the different groupings of the Quavers, Semiquavers, etc.; and by the emphatic marks of *Rf,* etc. placed over the notes."[3] Accent is distinguished from emphasis:

> In performing on the Piano Forte, a great difference seems to exist between them (accent and emphasis); since Accent always requires pressure immediately after the Note in struck, and Emphasis requires force at the very time of striking the Note. Thus Accent may be used in the most *Piano* passages, but Emphasis always supposes a certain degree of *Forte*.[4]

Although it may be argued that there is little effect from pressing the piano key after the note is struck, the performer feels a difference that may be conveyed to an audience. Although such pressure cannot affect the sound produced, because of the mechanism of the piano key, it may result in heightening the note by adding to its length. Callcott's description suggests that "accent" refers to sustaining the note, while "emphasis" requires stressing the attack of the note.

The word "accent" had been used in defining meter in seventeenth- and eighteenth-century treatises, more often in English sources than Continental. Butler used it to describe different kinds of measures (1636), and Alexander Malcolm used it to distinguish metrical groups (1721). The anonymous author of *A Philosophical Essay* (1677) says, "there is a loudness and briskness given to every other pulse, which makes it eminent," and also that "length and loudness is given to the Key notes."[5] This is an amplification of the usual seventeenth-century definition of measure organization.

Accent was certainly known and accepted in performance: for example, Mersenne describes drumming:

> Quelques-vns battent le Tambour si viste, que l'esprit, ou l'imagination ne peut comprendre la multitude des coups qui tombent sur la peau comme vne grefle tres-impestueuse, parmi laquelle les Tambours qui battent la quaisse en perfection frappent quelque-fois auec tant de violence, que son bruit imite celuy des mousquets, ou des canons, & que l'on admire comment vn simple parchemin peut en-

durer de si grands coups sans se creuer. En second lieu, que ces grands coups, qui excedent de beaucoup la force des autres, seruent pour marquer, & pour distinguer les mesures, & pour finir les cadences. L'on frappe aussi quelque-fois la peau proche des bords, mais le plus souuent au milieu, ce qui distingue vn peu les sons en les rendant plus clairs, ou plus plains.[6]

Some beat the drum so fast that the mind or the imagination cannot comprehend the multitude of blows that fall on the skin like a very violent hailstorm. Drummers who beat the drum perfectly strike some blows among the others with so much violence that the sound rivals that of muskets or cannons, and one wonders how a simple parchment can endure such great blows without splitting. Secondarily, these great blows, which exceed the force of the others by so much, serve to mark and distinguish measures and cadences. Sometimes the sounds may also be made a little clearer or plainer by striking the drum-head close to the edges, even though most strokes are made in the middle.

In the seventeenth century, definitions of measure organization usually did not include reference to accent or dynamic stress. Nevertheless, we assume that accent or stress was used for metrical articulation on those instruments capable of it. Accent in the seventeenth and early eighteenth centuries was one of many devices of measure articulation.

The three discussions of accent offered by Callcott, the *Philosophical Essay,* and Mersenne's drummer are quite different from one another. Johann Mattheson offers a definition that suggests that he understands accent as a gentle stress:

Ein Accent in den Noten ist der innerliche Gehalt und Nachdruck derselben/ welcher so placirt ist/ dass dadurch eine Note vor der andern/ ohne Ansehen ihrer äusserlichen Gestalt und gewöhnlichen Geltung/ zu gewissen Zeiten hervorraget. Das ist die *definitio.* Das Wort kommt her von *canere* und *ad,* als wolte man sagen: *ad canere,* mitsingen: weil solche Noten/ die dergleichen *accentum* haben/ natülicher Weise/ einem jeden dergestalt *eminenter* ins Gehör fallen/ dass er sie gleichsam mitzusingen/ und ihnen beyzustimmen genöthiget wird. Das ist die *Etymologia.*[7]

An accent on a note is its own inner content and emphasis, so placed that a note stands out from another, without consideration of its apparent size and its ordinary value in a given time. This is the definition. The word derives from *canere* and *ad,* as if to say *ad canere,* "singing together." Such a note, which is naturally accented, is eminent to the ear to such a degree that it invites you to accompany it and agree with it. That is the etymology.

Heinrich Christoph Koch favors a moderate stress for accent:

Man verstehe hier diessen Ausdruck Gewicht oder Nachdruck nicht unrecht, und glaube, dass ich derjenigen schlechten Spielart der Bogeninstrumente das Wort reden wolle, bey welcher man den Tönen, auf welchen schon von selbste vermöge der Tacteintheilung dieser Nachdruck vorhanden ist, einen so starken Nachdruck mit dem Bogen giebt, und die andern, denen dieser innere Nachdruck mangelt, so leichte mit der Boden abfertigt, dass die daraus entstehende Speilart dem Gange eines hinkenden gleich wird.[8]

Don't misunderstand this expression "weight" or "emphasis" and believe that I would apply these words to that bad kind of string playing that gives a very strong emphasis with the bow in spite of the fact that the notes themselves contain the actual division of beats, and plays the other notes, lacking this inner accent, so lightly that the consequent performance proceeds by a kind of hobble.

We can divide late eighteenth-century theorists into three categories: first, those who include accent as a part of the definition of *quantitas intrinseca;* second, those who give passing mention to measure organization equated with accent; and third, those who define the measure as identified by an accent imposed by the performer.

Matteson's use of the term *innerliche Gehalt* (inner content) associates his discussion of accent with *quantitas intrinseca.* The clarity of J. A. Scheibe's explanation of *quantitas intrinseca* comes from linking it with accent:

> Unsere eigene Empfindung lehret uns, wenn wir singen oder spielen, oder nur eine Musik anhören, dass die Noten, wenn sie schon dem äusserlichen Ausehen oder der äusserlichen Grösse nach, nach der man eine gegen die andere betrachtet, und gleichsam abweiget, gleich gross oder klein zu seyn scheinen, gleichwohl niemals von einerley oder einander ganz ähnlichen Grösse, Länge oder Kürze sind oder seyn können; ja, dass sogar niemals zwo Noten von einerley Gehalt oder Grösse einander innerlich vollig gleich sind. Wir müssen also diese Beschaffenheit und ungleich innerliche Grösse, diese sogenannte *Quantitatem intrinsecam* die insonderheit auf die Melodien, und dadurch auch auf die Harmonie einen grossen einfluss hat, vorzuglich aber in der Vokalmusik von äusserster Wichtigkeit ist, genau untersuchen, und soglich die Noten, eine gegen die andere, gehörig abwägen lernen.[9]
>
> Es ist schon angemerket worden, dass der allegemeinen Regel der Niederschlag eines Taktes lang, d.i. anschlagend, der Aufschlag aber kurz, d.i. durchgehend seyn sollte; allein ich habe zugleich gezeigt, dass diese Regel nicht eben ohne Ausnahme ist, oder sich doch wenigstens nicht auf alle Fälle und Taktarten schickt, wohl aber, dass der erste Theil des Aufschlages sowohl als des Niederschlages lang. der andere Theil beyder aber kurz wäre.
>
> Wenn ich also im Zweizweitheiltakte eine jede halbe Taktnote in zwo Viertheilnoten zertheile: so ist der erste Viertheilnote einer jeden halben Taktnote die anschlagende Note und also innerliche lang, und eine jede zwote Viertheilnote eben derselben halben Taktnote ist die durchgehende Note und also innerliche kurz; und zwar aus dieser Ursache, weil auf die erste Note der Accent oder der Ton fällt, welcher der folgenden zwoten Noten mangelt; denn zwo Noten von einerley Geltung können nicht alle beyde den Ton oder den Accent haben.[10]

When we play, sing, or only listen to music, our feeling tells us that in considering or weighing notes of the same appearance or size one against another, though they seem to be of equal duration, they are, or they give the impression of being, either longer or shorter, even though of entirely equal value or content. We must examine this unequal intrinsic size, the so-called *Quantitatem intrinsecam,* which has a great influence, especially on melody, and through it on harmony. It is particularly important that we learn to weigh the notes one against another in vocal music.

I have given the general rule that the downbeat of a measure should be long, that is struck; and the upbeat short, that is passing. But I have also shown that this rule is not without exception, or at least it is not so in all cases and measures, because the first part of the upbeat is sometimes as long as the first part of the downbeat, and the second parts of both are short. . . .

If each half note in 2/2 measure is divided into two quarter notes, the first quarter note is "struck" and therefore inwardly long, and the second quarter note is "passing" and therefore inwardly short, because the accent comes on the first note and is lacking on the second note. Therefore two notes of the same value cannot both have the accent.

We also find in Walther,[11] Adlung,[12] Kirnberger,[13] and Koch[14] that accent, "inner length," and the *quantitas intrinseca* were considered different terms for the same thing.

Adlung uses the word "accent" in relation to *thesis* and *arsis* and gives the impression that "accent" is a term of recent popularity with musicians:

> Heut zu Tage redet man viel von *accent*uirten Noten, wodurch die längern oder *in Thesi* stehenden verstanden werden. Diese Lehre heisst *de quantitate notarum intrinseca,* und hat sehr viel auf sich.[15]

> Nowadays there is much talk of accented notes, by which the long notes, those included in the down-beat are understood. This subject is called *Quantitas notarum intrinseca,* and is of great importance.

Daniel Gottlob Türk, a musician well aware of the traditions of eighteenth-century practice, explains the measure through accent; he even gives an example that places forte on the first quarter note, mezzoforte on the second, and so on, in order to clarify what he means.

> Anm. 3. Jede Taktart hat gute und schlechte Takttheile, das heisst, obgleich z. B. alle Viertel, ihrem äussern Werthe oder Dauer nach, einander gleich sind, wie in den nachstehenden Beyspielen, so liegt doch auf Einem mehr Nachdruck, (innerer Werth,) als auf dem Andern. Denn Jeder fühlt dass bey a) von zwey, und bey b) von drey Vierteln jedesmal das erste wichtiger ist, als das zweyte &c. [Ex. 6.1].

> Aus diesem Grunde werden auch die guten Takttheile innerlich lange, anschlagende, accentuirte &c. genannt. Beym Taktschlagen fallen sie in die Zeit des Niederschlagens (*thesis*).[16]

> Each measure has good and bad beats, which requires that among all quarter notes, although alike in their external value or duration (as in the following examples), some have more emphasis (inner value) than others. For everyone feels that in a) of each group of two notes, and in b) of each group of three, the first note is more important than the second, and so forth [Ex. 6.1]. For this reason, good beats are also said to be internally long, struck, or accented beats. In beating time, they occur on the downbeat (*thesis*).

EX. 6.1

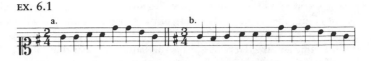

Tartini used the word "accent" but coupled it with "long and short."

Dalle cadenze ridotte a battuta nascono gli accenti musicali, cioè accenti lunghi, e brevi nello stesso senso, che sillabe lunghe, e brevi. . . . È certo, che noi abbiamo nella musica le note corrispondenti al valor delle sillabe, dato per esempio un dattilo nella parola bārbără, abbiamo in giustissima relazione una minima, e due semiminime, ₜ Bar băr ă ₜ perche la minima vale due semiminime, e però in precisione la minima è la silliba lunga, le due semiminime sono le due sillabe brevi. . . . Dunque appare, che adattando un dattilo a tre note musicali en genere, la prima delle quali vaglia il doppio delle due seguenti, sia conservata rogorosamente la natura di quantità delle tre sillabe; cioè la prima lunga, e le altre due brevi. Appare, ma non è. La cagione non dipende dal valor delle note, le quali rigorosamente ne'dati essempi corrispondono al valor delle date sillabe. Dipende da luogo della battuta, dove si porrano le tre note suddette. Sia il tempo ordinario, ch'e il più comune, e le tre sillabe siano espresse da una semiminime, e da due crome. Ecco in quanti luoghi della battuta di tempo ordinario è possibile la posizione [Ex. 6.2].

Altre posizione non sono possibili, perchè si torna alla prima. Ora è un fatto, che la prima, e la terza posizione risponde esattamente al valor delle sillabe. La seconda, e la quarta non risponde altrimente, perchè la seconda sillaba, ch'è breve, diventa lunga, e il risultato della pronunzia musicale ad onta della nota breve, e contro la volontà del musico è realmente bārbără. Le note musicali essendo sempre le stesse, il dattilo sempre. Lo stesso, e chiaro, che la ragione del cambiomento della sillaba breve in lunga è il luogo, e non altro.[17]

From meter regulated by the beat arise musical accents, that is to say long and short accents in the same sense as long and short syllables. . . . Given, for example, a dactylic foot [long, short, short] in the word *Bārbără*, we have an exact relationship to a half-note and two quarter notes, ₜ Bar băr ă ₜ , because the half-note is worth two quarters and the half note equals the long, and the quarters the two short syllables. . . . Therefore, adapting a dactyl in this manner, it appears that the first note is worth double the two following and thus the quantitative nature of the three syllables is rigorously preserved. It appears so, but it is not so. This doesn't depend on the value of the notes, which in this example rigorously correspond to the value of the given syllables, but on the position of the three notes in relation to the measure. In a measure of common time, using a quarter note and two eighths to express the three syllables we shall see how many positions these notes can occupy in the measure [Ex. 6.2].

EX. 6.2

Other positions are not possible because the next would repeat the first. Now it is a fact that the first and third positions correspond exactly to the value of the syllables. The second and the fourth do not, because the second syllable which is short becomes long; the result of this musical pronunciation, in spite of the short note, and against the will of the musician, is really Bār bār ă. As the musical notes are always the same and the dactyl is always the same, it is clear that the reason for the change of the short syllable into a long one is the placement [in the measure] and nothing else.

This discussion is nearly identical to the explanations of word-music accentuation given by Printz and Koch, and all use vocal accent in explaining the perception of meter in music. Tartini went on to describe the "long accent" as desirable, and he also gave an account of orchestral playing where:

> Per cui una Orchestra intiera per lo piu si accorda nell'accentare, o sia percuotere con maggior forza la prima nota di ciascun quarto del tempo ordinario, e molto più le due note del battere, e levare dal tempo alla breve, perchè o così se vede batter la misura dal direttore della Orchestra, o così ciascuno batte da se o co'l piede, o con la mente.[18]

> An entire orchestra comes together better by accenting, or striking with greater force, the first note of each quarter of ordinary time, and this is even more true for the two notes of the down and up beat of the tempo alla breve, whether the director of the orchestra is seen to beat the measure or whether each one beats it to himself with his foot, or in his mind.

The impression left by the preceding definitions is that the measure is governed by a perception of notes distinguished by "inner" length or brevity but enhanced by dynamic stress.

Let us now consider those late eighteenth-century writers who, in their brief mention of measure organization, indicated that accent alone defined metrical structure. Some writers were forced by limited space—in dictionaries, for example—to curtail their discussion of measure organization and to simplify it. Others seemed not to be interested in meter, almost as if they considered it to be inconsequential to overall rhythmic organization.

Rousseau's *Dictionnaire de musique* states succinctly:

> Des divers *temps* d'une measure, il y en a de plus sensibles, de plus marqués que d'autres, quoique de valeurs égales: le *temps* qui marque davantage s'appelle *temps fort;* celui qui marque moins s'appelle *temps foible:* C'est ce que M. Rameau, dans son *Traité d'Harmonie,* appelle *temps bon et temps mauvais.* Les *Temps* forts sont, le premier dans la mesure à deux *temps;* le premier et le troisième dans les mesures à trois et quatre: à l'égard du second *temps,* il est toujours foible dans toutes les mesures, et il en est de même du quatrième dans la mesure à quatres *temps.*[19]

> Of the different beats of a measure, there are some more prominent and stressed than the others, although they are of equal duration: The *beat* that is stressed is called *strong beat;* that which is less marked is called *weak beat.* These are what M. Rameau in his treatise on harmony calls *good beats* and *bad beats.*

The strong beats are the first in two-beat measures, and the first and third in three-
and four-beat measures. The second beat is always weak in all measures, and it is
the same with the fourth in the four-beat measure.

The difference between Rousseau's definition and that of his contemporary
Holden may be due to the space limitations of the *Dictionnaire*. The words
"strong" and "weak," without further qualification, convey an image of the
accent.

Charles Burney wrote this article for Dr. Rees's early nineteenth-century
Cyclopedia:

> Accent, in music. In the mechanism of melody, or measured musical tones,
> musicians have long agreed to regard the *first* and *third* notes of a bar, in common
> time, whether vocal or instrumental, as accented, and the *second* and *fourth* notes
> as unaccented. In triple time, divided into three portions, the *first* note and *last* are
> accented, the *second* unaccented. But these accents are variously modified; often to
> produce some comic effect, as wantonly limping, to ridicule lameness. If the *third*
> note in triple time is accented in serious music, it is always less forcibly marked
> than the first.[20]

Dr. Burney went on at length, but supplied no definition of "accent."

Ballière de Laissement,[21] Antoniotto,[22] Kollmann,[23] William Jones of Nayland,[24] and Momigny[25] also briefly discussed accentual measure organization
without defining accent. All of these writers expanded upon the subject of
larger rhythmical organization, such as phrase and period structure, which
held more interest for them than did meter.[26] Abbreviated treatment of measure
organization does not imply that these late eighteenth-century writers were
modernists in their musical outlook. Jones, in particular, preferred the music of
Handel, Corelli, and Geminiani to that of his own day.[27]

In the third category of eighteenth-century writers are those who define
the measure by an accent provided by the performer. This idea is increasingly
popular and demonstrates that quantitative meter is out of date by the end of
the eighteenth century.

The most explicit equation of accent with measure definition was by Leopold Mozart in his *Violinschule.* Perhaps he valued accent so highly because
the violin is capable of such elegant and varied dynamic stress.

> Meistens fällt der Accent der Ausdruck oder die Stärke des Tones auf die herr-
> schende oder anschlagende Note, welche die Italiäner *Nota buona* nennen. Diese
> anschlagende oder gute Noten sind merklich von einander unterschieden. Die son-
> derbar herrschende Noten sind folgende: in iedem Tact die das erste Viertheil an-
> schlagende Note; die erste Note des halben Tactes oder dritten Viertheils im Vier-
> viertheiltacte; die erste Note des ersten und vierten Viertheils 6/4 und 6/8 Tacte;
> und die erste Note des ersten, vierten, siebenten und zehenden Viertheils im 12/8
> Tacte. Diese nun mögen jene anschlagende Noten heissen, auf die allemal die

meiste Stärke des Tones fällt: wenn anders der Componist keinen andern Ausdruck hingesetzet hat. Bey dem gemeinen Accompagnieren einer Arie oder einer Concertstimme, wo meistens nur Achttheilnoten oder Sechszehntheilnoten vorkommen, werden sie itzt meistens abgesöndert hingeschrieben, oder wenigst Anfangs ein paar Täcte mit einem kleinen Striche bemerket [Ex. 6.3]. Man muss also auf solche Art fortfahren die erste Note stark anzustossen, bis eine Abänderung vorkömmt.

Die andern guten Noten sind die, welche zwar allezeit durch eine kleine Stärke von den übrigen unterschieden sind; bey denen man aber die Stärke sehr gemässiget anbringen muss. Es sind nämlich die Viertheilnoten und Achttheilnoten im Allabreve Tacte, und die Viertheilnoten in dem so genannten halben Trippel; ferner die Achttheilnoten und Sechzehntheilnoten im geraden und auch im 2/4 und 3/4 Tacte; und endlich die Sechzehntheilnoten im 3/8 und 6/8 u. s. f. Wenn nun dergleichen mehrere Noten nacheinander folgen, über deren zwo und zwo ein Bogen stehet: so fällt auf die erste der zwoen der Accent, und sie wird nicht nur etwas stärker angespielet, sondern auch etwas länger angehalten; die zwote aber wird ganz gelind, und still, auch etwas später daran geschleiset. . . . Es sind aber auch oft 3, 4, und noch mehrere Noten durch einen solchen Bogen und Halbcirkel zusammen verbunden. In solchem Falle muss man die erste derselben etwas stärker anstossen, und ein wenig länger anhalten, die übrigen hingegen durch Abnehmung der Stärke immer stiller, ohne mindesten Nachdruck, in dem nämlichen Striche daran schleifen.[28]

EX. 6.3

Generally the expressive accent or stress falls on the predominant or struck note, which the Italians call *Nota buona*. These struck or good notes, however, differ perceptibly from each other. The specially predominant notes are as follows: in every measure, the first note of the first quarter of the measure is a struck note; the first note of the half-bar or third quarter in four-quarter time; the first note of the first and fourth quarters in 6/4 time and 6/8 time; and the first note of the first, fourth, seventh and tenth quarters in 12/8 time. Each of these may be called struck notes, the ones on which the chief stress always falls if the composer has indicated no other expression. In the ordinary accompaniment to an aria or a concert piece, where for the most part only eighths or sixteenths occur, they are now usually written detached, or at the least, a few bars at the beginning are marked with a small stroke [Ex. 6.3]. One must continue to accent the first note strongly in the same manner until a change occurs.

The other good notes are those which are always distinguished from the remainder by a small stress, but on which the stress must be applied with great moderation. They are, namely, quarters and eighths in allabreve time, and quarters in the so-called half-note triple; further, there are eighths and sixteenths in common time and also in 2/4 and 3/4 time: and finally sixteenths in 3/8 and 6/8 time, and so on. Now if several notes of this kind follow each other, over which, two by two a slur is placed, then the accent falls on the first of the two, and it is not only played somewhat louder, but also sustained rather longer; while the second is slurred on to it quite smoothly and quietly and somewhat late. . . . But often three, four and even more notes are bound together by a slur and half circle. In this case, the first must be somewhat more strongly accented and sustained longer; the others on the contrary, are slurred in the same stroke with a diminishing tone, more and more quietly without the slightest accent.

Leopold Mozart's insistent use of the words "accent" and "stress" and the dynamic indications in his musical examples are striking. He limited his *forte* to mean "played rather more strongly," and there are so many places where accents are to be played in his examples that the effect of any individual accent seems diminished. His directions about the performance of slurs are of special interest since such phrasing marks were not often used before the mid-eighteenth century. The similarity of Leopold Mozart's bowing directions to those of Muffat has been mentioned, but Muffat did not use the word "accent" in defining meter.

William Tans'ur advocated the imposition of accent as a means of measure organization:

> This is what is called the *Accented,* and *Unaccented parts of the Measure;* which the *Italians* call Tempo Buono, or Time-Good; and Tempo-Cattivo, or Time or Measure-Bad; that is to say, the *good* and *bad,* parts of the *Measure,* etc.
>
> In Common Time, the first Notes of the *beginning of a Bar,* and the first Notes of the *last half* of the Bar is the *Accented* Part; that is, the first and third *Crotchet* of every *Bar,* the rest being the *Unaccented Parts:* but in Tripla-Time (where notes go by *three* and *three*) the *first* of the three is the *accented part,* and the rest the *unaccented.*
>
> The accented Parts should be always as *full* of *Harmony* as possible, and as void of *Discords* as may be, in order to render the *Composition* the more *affecting:* but the *unaccented parts* may consist of *Discords,* and the like, without any great offence to the Ear, etc. This being a *part of music,* that few or no *Authors* have very rarely mentioned; although it is the whole *Ornament* and *Spirit* of every *Composition,* especially when any person performs alone.
>
> In Common Time, remember well by Heart,
> The first and third is the accented part:
> And if your Music Tripla-Time should be,
> Your Accent is the first of ev'ry three [29]

By such verses, Tans'ur attempted to make elementary musical concepts memorable to the student. Tans'ur's book was widely read; many young musicians learned from him to impose accent as the sole indication of measure organization.

Theorists of the later eighteenth century became much more interested in defining phrase structure and less interested in musical meter. Perhaps the growing number of musical amateurs, the readers of Tans'ur's music primers, found the simplified concepts of an accentual measure easier to learn.

A rich variety of articulation techniques was known to seventeenth- and eighteenth-century performers. The right pronunciation of the musical styles of the time included the most subtle and artful devices, which seem to be wonderfully effective on the instruments of their own time. These devices, however, are less effective when attempted on modern instruments. The performers of the late eighteenth century employed accent in addition to these techniques and evolved a dramatic, forceful style suitable to the music of C. P. E. Bach, Haydn, Mozart, and Beethoven.

Although meter may seem to be a comparatively small element of a performance style, the metrical impulse in music is fundamental. A change such as the use of dynamic accent can strike a listener as profound. If Clementi's comment about the predominance of a new legato style in the early years of the nineteenth century is reliable, accentuation must have become necessary to clarify meter and to mark important harmonic and melodic points because of the lack of articulation silences. We may be able to sense the quality of this new style of performance, smoothly lyrical with heightened dynamic stress, and also to see more clearly an earlier performance style that used dynamic accent rarely or not at all.

Quantitative articulation employed many and varied techniques, carefully weighed note durations and silences and delicate differences in the beginnings and endings of notes brought about by bowings, tonguings, fingerings, and tone color. The technique taught to beginning performers was securely based on a recognition of meter.

Singing style offered the important model of word articulation to instrumentalists; with more limited expressive capacities than the voice, instruments developed elaborate and complicated techniques in order to compete in clarity and expressiveness. Pronunciation and meter need to be balanced by the lyric and dramatic impulses of music; a performer first must establish a firm foundation of metrical order upon which to raise the great arch of expressive song.

APPENDIX

Rhythmopoeia According to Johann Mattheson and Wolfgang Caspar Printz

RHYTHMOPOEIA ACCORDING TO JOHANN MATTHESON

Mehr dreisylbige Füsse.

10) **Amphimacer,** - υ -.
Von den Feldschlachten und Gesechten also genannt, weil er auf kriegerischen Instrumenten Dienste gethan hat, und solche auch noch zu thun fähig ist: ab ἀμφὶ, circum; & μάχομαι, pugno. Hat eine lange, eine kurtze und wiederum eine lange Sylbe.

allegro.

§. 33.

11) **Amphibrachys,** υ - υ.
Von ἀμφὶ, circum, & βραχὺς, brevis, weil eine lange Sylbe hier mit zwo kurtzen umgeben wird, welches itzo die höchste Mode ist. Er wurde von der Insel Creta auch **Creticus** genannt.

vivace.

§. 34.

12) **Palymbacchius,** - - υ.
Von πάλιν, rursus; und βάχχιος, d. i. ein umgekehrter **Bacchius:** denn er führet zween lange und darauf einen kurtzen Klang; so wie jener **Bacchius** einen kurtzen und zween lange hat.

andante.

§. 35.

Vierfylbige Klang-Füsse.

13) **Pæon,** der erste, - υ υ υ.
Von παιάν, hymnus, weil er den Lobgesängen gewidmet war. Uns dienet er in Ouvertüren und Entreen. Er bestehet aus einer langen und drey kurtzen Noten.

§. 36.

14) **Pæon,** der andre, υ - υ υ.
Dessen erster Klang ist kurtz, der zweite lang, und die beiden letzten sind wiederum kurtz.

§. 37.

15) **Pæon,** der dritte, υ υ - υ.
Dessen beide ersten Klänge kurtz, der dritte lang, und der letzte wieder kurtz.

§. 38.

16) **Pæon,** der vierte, υ υ υ -.
Hat erst drey kurtze, und zuletzt einen langen Klang. Diese vier Pæones sind alle zu Lobgesängen gebraucht worden; taugen auch noch sehr wol dazu.

§. 39.

17) **Epitritus,** der erste, υ - - -
a τρίτος, verto, & ἐπὶ, super: weil man über seinen vier Sylben auch vier Umkehrungen anstellet. Dieser bestehet aus einem kurtzen, und dreien darauf folgenden langen Klängen.

§. 40.

18) **Epitritus, der zweite, - ᴗ - -.**
Hat erst einen langen, darauf einen kurtzen, und zuletzt zween lange Klänge.

§. 41.

19) **Epitritus, der dritte, - - ᴗ -.**
Bestehet aus zween langen Klängen, so dann einem kurtzen und endlich einem abermahligen langen Klange.

§. 42.

20) **Epitritus, der vierte, - - - ᴗ.**
Ist aus dreien langen und einem kurtzen zusammengesetzet.

§. 43.

21) **Ionicus, a majori, - - ᴗ ᴗ.**
Ist ein nach der Landschafft Jonien bekannter und zum Tantzen sehr bequemer Klangfuß. Der Zusatz a majori bedeutet, das die beeden langen Sylben vorangehen und die beeden kurtzen folgen.

§. 44.

22) **Ionicus, a minori, ᴗ ᴗ - -.**
Da gehen die beiden kurtzen Klänge voran, und die beiden langen schliessen. Solches bedeutet der Zusatz: a minori, und ist also die Umkehrung des vorhergehenden Fusses.

§. 45.

23) **Antispastus, ᴗ - - ᴗ.**
Von σπάω, traho, und ἀντὶ, contra, weil die Sylben oder Klänge gleichsam gegen einander gezogen werden: deren erste und letzte kurtz, die mittlern aber lang sind.

§. 46.

24) **Choriambus, - ᴗ ᴗ -.**
Vom Choräo und Jambo zusammengefüget, dabey die ersten und letzten Klänge lang, die mittlern aber kurtz sind.

§. 47.

25) **Proceleusmaticus, ᴗ ᴗ ᴗ ᴗ.**
Von κελεύω, jubeo, deutet ein befehlendes, aufmunterndes Geschrey der Schiffleute an, clamorem hortatorium nautarum. Es bestehet dieser Fuß aus vier kurtzen Klängen.

§. 48.

26) **Ditrochæus, - ᴗ - ᴗ.**
Ein doppelter Trochäus, so wie der Dijambus und Dispondäus nur verdoppelte Jambi und Spondäi sind, die wir eben darum nicht mit in die Rechnung bringen. Der Ditrochäus erscheinet in dessen hier auf andre Art, als der einfache oben §. 6 No. 3, wenn er verdoppelt wird.

RHYTHMOPOEIA ACCORDING TO
WOLFGANG CASPAR PRINTZ

NOTES

1. The Origins of the Measure in the Seventeenth Century

1. Sebald Heyden, *De arte canendi* (1540), trans. Clement A. Miller (Rome, 1972), pp. 19–20.

2. J. A. Bank, *Tactus, Tempo and Notation in Mensural Music from the 13th to the 17th Century* (Amsterdam, 1972), pp. 113–15.

3. *Andreas Ornithoparchus his Micrologus . . . [trans.] by John Dowland lutenist* (London, 1609). Book II, chap. 6, p. 46. Reprinted in *A Compendium of Musical Practice*, ed. Gustave Reese and Steven Ledbetter (New York, 1973), p. 166.

4. For example, Bartolomé Ramos de Pareja, *Musica practica* (Bologna, 1482), ed. J. Wolf in *Publicationen der Internationalen Musikgesellschaft*, Beihefte. Folge 1 (Leipzig, 1901), p. 83; Franchinus Gaffurius, *Practica musicae* (Milan, 1496), Lib. II, cap. 3; Marin Mersenne, *Harmonie universelle* (Paris, 1636; facsimile ed., Paris, 1963), Livre cinquiesme de la composition, Prop. XI, p. 324v.; and Johann Rudolf Ahle, *Kurze/ doch deutliche Anleitung zu der lieblich- und löblichen Singekunst* (Muhlhausen, 1690), p. 34.

5. Andreas Ornithoparchus, *Micrologus*, chap. 6, p. 46.

6. Ibid.

7. Ibid.

8. Gioseffo Zarlino, *The Art of Counterpoint*, trans. Marco and Palisca, pp. 118–19.

9. Mersenne, *Harmonie universelle*, Livre cinquiesme de la composition, Proposition XI, p. 324.

10. Ibid., pp. 324–25.

11. Agostino Pisa, *Battuta della musica dichiarata* (Rome, 1611). Facsimile edition, ed. Walther Dürr (Bologna, 1965). See also Putnam Aldrich's *Rhythm in Seventeenth-Century Italian Monody* (New York, 1966), p. 25.

12. Pier Francesco Valentini, "Trattato della battuta musicale" (Rome: Vatican Library Ms. Barb. lat. 4417, 1643). See also Margaret Murata's "P. F. Valentini on Tactus and Proportion." Professor Murata kindly allowed me to see her article before it was published in the Proceedings of the Frescobaldi Quadricentennial, Madison, Wisconsin.

13. Pier Francesco Valentini, "Battuta," p. 76, para. 154.

14. Ibid., p. 138, para. 230.

15. Ibid., p. 27, para. 51.

16. Ibid., p. 34, para. 64, and p. 62, para. 129.

17. Ibid., pp. 44–45, para. 90, and p. 138, para. 230.

18. William Barley, *A new booke of tabliture* (London, 1596), p. 4 verso.

19. Thomas Ravenscroft, *A briefe discourse of the true (but neglected) use of charact'ring the degrees by their perfection, imperfection, and diminution in measurable musicke, against the common practice and custom of these times* (London, 1614), p. 2.

20. Christopher Simpson, *A compendium of practical musick* (London, 1667), pp. 18–19.

21. Francesco Piovesana Sacilese, *Misure harmoniche regolate* (Venice, 1627), p. 60, cited in Carl Dahlhaus, "Zur Geschichte des Taktschlagens im frühen 17. Jahrhundert," in *Studies in Renaissance and Baroque Music in Honor of Arthur Mendel*, ed. Robert Marshall (Kassel, 1974), pp. 117–23.

22. Lorenzo Penna, *Li primi albori musicali* (4th ed., Bologna, 1684), p. 36. See also Georg Schünemann, *Geschichte des Dirigierens* (Leipzig, 1913), pp. 122f.

23. Johann Quirsfeld, *Breviarum musicum* (Dresden, 1688), p. 17.

24. Daniel Merck, *Compendium musicae instrumentalis chelicae* (Augsburg, 1659), pp. 5–6.

25. Curt Sachs, *Rhythm and Tempo* (New York, 1953), p. 223.

26. Ravenscroft, *A brief discourse,* p. 19.

27. Wolfgang Caspar Printz, *Compendium musicae signatoriae & modulatoriae vocalis* (Dresden, 1689), unpaginated.

28. De La Voye-Mignot, *Traité de musique* (Paris, 1656), p. 13.

29. Henry Purcell, *A choice collection of lessons for the harpischord or spinnet* (London, 1696), unpaginated.

30. Carl Dahlhaus, "Zur Entstehung des modernen Taktsystems im 17. Jahrhundert," *Archiv für Musikwissenschaft* 18 (1961): 227–29.

31. Bank, *Tactus, Tempo and Notation,* p. 249.

32. This interpretation of Praetorius's exposition is in agreement with that of Dahlhaus's article cited in n. 30, pp. 229–30, but not with that of Hans Otto Hieckel in "Der Madrigal- und Motettentypus in der Mensurallehre des Michael Praetorius," *Archiv für Musikwissenschaft* 19 and 20 (1962–63): 40–55.

33. Michael Praetorius, *Syntagma musicum* (Wolfenbüttel, 1619), III, cap. vii, p. 49.

34. Ibid., III, pp. 50–51.

35. See Irmgard Herrmann-Bengen, *Tempobezeichnungen, Ursprung, Wandel, im 17. und 18. Jahrhundert* (Tutzing, 1959), pp. 44–48.

36. Georg Quitschreiber, *Musikbuchlein für die Jugend* (Jena, 1607), chaps. IV, VII.

37. These include Anon., *Brevia mvsicae rvdimenta latino belgicae* (Amsterdam, 1591; reprinted 1621), chap. X; Nikolaus Gengenbach, *Musica nova, newe Singekunst* (Leipzig, 1626), pp. 78–79; Joan Albert Ban, *Zangh-Bloemzel* (Amsterdam, 1642); De La Voye-Mignot, *Traité de musique;* Wolfgang Hase, *Grundliche Einführung in die edle Musik* (Gosslar, 1657); Johann Quirsfeld, *Breviarum musicum;* Wolfgang Caspar Printz, *Compendium musicae signatoriae;* Giovanni Bononcini, *Musico prattico* (Bologna, 1673); Johann Rudolf Ahle, *Kurze doch deutliche Anleitung zu der lieblich- und löblichen Singekunst* (Mülhausen, 1690); Georg Muffat, Preface to *Florilegium primum, DTOe,* Band I, 2 Hälfte (Wien, 1894); and John Playford, *Introduction to the skill of musick* (London, 1697).

38. Daniel Speer, *Grund-richtiger/ kurtz/ leicht/ und nöthiger Unterricht der musikalischen Kunst* (Ulm, 1687), p. 33.

39. Merck, *Compendium musicae,* p. 6.

40. Saint Lambert, *Les Principes du clavecin, contenant une explication exacte de toute ce qui concerne la tablature & le clavier* (Paris, 1702), p. 18. Trans. Rebecca Harris-Warrick, *Principles of the Harpsichord by Monsieur de Saint Lambert* (Cambridge, 1984), p. 37. The translation used here is slightly different.

41. De La Voye-Mignot, *Traité,* p. 12.

42. Antoine du Cousu, *La musique universelle* (Paris, 1658), p. 60.

43. This example is taken from Philidor's 1690 Ms. copy, the earliest known source of the music for this ballet. (Paris: Bibliothèque du Conservatoire Ms. Rés. F. 514 [R. 1822]), p. 31.

44. Jean Rousseau, *Methode claire, certaine et facile pour apprendre à chanter la musique* (Paris, 1683), p. 33.

45. Perrine, *Livre de musique pour le lut* (Paris, 1679), p. 48.

46. Etienne Loulié, *Elemens ou principes de musique* (Paris, 1696), p. 32.; trans. Albert Cohen, *Elements or Principles of Music* (Brooklyn, 1965), p. 27.

47. Charles Masson, *Nouveau traité des règles pour la composition de la musique* (Paris, 1705), p. 7.

48. Georg Muffat, Preface to *Florilegium primum,* ed. Heinrich Rietsch. Denkmäler der Tonkunst in Österreich, II Band, Zweite Hälfte (Vienna: Artaria, 1895).

49. Etienne Loulié, *Elements,* pp. 27–30 of Albert Cohen's translation.

50. R. Peter Wolf, "Metrical Relationships in French Recitative of the Seventeenth and Eighteenth Centuries," *Recherches sur la Musique Française Classique* 18 (1978): 29–49.

51. Georg Falck, *Idea boni cantoris* (Nürnberg, 1688), pp. 63–65.

52. Printz, *Compendium musicae signatoriae,* p. 17.

53. Masson, *Nouveau traité,* p. 7.

54. Pier Francesco Valentini, "Trattato del tempo, e del modo, e della prolatione." (Rome: Vatican Library Ms. Barb. lat. 4419, 1643), pp. 300–459.

55. Dahlhaus, "Modernen Taktsystems," pp. 230–36.

56. This classification of proportions by ancient mathematical terminology is fully explained by Thomas Morley in the *Annotations* to *A plaine and easie introduction to practicall musicke* (London, 1597). The annotation refers to p. 27, vers. 18 in the original edition, and is found on pp. 127–28 of the modern edition by R. Alec Harman (New York, 1971).

57. Bononcini, *Musico prattico,* p. 14.

58. Michael Praetorius, *Syntagma musicum,* III, pp. 52–54.

59. Ibid., p. 79, diagram.

60. Dahlhaus, "Modernen Taktsystems," pp. 232–33.

61. Michael Praetorius, *Syntagma musicum* III, pp. 73–78.

62. Bononcini, *Musico prattico,* pp. 20–23.

63. Penna, *Li primi albori,* pp. 36–40.

64. Ibid., p. 40.

65. This is called "void notation" in the *New Grove Dictionary,* vol. 13, p. 377.

66. Wolfgang Caspar Printz, *Compendium musicae signatoriae,* 2d ed. (Dresden, 1714), p. 16.

67. Bononcini, *Musico prattico* p. 11.

68. Ibid., pp. 17–24.

69. Girolamo Frescobaldi, *Il primo libro di capricci* (Rome, 1624). From the "avvertimento," or preface, reprinted in Sartori, *Bibliografia della musica strumentale italiana stampata in Italia fino al 1700* (Florence, 1952), p. 295–96. See also Frederick Hammond, *Girolamo Frescobaldi* (Cambridge, Mass., 1983), p. 226–27.

70. Giovan Giacomo Carissimi, *Ars cantandi; Das ist richtiger und aussfürlicher Weg/ die Jugend aus dem rechten Grund in der Sing Kunst zu unterrichten* (Augspurg, 1696), p. 16.

71. Ibid., p. 15.

72. Printz, *Compendium musicae signatoriae,* chap. 4, p. 17. Repeated unchanged in the second edition of 1714.

73. Loulié, *Elements,* p. 29.

74. Printz, *Compendium musicae signatoriae,* in both first and second editions, p. 17.

75. Jean Rousseau, *Méthode . . . pour apprendre à chanter* (Paris, 1683), pp. 33–45.

76. Ibid., p. 36.

77. Merck, *Compendium musicae,* p. 11.

78. Ibid., p. 6.

79. Loulié, *Elements,* p. 29.

80. Oliver Strunk, *Source Readings* (New York, 1950), p. 444.

81. Saint Lambert, *Principles of the Harpsichord,* p. 45.

82. Ibid.

83. William Bathe, *A briefe introduction to the skill of song* (London, [1596]).

84. *A new and easie method to learn to sing by book: Whereby one (who hath a good Voice and Ear) may, without other help learn to sing true by Notes.* (London, 1686), p. 47.

85. John Playford, *An introduction to the skill of musick* (London, 1697), p. 9.

86. Thomas Mace, *Musick's monument* (London, 1676), and the Manchester Ms., ca. 1660, in the Henry Watson Music Library of the Central Library, Manchester, England.

87. Charls Butler, *The principles of musik* (London, 1636), p. 25.

88. Ibid., p. 26.

89. Herrmann-Bengen, *Tempobezeichnungen*, pp. 40–75.

90. Merck, *Compendium musicae*, p. 16.

2. Time Signatures in the Eighteenth Century

1. Etienne Loulié, *Elements or Principles of Music*, trans. Albert Cohen (Brooklyn, 1965), pp. 26–33, 59–62.

2. Michel Pignolet de Montéclair, *Nouvelle méthode pour apprendre la musique* (Paris, 1709), p. 10. This is the method used by Zaccaria Tevo in *Il musico testore* (Venice, 1706), pp. 91–99.

3. Montéclair, *Nouvelle méthode*, p. 15.

4. Pierre Dupont, *Principes de musique* (Paris, 1718), p. 16.

5. François David, *Méthode nouvelle* (Paris, 1732), pp. 22–28.

6. In the *Dictionnaire de musique*, 1768, s.v. "Mesure," vol. 1, pp. 417–23, but not in his *Projet concernant de nouveau signes pour la musique*, 1742.

7. Vincenzo Manfredini, *Regole armoniche o sieno precetti ragionati* (Venice, 1775), pp. 2–3.

8. J. F. Démotz de la Salle, *Méthode de musique* (Paris, 1728), pp. 154, 160.

9. Borin, *La musique théorique et pratique dans son ordre naturel* (Paris, 1722), pp. 26–28.

10. Michel Corrette, *L'École d'Orphée* (Paris, 1738), p. 2; and *Le parfait maître à chanter* (Paris, 1758), p. 12.

11. Démotz de la Salle, *Méthode de musique*, pp. 154–74.

12. Borin, *La musique théorique et pratique*, pp. 28–29.

13. Alexander Malcolm, *A treatise of musick; speculative, practical and historical* (Edinburgh, 1721), p. 390.

14. Ibid., p. 397–98.

15. Ibid., pp. 403–404.

16. Ibid., p. 402.

17. Ibid., p. 403.

18. William Turner, *Sound anatomiz'd in a philosophical essay on musick* (London, 1734), p. 22. John Stickney's *The gentleman and lady's musical companion* (Newbury-port, Massachusetts, 1774) repeats this, p. 7.

19. William Turner, *Sound anatomiz'd*, pp. 26–27.

20. Ibid., pp. 22–27.

21. William Tans'ur, *A musical grammar and dictionary or a general introduction to the whole art of music* (London, 1746), p. 64. Cited from the edition of 1829.

22. James Grassineau, *A musical dictionary* (London, 1740), p. 281.

23. Ibid.

24. Ibid., p. 128.

25. Ibid., p. 292.

26. Ibid., p. 302.

27. Peter Prelleur, *The modern music-master, or the universal musician* (London, 1731).

28. John Holden, *An essay towards a rational system of music* (Glasgow, 1770).

29. Joshua Steele, *Prosodia rationalis, or an essay towards establishing the melody and measure of speech* (London, 1779), p. 22.

30. Stickney, *Musical companion*, pp. 6–7.

31. J. P. Rameau, *A treatise of music, containing the principles of composition* (London, 1752), pp. 5–6.

32. Giorgio Antoniotto, *L'arte armonica, or a treatise on the composition of musick* (London, 1760), plate 5.

33. John Wall Callcott, *A musical grammar* (London, 1806), pp. 229–36.

34. A. C. F. Kollmann, *An essay on musical harmony* (London, 1796), pp. 73–75.

35. Elias Mann, *The Northampton collection of sacred harmony* (Northampton, Mass., 1797), pp. 5–6.

36. Johann Peter Sperling, *Principia musicae* (Bautzen, 1705), p. 47.

37. Ibid., p. 53.

38. Ibid.

39. Ibid., p. 66.

40. Martin Heinrich Fuhrmann, *Musikalischer Trichter* (Frankfort an der Spree, 1706), p. 44.

41. Johann Gottfried Walther, *Praecepta der Musikalischen Composition 1702* (Leipzig, 1955), pp. 28–33.

42. Johann Gottfried Walther, *Musikalisches Lexikon* (1732), pp. 598, 616–18.

43. Ibid., p. 617.

44. Mattheson's principal discussion of meter and time signatures is found in *Das neu-eröffnete Orchestre* (Hamburg, 1713), Pars Prima, chap. III, "Vom *Tacte* insonderheit," pp. 76–89. The reader of *Der vollkommene Capellmeister,* his great compendium (Hamburg, 1739), pp. 171–72, is referred to this earlier work for its discussion of meter.

45. Mattheson, *Der vollkommene Capellmeister*, p. 172.

46. Mattheson, *Orchestre*, pp. 80–81.

47. Ibid., p. 91.

48. J. F. B. C. Maier, *Museum musicum theoretico practicum* (Nürnberg, 1732), pp. 9–10.

49. Franz Anton Maichelbeck, *Die auf dem Clavier lehrende Caecilia* (Augsburg, 1738), pars prima, caput I.

50. J. P. Eisel, *Musicus autodidaktos oder der sich selbst informirende Musikus* (Erfurt, 1738), pp. 16–17.

51. Joseph Joachim Benedict Münster, *Musices instructio* (Augsburg, 1748).

52. Jacob Adlung, *Anleitung zu der musikalische Gelahrtheit* (Erfurt, 1758), pp. 205–20.

53. Johann Joachim Quantz, *Versuch einer Anweisung die Flöte traversière zu spielen* (Berlin, 1752), pp. 55–56.

54. Leopold Mozart, *Versuch einer Grundlichen Violinschule* (Augsburg, 1756); trans. E. Knocker (London, 1948), pp. 31–33.

55. Ibid., p. 32.

56. Friedrich Wilhelm Marpurg, *Anleitung zum Clavierspielen* (Berlin, 1755), pp. 19–20.

57. Johann Adam Hiller, *Answeisung zum Musikalisch-richtigen Gesange* (Leipzig, 1774), p. 125.

58. Christian Kalkbrenner, *Theorie der Tonkunst* (Berlin, 1789), p. 119.

59. Johann Philipp Kirnberger, *Die Kunst des reinen Satzes in der Musik* (Berlin, 1771–79), Zweyter Theil, p. 117. English trans., David Beach and Jurgen Thym (New Haven, 1982), p. 385.

60. Ibid., p. 106; p. 377 in the translation.

61. Ibid., p. 130; p. 396 in the translation.

62. Heinrich Christoph Koch, *Versuch einer Anleitung zur Composition* (Leipzig,

1787), Zweyter Theil, pp. 288–332. Late eighteenth-century writers who continue this classification are Wolf (*Musikalische Unterricht*, 1788) and Löhlein (*Klavierschule*, 1765).

63. J. A. Scheibe, *Ueber die Musikalische Composition* (Leipzig, 1773), vol I., chap. 5.

64. Jean-Philippe Rameau, *Traité de l'harmonie réduite à ses principes naturels* (Paris, 1722), II, pp. 151–52.

65. Ibid., p. 152–53.

66. Ibid., p. 156.

67. Ibid., p. 157.

68. Michel Pignolet de Montéclair, *Principes de musique* (Paris, 1736), p. 116.

69. Jean-Jacques Rousseau, *Projet concernant de nouveau signes pour la musique,* in *Oeuvres complettes de J.-J. Rousseau* (Paris, 1824), vol. 11, pp. 12–13.

70. Ibid., pp. 13–14.

71. Joseph de Lacassagne, *Traité générale des élémens du chant* (Paris, 1766), p. 39.

72. Ibid., p. 40.

73. Ibid., p. 99.

74. Pascal Boyer, *Lettre à monsieur Diderot, sur le projet de l'unité de clef dans la musique et la réforme des mesures, proposés par M. l'Abbé La Cassagne* (Amsterdam, 1767).

75. Jean-Benjamin de Laborde, *Essai sur la musique ancienne et moderne* (Paris, 1780), vol. III, p. 597.

76. François Joseph Fétis, *Biographie universelle des musiciens* (Paris, 1883), Tome II, p. 26.

77. Frédéric Thiémé, *Nouvelle théorie sur les différens mouvemens des airs, fondée sur la pratique de la musique moderne* (Paris, 1801), pp. 36–46.

78. Malcom, *Treatise of musick,* p. 397.

79. Turner, *Sound anatomiz'd, ,* p. 20.

80. Prelleur, *Modern music-master,* no pagination.

81. Maier, *Museum musicum,* p. 16.

82. David, *Méthode nouvelle,* p. 23.

83. Rameau, *A treatise of music,* p. 5.

84. Grassineau, *Dictionary,* p. 282.

85. Kirnberger, *Reinen Satzes,* p. 118, trans. p. 386.

86. Borin, *Musique théorique et pratique,* p. 27.

87. Démotz de la Salle, *Méthode de musique,* p. 156.

88. Corrette, *Ecole d'Orphée,* p. 4.

89. Tans'ur, *A musical grammar,* p. 53.

90. Stickney, *Musical companion.*

91. Sébastien de Brossard, *Dictionnaire.*

92. Quantz, *Versuch,* pp. 264, 270.

93. Ibid., p. 270.

94. David, *Méthode nouvelle,* p. 23.

95. Corrette, *Ecole d'Orphée,* p. 3.

96. Mattheson, *Orchestre,* p. 79.

97. Maier, *Museum musicum,* pp. 9–10.

98. Mattheson, *Orchestre,* p. 79.

99. Corrette, *Ecole d'Orphée,* p. 4.

100. Lacassagne, *Traité générale,* pp. 147–48.

101. Quantz, *Versuch,* p. 264.

102. Kirnberger, *Reinen Satzes,* p. 118, trans. p. 387.

103. Tans'ur, *A musical grammar,* p. 56.

104. Turner, *Sound anatomiz'd,* p. 22.

105. Mattheson, *Orchestre,* p. 86.

106. Corrette, *Ecole d'Orphée*, p. 5.
107. Tans'ur, *A musical grammar*, p. 56.
108. Kirnberger, *Reinen Satzes*, p. 127, trans. p. 394.
109. Turner, *Sound anatomiz'd*, p. 27.
110. Grassineau, *Dictionary*, p. 295.
111. Démotz de la Salle, *Méthode de musique*, p. 155.
112. Corrette, *Ecole d'Orphée*, p. 4.
113. Grassineau, *Dictionary*, p. 295.
114. Mattheson, *Orchestre*, p. 86.
115. Maier, *Museum musicum*, p. 11.
116. Corrette, *Ecole d'Orphée*, p. 4.
117. Tans'ur, *A musical grammar*, p. 57.
118. Grassineau, *Dictionary*, p. 295.
119. Kirnberger, *Reinen Satzes*, p. 128, trans. p. 396.
120. Mattheson, *Orchestre*, p. 87.
121. Maier, *Museum musicum*, p. 11.
122. Grassineau, *Dictionary*, p. 296.
123. Tans'ur, *A musical grammar*, p. 62.
124. Corrette, *Ecole d'Orphée*, p. 5.
125. Kirnberger, *Reinen Satzes*, p. 130, trans. p. 397.
126. Mattheson, *Orchestre*, p. 80.
127. Maier, *Museum musicum*, p. 10.
128. Corrette, *Ecole d'Orphée*, p. 5.
129. Lacassagne, *Traité générale*, p. 147.
130. Grassineau, *Dictionary*, p. 299.
131. Tans'ur, *A musical grammar*, p. 62.
132. Grassineau, *Dictionary*, p. 299.
133. Mattheson, *Orchestre*, p. 80.
134. Corrette, *Ecole d'Orphée*, p. 4.
135. Lacassagne, *Traité générale*, p. 147.
136. Tans'ur, *A musical grammar*, p. 62.
137. Corrette, *Ecole d'Orphée*, p. 5.
138. Grassineau, *Dictionary*, p. 297.
139. Tans'ur, *A musical grammar*, p. 62.
140. Kirnberger, *Reinen Satzes*, p. 129, trans. p. 396.
141. Grassineau, *Dictionary*, p. 301.
142. Turner, *Sound anatomiz'd*, p. 26.
143. Mattheson, *Orchestre*, p. 81.

3. *Rhythmopoeia:* Quantitative Meters in Poetry and Music

1. C. F. Abdy Williams, *The Aristoxenian Theory of Musical Rhythm* (Cambridge, England, 1911), p. 26.
2. See Richard L. Crocker, "*Musica Rhythmica* and *Musica Metrica* in Antique and Medieval Theory," *Journal of Music Theory* 2 (April 1958): 2–23.
3. D. P. Walker, "Musical Humanism in the 16th and Early 17th Centuries," a series of articles in *Music Review* 2 (1941) and 3 (1942); and a series of articles on various aspects of *musique mesurée à l'antique* in *Musica Disciplina* 1–4 (1947–50).
4. Gustave Reese, *Music in the Renaissance* (New York, 1954), p. 705.
5. Rochus von Liliencron, "Die horazischen Metren in deutschen Kompositionen des 16 Jdts," *Vierteljahrschrift für Musikwissenschaft* (1884): 22–91. Tritonius's, Senfl's, and Hofhaimer's settings are reprinted in this article.
6. Benedikt Widmann, "Die Composition der Psalmen von Statius Olthof," *Vierteljahrschrift für Musikwissenschaft* (1889): 290–321.
7. Rochus von Liliencron, "Die Chorgesänge des lateinisch-deutschen Schuldra-

mas in XVI Jdt," *Vierteljahrschrift für Musikwissenschaft* (1890): 309–87. A publication as late as 1620 is listed here. See also: F. W. Sternfeld, "Music in the Schools of the Reformation," *Musica Disciplina* 2 (1948): 99, and Oliver Strunk, "Vergil in Music," *The Musical Quarterly* 16 (1930):482.

8. Athanasius Kircher, *Musurgia universalis* (Rome, 1650), "De pedibus Rhythmorum sive Metrorum," Tome II, pp. 30–70.

9. Walker, "Musical Humanism," *Music Review* 2 (1941): 4.

10. Ibid., p. 9.

11. *Quastiones celiberrimae in genesim* (Paris, 1623), and *Harmonie universelle* (Paris, 1636), VI, XVIII.

12. Walker, "Musical Humanism," pp. 114–15.

13. Ibid., p. 289.

14. Ibid., p. 295.

15. Ibid., pp. 302–303.

16. Marin Mersenne, *Harmonie universelle* (Paris, 1636), VI, p. 18.

17. D. P. Walker, "The Aims of Baif's *Academie de Poésie et de Musique*," *Journal of Renaissance and Baroque Music* 1 (1947): 91.

18. Marin Mersenne, *Harmonie universelle*, Livre second des chants, pp. 177–78.

19. Ibid., Livre sixiesme de L'art de Bien Chanter, Seconde Partie de l'art d'embellir la voix, les recits, les airs, ov les chants, p. 403.

20. Ibid., pp. 397–98.

21. Ibid., p. 376.

22. Ibid., Livre second des chants, pp. 167–68.

23. Johann Mattheson, *Der vollkommene Capellmeister* (Hamburg, 1739), pp. 161–64.

24. *Traité de la musique qui découvre les règles les plus rares de la théorie musicale et de la composition instrumentale* (1736), cited in Carl Alette's "Theories of Rhythm" (Ph.D. diss., University of Rochester, 1954), p. 162.

25. Mattheson, *Vollkommene Capellmeister*, pp. 160–70.

26. Ibid., pp. 224–25.

27. Ibid., p. 170.

28. Ibid., pp. 147–48.

29. Ibid., p. 147, para. 93.

30. Ibid., p. 171. Mattheson seems to be using the word *tact* here in its original mensural significance rather than in its newer meaning as measure.

31. Our perception of a unit of meter begins with *arsis*, the more dynamic pulse, and ends with *thesis*, the more reposeful pulse. Notation, however, places *thesis* after the bar line, first in the measure, and *arsis* last in the measure. What we perceive as a unit is therefore indicated across bar lines, not between them.

32. Wolfgang Caspar Printz, *Phrynis Mitilenaeus, oder satyrischer Componist* (Dresden and Leipzig, 1696), part III, chapter XII.

33. Ibid., p. 110.

34. Johann Adolf Scheibe, *Der critische Musikus. Neue, vermehrte und verbesserte Auflage* (Leipzig, 1745), Das 37te Stück, 12 May 1739, pp. 342 ff.

35. Lorenz Chr. Mizler von Kolof, *Neu-eröffnete Musikalische Bibliothek*, IV Bd. (Leipzig, 1739–54), III, p. 393, para. 43, in a review by Schröter of the article by Scheibe.

36. Marin Mersenne, *Harmonie universelle*, Embellissement des chants, p. 402.

37. In *Harmonie universelle*, Livre Septiesme des instruments de percussion, p. 59, Mersenne quotes Doni, who calls hesychastic music grave and moderate.

38. Mersenne, *Harmonie universelle*, p. 402.

39. Isaac Vossius, *De poematum cantu et viribus rhythmi* (London, 1673), pp. 73–75. The English translation is from John Brown's *A dissertation on the rise, union, and power, the progressions, separations and corruptions, of poetry and music* (London, 1763), pp. 72–73.

40. Mattheson, *Vollkommene Capellmeister,* pp. 210–34.

41. Ibid., p. 166, para. 22; p. 169.

42. Ibid., pp. 167, 166, 168, 170, 168, 169.

43. Jean-Jacques Rousseau, *Dictionnaire de musique* (Paris, 1768), in *Oeuvres complettes de J.-J. Rousseau* (Paris, 1824), vol. 13, pp. 144–45, 147.

44. Ibid., pp. 144–45.

45. Ibid., p. 146.

46. Ibid., p. 147.

47. Ibid., pp. 148–49.

48. See J. A. Hiller, *Anweisung zum musikalisch-richtigen Gesange* (Leipzig, 1774), ch. XIV, pp. 190 ff., and J. A. Scheibe, *Critischer Musikus,* p. 342.

49. John Wall Callcott, *A musical grammar,* p. 241.

50. Ibid., p. 245.

51. Charles Burney, *The present state of music in Germany, the Netherlands, and United Provinces, or The journal of a tour through those countries, undertaken to collect materials for a general history of music* (London, 1775), pp. 159–60.

4. *Quantitas Intrinseca:* The Perception of Meter

1. John Holden, *An essay towards a rational system of music* (Glasgow, 1770), pp. 26, 32–33.

2. Joshua Steele, *Prosodia rationalis or an essay towards establishing the melody and measure of speech* (London, 1779), pp. 11–12, 20–21, 68.

3. Wolfgang Caspar Printz, *Phrynis Mitilenaeus oder Satyrischer Componist* (Dresden, 1696), p. 18.

4. Johann David Heinichen, *Der General Bass in der Composition* (Dresden 1728), p. 257.

5. Johann Adolf Scheibe, *Der critische Musikus. Neue, vermehrter, und verbesserte Auflage* (Leipzig, 1745), Das 37te Stück, 12 May 1739, p. 346.

6. Girolamo Diruta, *Il transilvano* (Venice, 1625), Prima Parte, pp. 6–7.

7. Other musicians identified good and bad fingers differently but nevertheless based their systems on a similar perception of metrical order.

8. Lorenzo Penna, *Li primi albori musicali* (Bologna, 1672), pp. 38ff.

9. Leopold Mozart, *Versuch einer grundlichen Violinschule* (Augsburg, 1756), trans. Editha Knocker, *A Treatise on the fundamental principles of violin playing* (London, 1948), p. 219. Friedrich W. Marpurg, *Anleitung zum Clavierspielen* (Berlin, 1755), chap. V, p. 18; trans. and annotated by Elizabeth Hays (Ph.D. diss., Stanford University, 1977), Book I, pp. V, 9–26. Georg Simon Löhlein, *Clavierschule* (Leipzig und Zullichau, 1779), p. 52. Daniel Gottlob Türk, *Klavierschule, oder Anweisung zum Klavierspielen für Lehrer und Lernende* (Leipzig, 1789), p. 81; trans. Raymond Haggh, *School of Clavier Playing* (Lincoln, Nebraska, 1982), p. 90. He has translated *gute* and *schlechte takttheile* as "strong and weak" beats. Pier Francesco Tosi, *Anleitung zur Singekunst. Aus dem Italienischen . . . mit Erläuterungen und Zusatzen von J. F. Agricola* (Berlin, 1757), zweite Hauptstuck, p. 73.

10. Susan Wollenberg, "Georg Muffat," *New Grove Dictionary,* vol. 12, pp. 760–61.

11. Georg Muffat, Preface to *Florilegium secundum,* Denkmäler der Tonkunst in Österreich, Jahrg. II/2, Band 4, pp. 13, 26, 39, 50. See also Kenneth Cooper and Julius Zsako, "Georg Muffat's Observations on the Lully Style of Performance," *MQ* 53 (1967): 239. My translation reflects the Italian and German more closely than the French version, which seems to have been the basis of that of Cooper and Zsako.

12. Johann Gottfried Walther, *Musikalisches Lexikon,* 1732, p. 507.

13. Ibid., p. 598.

14. Johann Adam Hiller, *Anweisung zum musikalisch-richtigen Gesange* (Leipzig, 1774), pp. 47–48.

5. Articulation of Quantitative Meter

1. *Notes inégales* is a topic that has inspired much research and writing in the past thirty years, and this account of it as a part of metrical articulation will be brief. David Fuller's article on *Notes inégales* in *The New Grove Dictionary*, VI, gives an excellent and current account of the subject with a comprehensive bibliography. Frederick Neumann's article "The French *Inégales,* Quantz, and Bach," *JAMS* 18 (1965): 313–58, is a thorough investigation of the topic devoted to demonstrating that *notes inégales* was exclusively a French performance practice.

2. Loys Bourgeois, *Le droit chemin de musique* (Geneva, 1550).

3. Diego Ortiz, *Trattado de glosas sobre clausulas y otros generos de puntos en la musica de violones, Roma 1553* (Kassel, 1936), p. 48.

4. Tomás de Santa Maria, *Libro llamado Arte de tañer fantasia* (Valladolid, 1565) fol. 45v–46r.

5. *Le nuove musiche* [1602], trans. John Playford and Oliver Strunk in *Source Readings in Music History* (New York, 1950), p. 380.

6. Benigne de Bacilly, *Remarques curieuses sur l'art de bien chanter* (Paris, 1668), pp. 229–30, 232–33.

7. Marin Marais, *Pieces de violes, livre Ier* (Paris, 1686), preface.

8. Jean Rousseau, *Traité de la viole* (Paris, 1687), p. 114.

9. Etienne Loulié, *Elemens ou principes de musique, mis dans un nouvel ordre* (Paris, 1696), p. 32.

10. Ibid., pp. 33–35.

11. Ibid., p. 62.

12. Cited in Bruce Haynes, "Johann Sebastian Bach's Pitch Standards: The Woodwind Perspective," *Journal of the American Musical Instrument Society* XI (1985): 62–63.

13. Georg Muffat, *Florilegium secundum*, ed. H. Rietsch ("Denkmäler der Tonkunst in Österreich." Band II, zweite hälfte; Wien, 1895), pp. 11, 24, 37, and 48. This translation considers Muffat's prefaces in Latin, Italian, and German as well as in French.

14. Johann Gottfried Walther, *Musikalisches Lexikon* 1732, p. 372.

15. *Versuch einer Anweisung die flöte traversière zu speilen*, 1752, p. 105. Trans. Edward R. Reilly, *On Playing the Flute* (New York, 1966), p. 123.

16. Quantz, *Versuch*, pp. 105–106.

17. Daniel Gottlob Türk, *Klavierschule, oder Anweisung zum Klavierspielen* (Leipzig, 1789). This is in chapter 5, part three, paragraph 23, and is on pp. 311–12 of Raymond Haggh's English translation, *School of Clavier Playing* (Lincoln, 1982).

18. Jane Arger, *Les agréments et le rythme* (Paris, 1917).

19. François Couperin, *L'Art de toucher le clavecin* (Paris, 1716–17), p. 39.

20. Pierre Marcou, *Elémens théoriques et pratiques de musique* (Paris, 1782), pp. 35–36.

21. Friedrich W. Marpurg, *Anleitung zum Clavierspielen* (Berlin, 1755), p. 29. Marpurg omits this paragraph from the French edition, *Principes du clavecin* (Berlin, 1756), p. 34. Mark Lindley cites this in his essay "Keyboard Technique and Articulation: Evidence for the Performance Practices of Bach, Handel, and Scarlatti," in *Bach, Handel, Scarlatti Tercentenary Essays*, ed. Peter Williams (Cambridge, 1985), p. 220.

22. Türk, *Klavierschule*, Haggh trans., chap. 6, part 3, para. 38–40, pp. 344–45.

23. François Couperin, *L'art de toucher le clavecin* (Paris, 1716), ed. and trans. Margery Halford (New York, 1974). Couperin advocated finger-substitutions in *La Milordine*, p. 51, in order to allow legato connections and overlapping harmonies in the *Premier prelude*, p. 56. A new method of fingering parallel thirds (p. 42) facilitated a degree of legato that was not obtainable by the old method. Rameau's directions for the performance of *appuys* in the *port de voix* and the *coulez* are found in the *table* of the *Pieces de clavecin* (Paris, 1724).

24. Girolamo Diruta, *Il transilvano* (Venice, 1593), p. 6r. See also Edward John Soehnlein, "Diruta on the Art of Keyboard Playing" (Ph.D. diss., University of Michigan, 1975), pp. 135–43, and Julane Rodgers, "Early Keyboard Fingering, ca. 1520–1620" (D.M.A. diss., University of Oregon, 1971), pp. 278–98. A summary of Diruta's discussion and extensive examples of his scale fingerings are included in Sandra Soderlund's *Organ Technique, an Historical Approach* (Chapel Hill, 1980; 2d ed. 1986), pp. 35–54.

25. From Soderlund's *Organ Technique*, p. 51.

26. British Library Add. Ms. 29485 (ca. 1600).

27. Harald Vogel, liner notes for Organa recording 3005, "The Fisk Organ at Wellesley College, a Revival of the Meantone Tradition."

28. Rodgers, "Early Keyboard Fingering," p. 89.

29. Robert Parkins, "Keyboard Fingering in Early Spanish Sources," *Early Music* 11, no. 3 (July 1983): 323–31.

30. Rodgers, "Early Keyboard Fingering," p. 159.

31. Peter Williams, *The Organ Music of Bach III, A Background* (Cambridge, 1984), pp. 215–16.

32. Mark Lindley, "An Introduction to Alessandro Scarlatti's *Toccata prima*," *Early Music* 10, no. 3 (July 1982): 333–39.

33. *Versuch*, p. 17. Quoted in Williams, *Organ Music of Bach III*, p. 215.

34. Quoted in Lindley's essay "Keyboard Technique," p. 217.

35. Williams, *The Organ Music of Bach III*, chap. 24, "Fingering," pp. 212–25.

36. *Klavierschule*, Haggh trans., chap. 2, para. 8–9, pp. 133–36.

37. Carl Czerny, *Erinnerungen aus meinem Leben*, ed. Walter Kolneder, Sammlung Musikwissenschaftlicher Abhandlungen, bd. 46 (Strasbourg-Baden-Baden: Verlag Heitz GMBH, 1968), p. 15.

38. Muzio Clementi, *Introduction to the Art of Playing on the Piano Forte* (London, 1801), pp. 8–9. Cited in Christopher Kite, "The day has still to come when Mozart on a Steinway will be regarded . . . as necessarily a kind of transcription," *Early Music* 13, no. 1 (February 1985): 55.

39. Richard Erig and Veronika Gutmann, *Italienische Diminutionen die zwischen 1553 und 1638 mehrmals bearbeiten Sätze* (Zurich, 1979). Band I, Prattica Musicale, Veröffentlichungen der Schola Cantorum Basiliensis, p. 32. An essay on wind articulations is on pp. 30–44 in both German and English.

40. Erig, *Italienische Diminutionen*, p. 36.

41. Jean Pierre Freillon Poncein, *La Veritable manière d'apprendre a jouer en perfection du hautbois, de la flûte, et du flageolet, avec les principes de la musique pour les voix et pour toutes sortes d'instruments* (Paris, 1700), pp. 15–17.

42. Jacques Martin Hotteterre, *Principes de la flute traversiere, ou la flute d'Allemagne, de la flute douce, et du haut-bois* (Paris, 1707), pp. 21–23.

43. Ibid., pp. 26–27.

44. Quantz, *Versuch*, pp. 66–71/*On Playing the Flute*, pp. 71–86.

45. Ibid., pp. 64–65/74–75.

46. Ibid., pp. 136–51/162–78.

47. Published in 1707, with editions in 1713, 1720, 1722, 1741, and (with additions by Bailleux) 1765. A Dutch translation was printed in 1728, an English translation in 1729. Peter Prelleur pirated parts of it in *The modern music master* in 1731, and it was pirated again in *The compleat tutor for the German flute*, printed by John Simpson (n.d.). David Lasocki's introduction to his translation of the *Principes* (New York, 1968) cites these editions and contains much useful information.

48. Published in 1752, with editions in 1780 and 1789. It was translated into French, Dutch, and an abridged English version, according to Thomas Warner's *Annotated Bibliography of Woodwind Instruction Books, 1600–1830*, (Detroit, 1967), p. 21.

49. See Betty Bang Mather's *Interpretation of French Music from 1675 to 1775 for Woodwind and Other Performers* (New York, 1973), "The New Tongue Strokes," pp. 45–50.

50. See Rebecca Harris-Warrick, "Newest Instructions for the German Flute" (D.M.A. Final Project, Stanford University, 1977), pp. 96–97.

51. Marin Mersenne, *Harmonie universelle*, Livre IV, p. 204.

52. Jean Rousseau, *Traité de la viole* (Paris, 1687).

53. Johan H. D. Bol, *La basse de viole du temps de Marin Mersenne et d'Antoine Forqueray* (Bilthoven, 1973), pp. 102–20.

54. Sylvestro Ganassi dal Fontego, *Regola rubertina* and *Lettione seconda* (Venice, 1542 and 1543).

55. Mersenne, *Harmonie universelle*, Livre IV, pp. 198–204.

56. Christopher Simpson, *The division-viol* (London, 1667).

57. Danoville, *L'art de toucher les dessus et basse de viole* (Paris, 1687).

58. Johann Andreas Herbst, *Musica prattica* (Frankfurt, 1653).

59. Gasparo Zannetti, *Il scolaro di Gasparo Zannetti per imparar a suonare di violino et altri stromenti* (Milan, 1645).

60. Georg Muffat, preface to *Florilegium secundum* (Passau, 1698).

61. Muffat's rules are quoted from "Georg Muffat's Observations on the Lully Style of Performance," trans. Kenneth Cooper and Julius Zsako, MQ 53 (April 1967): 224–28.

62. Georg Muffat, foreword to *Auserlesene . . . Instrumental-Music*, cited by David Boyden, *The History of Violin Playing from its Origins to 1761* (London, 1965), p. 257.

63. Boyden, *History of Violin Playing*, pp. 162–63.

64. Pierre Dupont, *Méthode de violon: Principes de violon par demande et par réponse* (Paris, 1713).

65. Michel Pignolet de Montéclair, *Méthode facile pour apprendre à jouer du violon* (Paris, 1711).

66. Marc Pincherle, *La Technique du violon chez les premiers sonatistes français* (Geneva, 1974), pp. 19–20. A reprint of articles in S.I.M. 1911.

67. Quantz, *Versuch*, p. 192, para. 10.

68. Leopold Mozart, *Versuch einer Grundlichen Violinschule* [1756], Dritte vermehrte Auflage (Augsburg, 1787), pp. 102–109. Trans. E. Knocker, *A Treatise on the Fundamental Principles of Violin Playing* (London, 1948), pp. 96–102.

69. Francesco Geminiani, *The art of playing on the violin*, ed. David D. Boyden, facs. ed. (London, [1952]), p. 4, example VIII.

70. Ibid., p. 9.

71. Boyden, *History of Violin Playing*, pp. 157–70, 256–71.

72. Robin Stowell, "Violin Bowing in Transition," *Early Music* 12, no. 3 (August 1984): 324–25.

73. Hubert Le Blanc, *Défense de la basse de viole contre les entreprises du violon et les prétensions du violoncel* (Amsterdam, 1740), p. 23.

74. Etienne Loulié, "Méthode pour apprendre a jouer la violle," ca. 1700. Ms. Bibl. Nat. Paris, fonds fr. n. a. 6355, fol. 210–22.

75. John Hsu, *A Handbook of French Baroque Viol Technique* (New York, 1981), pp. 2–5.

76. Engramelle's work has been briefly discussed in Hans-Peter Schmitz's *Die Tontechnik des Pere Engrammele*, no. 8 of Musikwissenschaftliche Arbeiten, herausgegeben von der Gesellschaft für Musikforschung (Kassel und Basel, 1953). David Fuller's *Mechanical Musical Instruments as a Source for the Study of 'Notes Inégales'* (Cleveland Heights, 1974), is an important and useful study of the topic. The companion tape to the present volume performs the musical examples from *La tonotechnie* as realized with the help of a computer program by Roland Hutchinson. Douglas Keislar and the

Center for Computer Research in Acoustics and Music at Stanford University created the tone quality and the note shapes of the music.

77. The plates are from Dom François Bédos de Celles's *L'art du facteur d'orgues,* Quatrième Partie (Paris, 1776–78).

78. Marie-Dominique-Joseph Engramelle, *La tonotechnie,* pp. 20–22.

79. Bédos de Celles, *L'art du facteur d'orgues,* Quatrième Partie, p. 628.

80. Engramelle, *La tonotechnie,* pp. 23–25.

81. Ibid., pp. 30–33.

82. They are Loulié, *Elemens ou principes* (1696); L'Affilard, *Principes très faciles* (1697, 1705); Saint Lambert, *Les principes du clavecin* (1702); Hotteterre, *Principes de la flûte traversière* (1707); Montéclair, *Nouvelle méthode* (1709); Couperin, *L'art de toucher* (1717); Démotz de la Salle, *Méthode de musique* (1728); Vague, *L'art d'apprendre la musique* (1733); David, *Méthode nouvelle* (1737); Bordet, *Méthode raisonnée* (1755); Villeneuve, *Nouvelle méthode très courte* (1756); Bordier, *Nouvelle méthode* (1760); and Rollet, *Méthode pour apprendre la musique* (1769).

83. Engramelle, *La tonotechnie,* pp. 33–34.

84. Ibid., p. 230.

6. Accent as Measure Articulation and as Measure Definition

1. John Wall Callcott, *A musical grammar* (London, 1806), para. 81, p. 41.

2. Ibid., pp. 230–31.

3. Ibid., para. 528, p. 238.

4. Ibid., para. 529, p. 238.

5. [Francis North?], *A Philosophical essay of musick directed to a friend* (London, 1677), pp. 33–35.

6. Marin Mersenne, *Harmonie universelle* (Paris, 1636), Livre septiesme des instruments de percussion, p. 56.

7. Johann Mattheson, *Critica musica* (Hamburg, May 1722), p. 43.

8. Heinrich Christoph Koch, *Versuch einer Anleitung zur Composition* (Leipzig, 1782–83), vol. II, p. 280, fn.

9. Johann Adolf Scheibe, *Ueber die musikalische Composition. Erster Theil: die Theorie der Melodie und Harmonie* (Leipzig, 1773), p. 225.

10. Ibid., pp. 230–31.

11. Johann Gottfried Walther, *Praecepta der Musikalischen Composition,* pp. 34–36.

12. Jacob Adlung, *Anleitung zu der musikalische Gelahrtheit* (Erfurt, 1758), p. 206, fn.

13. Johann Philipp Kirnberger, *Die Kunst des reinen Satzes* (Berlin, 1771–76), Vierter Abschnitt, 105.

14. Koch, *Versuch,* vol. II, p. 273.

15. Adlung, *Anleitung,* p. 206, fn. c.

16. Daniel Gottlob Türk, *Klavierschule* (1789), p. 91.

17. Giuseppe Tartini, *Trattato di Musica secondo la vera scienza dell'armonia* (Padua, 1754), pp. 115–16.

18. Ibid., p. 117.

19. Jean-Jacques Rousseau, *Dictionnaire de musique,* vols. 12 and 13 of *Oeuvres Complettes de J.-J. Rousseau* (Paris, 1824), vol. 13, p. 277.

20. Charles Burney, Music articles in *The Cyclopedia; or Universal Dictionary of Arts, Sciences and Literature,* ed. A. Rees, 45 vols. (London, 1819), vol. 1, s.v. *Accent. Grove's Dictionary* (art. on Burney) indicates these articles were written beginning in 1801.

21. Charles Louis Denis Ballière de Laissement, *Théorie de la musique* (Paris, 1764), p. 43, para. 88.

22. Giorgio Antoniotto, *L'Arte Armonica or a treatise on the composition of musick* (London, 1760).

23. A. C. F. Kollmann, *An essay on musical harmony* (London, 1796), pp. 73 ff.

24. William Jones of Nayland, *A treatise on the art of music* (Colchester, 1784), p. 45.

25. Jérome-Joseph de Momigny, *Cours complet d'harmonie et de composition,* 3 vols. (Paris, 1806), vol. I, p. 138.

26. Leonard Ratner remarks, "The definition of these principles (of phrase structure), new in the history of music theory, especially in connection with the period, is the important contribution of the theorists of the late eighteenth century," in "Eighteenth-Century Theories of Musical Period Structure," MQ 42 (1956): 454.

27. Jones of Nayland, *Treatise,* p. 49.

Handel and Corelli are distinct in their ideas, and clear in the design of their accents and measures; Geminiani is rather more obscure and irregular. His fancy was various and elegant, his expression as a composer extremely pathetic, and he had a great practical knowledge of Harmony; but he seems to have wanted an arithmetic Head—As for Haydn and Boccherini, who merit a first place among the Moderns for invention, they are sometimes so desultory and unaccountable in their way of treating a subject; that they may be reckoned among the wild warblers of the wood: and they seem to differ from some pieces of *Handel,* as the Talk and the Laughter of the Tea-Table (where, perhaps, neither wit nor invention are wanting) differs from the oratory of the Bar and Pulpit.

28. Leopold Mozart, *Versuch einer Grundlichen Violinschule* [1756], Dritte verhehrte Auflage (Augsburg, 1787), pp. 261–63.

29. William Tans'ur, *A musical grammar and dictionary: or a general introduction to the whole of music* (London, 1819), pp. 27–28 [1st ed., 1746].

BIBLIOGRAPHY

Adlung, Jacob. *Anleitung zu der musikalischen Gelahrtheit 1758.* Faksimile-Nachdruck, ed. H. J. Moser. Documenta musicologica. 1. Reihe: Druckschriften Faksimiles 4. Kassel und Basel: Bärenreiter-Verlag, 1943.

Ahle, Johann Rudolf. *Kurze/ doch deutliche Anleitung zu der lieblich- und löblichen Singekunst, vor vielen jahren verfasset und geordnet für die anfahende Jugend der Mühlheusischen Statt- und Land-Schulen/ und etliche mahl herausgegeben von Johan Rudolf Ahlen; itzund aber/ so wohl denen lehr- als lernenden zu beliebiger Nachricht/ mit ergetz- und nützlichen/ teils auch nöthigen Anmerkungen vermehret/ und nach vielfältigem begehren aufs neue zum drukke befördert durch des seel. Verfassers Sohn Johan Georg Ahlen/ R. G. P.* Mühlhausen: in Verlegung des Vermehrers/ gedrukt durch Christian Pauli, 1690.

Aldrich, Putnam. "'Rhythmic Harmony' as Taught by Johann Philipp Kirnberger." In *Studies in Eighteenth-Century Music,* ed. H. C. Robbins Landon. New York and London: Oxford University Press, 1970.

———. *Rhythm in Seventeenth-Century Italian Monody.* New York: W. W. Norton, 1966.

Alette, Carl. "Theories of rhythm." Ph.D. diss., University of Rochester, 1951.

Alstedius, Johannes Henricus. *Templum musicum, or the musical synopses of the learned and famous Johannes-Henricus-Alstedius being a compendium of the rudiments both of the mathematical and practical part of musick faithfully translated out of Latin by John Birchensha* [Book IV: *Musica* of *Elementale Mathematicum,* 1611]. Trans. John Birchensha. London: Printed by W. Godbid for Peter Dring, 1664.

Antoniotto, Giorgio, *L'Arte armonica, or a treatise on the composition of musick.* London: John Johnson, 1760.

Apel, Willi. *Harvard Dictionary of Music.* 2d ed. Cambridge, Mass.: Harvard University Press, 1969.

———. *The Notation of Polyphonic Music, 900–1600.* 4th ed. Cambridge, Mass.: The Medieval Academy of America, 1949.

Arbeau, Thoinot [Jehan Tabourot]. *Orchesography, a treatise in the form of a dialogue whereby all may easily learn and practice the honorable exercise of dancing* [1588]. Trans. Mary Stewart Evans. New York: Kamin Dance Publishers, 1948.

Arger, Jane. *Les agréments et le rythme: leur représentation graphique dans la musique vocale française du XVIIIe siècle.* Paris: Rouart, Lerolle & Cie. [1917].

Artusi, Giovanni Maria. *L'Arte del contrapunto* 1586. Facs. of 1598 ed., Hildesheim: Georg Olms Verlag, 1969.

———. *L'Artusi overo delle imperfettioni della moderna musica ragionamenti dui,* Venice 1600. Facs. ed., Bologna: Forni, 1968.

Ashworth, John. "A Commentary on Freedom and Taste in Continuo Accompaniment: As Described by Saint-Lambert in the *Nouveau traité de l'accompagnement,* and Applied to 'Orphée', a Cantata by Louis Nicholas Clérambault." D.M.A. paper, Stanford University, 1977.

Auda, Antoine. "Le 'tactus' dans le messe 'l'homme armé' de Palestrina." *Acta Musicologica* (1942): 27–73.

Babitz, Sol. "'Concerning the Length of Time that Every Note Must be Held.'" *Music Review* 28 (1967): 21–37.

———. "On Using J. S. Bach's Keyboard Fingerings." *Music and Letters* (1962): 123–28.

————. "A Problem of Rhythm in Baroque Music." *Musical Quarterly* 38 (1952): 533–65.

Bach, Carl Philipp Emanuel. *Versuch über die wahre Art, das Clavier zu spielen.* Berlin, 1759. *Essay on the True Art of Playing Keyboard Instruments.* Trans. William J. Mitchell. New York: W. W. Norton, 1949.

Bacilly, Bénigne de. *L'Art de bien chanter augmenté d'un discours qui sert de réponse à la critique de ce traité.* Paris: Ballard, 1679.

————. *Remarqves cvrievses svr l'art de bien chanter, et particvlierement povr ce qvi regarde le chant françois. Ouvrage fort vtile à ceux qui aspirent à la methode de chanter, sur tout à bien prononcer les paroles auec toute la finesse & toute la force necessaire; & à bien obseruer la quantité des syllables & ne point confondre les longues & les brefues, suivant les regles qui en sont établies dans ce traité.* Paris: Ballard, 1668. *A Commentary upon the Art of Proper Singing.* Trans. Austin Caswell. Brooklyn: Institute of Medieval Music, 1968.

Bailleux, Antoine. *Méthode pour apprendre la musique vocale et instrumentale.* Paris, 1770.

Ballière de Laissement, Charles Louis Denis. *Théorie de la musique.* Paris: Didot le jeune, 1764.

Ban, Ioan Albert. *Zangh-Bloemzel & Kort Sangh-Bericht 1642.* Ed. Frits Noske. Early Music Theory in the Low Countries, vol. 1. Amsterdam: Frits Knuf, 1969.

Bank, J. A. *Tactus, Tempo, and Notation in Mensural Music from the 13th to the 17th Century.* Amsterdam: Annie Bank, 1972.

Barley, William. *A new book of tabliture.* London: Wm. Barley, 1596.

Bathe, William. *A brief introduction to the skill of song.* London: Thos. East, [1596].

Bayly, Anselm. *A practical treatise on singing and playing with just expression and real elegance.* London, 1771.

Bedos de Celles, François. *L'Art du facteur d'orgues.* Paris: L. F. Delatour, 1766–78. Faksimile-Nachdruck, ed. Christhard Mahrenholz. Documenta musicologica. 1. Reihe: Druckschriften-Faksimiles, 24, 25, 26. Kassel: Bärenreiter-Verlag, 1963–66.

Beicken, Suzanne. "Johann Hiller's *Anweisung zum musikalisch-zierlichen Gesange,* 1780: a Translation and Commentary." Ph.D. diss., Stanford University, 1980.

Bernhard, Christoph. "Von der Sing-kunst oder Manier" (ms., ca. 1650). Trans. Walter Hilse in *The Music Forum* 3 (1973): 1–29.

Béthizy, Jean Laurent de. *Exposition de la théorie et de la pratique de la musique.* Paris, 1764.

Beyschlag, Adolf. *Die Ornamentik der Musik.* 2 Auflage. Leipzig: Breitkopf und Härtel, 1953.

Blumenfeld, Harold. *The Syntagma Musicum of Michael Praetorius. Vol. 2. De Organographia First and Second Parts.* New York: Bärenreiter, 1962.

Boal, Ellen TeSelle. "Purcell's Clock Tempos and the Fantasias." *Journal of the Viola da Gamba Society of America* 20 (Dec. 1983): 24–39.

Bol, Johan Hendrik Daniel. *La basse de viole du temps de Marin Marais et d'Antoine Forqueray.* Utrechtse Bijdragen tot de Muziekwetenschap, no. 7. Bilthoven: A. B. Creyghton, 1973.

Bononcini, Giovanni Maria. *Musico prattico che brevemente dimostra il modo di giungere alla perfetta cognizione di tutte quelle cose, che concorrono alla composizione di i canti, e di ciò ch'all' arte del contrapunto si ricerca.* Bologna: per Giacomo Monti, 1673.

Bordet. *Méthode raisonnée pour apprendre la musique.* Paris [1755].

Bordier, Louis Charles. *Nouvelle méthode de musique.* Paris [1760].

Borin [formerly attributed to Didier Saurin]. *La musique theorique, et pratique, dans son ordre naturel: nouveaux principes par mr. XXXXX.* Paris: J. B. C. Ballard, 1722.

Borrel, Eugène. "Les notes inégales dans l'ancienne musique française." *Revue de musicologie* 12 (Nov. 1931): 278–89.

Bourgeois, Loys. *Le droict chemin de musique,* Genf 1550. Faksimile-Nachdruck, ed. A. Gaillard. Documenta musicologica, 1. Reihe: Druckschriften-Faksimiles, 6. Kassel und Basel: Bärenreiter-Verlag, 1954.

Boyden, David. *The History of Violin Playing from its Origins to 1761.* London: Oxford University Press, 1965.

Boyer, Pascal. *Lettre à M. Diderot sur le projet de l'unité de clef dans la musique, & de la réforme des mesures proposées par M. Lacassagne.* Amsterdam, 1767.

Brelet, Gisèle. *Le Temps musicale.* Paris: Presses Universitaires de France, 1949.

Brevia musicae rvdimenta latino belgicae ex prolixioribus mvsicorvm praeciptis excerpta 1605. Ed. Frits Noske. Early Music Theory in the Low Countries, vol. 3. Amsterdam: Frits Knuf, 1973.

Brijon, C. R. *Réflexions sur la musique, et la vraie manière de l'éxécuter sur le violon.* Paris, 1763. Facs. ed., Geneva: Minkoff, 1972.

Brossard, Sébastien de. *Dictionaire de musique, contenant une explication des termes grecs, latins, italiens, & françois les plus usitez dans la musique. A l'occasion desquels on rapporte ce qu'il y a de plus curieux, & de plus necessaire à sçavoir; tant pour l'histoire & la theorie, que pour la composition, & la pratique ancienne & moderne de la musique vocale, instrumentale, plaine, simple, figurée &c. Ensemble, une table alphabetique des termes françois qui sont dans le corps de l'ouvrage . . . Un traité de la maniere de bien prononcer, sur sur tout en chantant, les termes italiens, latins, & françois. Et un catalogue de plus de 900 auteurs qui ont écrit sur la musique, en toutes sortes de temps, de pays, et de langues.* Paris: Ballard, 1703.

Brown, John. *A dissertation on the rise, union, and power, the progression, separations, and corruptions, of poetry and music.* London, 1763.

Buelow, George J. *Thorough-Bass Accompaniment According to Johann David Heinichen.* Berkeley: University of California Press, 1966.

Bukofzer, Manfred F. *Music in the Baroque Era, from Monteverdi to Bach.* New York: W. W. Norton, 1947.

Burchill, James. "St.-Lambert's *Nouveau traité de l'accompagnement:* A Translation with Commentary." Ph.D. diss., Eastman School of Music, 1979.

Burney, Charles. "Accent, in music." In *The Cyclopedia; or universal dictionary of arts, sciences, and literature.* Ed. Abraham Rees. London: 1819.

———. *An eighteenth-century musical tour in France, Italy, central Europe and the Netherlands; being Dr. Charles Burney's account of his musical experiences.* Ed. Percy A. Scholes. London: Oxford University Press, 1959.

———. *A general history of music from the earliest ages to the present period (1789).* Ed. Frank Mercer. New York: Dover Publications, 1957.

———. *The present state of music in France and Italy.* London: T. Beckett, 1773.

———. *The present state of music in Germany, the Netherlands, and the United Provinces.* London: T. Beckett, 1773.

Burwell, Mary. Ms. of Lute Music. Ed. Roger Spencer. Facs. ed., Leeds: Boethius Press, 1974.

Buterne, Charles. *Méthode pour apprendre la musique vocale et instrumentale.* Rouen, 1752.

Butler, Charls. *The principles of musik, in singing and setting: with the two-fold use thereof, (ecclesiasticall and civil).* London: John Haviland for the author, 1636. Facs. ed., New York: Da Capo Press, 1970.

Buttstett, Johann Heinrich. *Ut mi sol re fa la tota Musica et Harmonia aeterna oder neu-eröffnetes, altes, wahres, einziges, und ewiges Fundamentum Musices.* Erfurt: Werther, 1716.

Caccini, Giulio. Preface to *Le nuove musiche* [1602]. In *Source Readings in Music History from Classical Antiquity through the Romantic Era.* Ed. Oliver Strunk. Trans. John Playford. New York: W. W. Norton, 1950.

Cajon, A. F. *Les Eléments de musique avec des leçons a une et 2 voix.* Paris, 1772.

Callcott, John Wall. *A musical grammar, in four parts, I. Notation, II. Melody, III. Harmony, IV. Rhythm*. London: B. Macmillan, 1806.

Carissimi, Giovanni Giacomo. *Ars cantandi; das ist Richtiger und Aussfürlicher Weg/ die Jugend aus dem rechten Grund in der Sing Kunst zu unterrichten: durch Weiland den Weltberühmten Musicum herrn Giovan Giacomo Carissimi. In Welscher Sprach aufgesetzt: nunmehro aus denselben aber von einem Music-freund in unsere Mutter-Sprach gebracht/ und/ so vil möglich/ deutlich gegeben. Allen Liebhabern der Musik, meistens aber den Lehr-Meistern zu besserer Bequemlichkeit/ und der Jugend zu leichterem Begriff und behäglichkeit/ im Druck gegeben*. Augsburg: Jacob Koppmayer, 1696.

Carse, Adam. *The Orchestra in the XVIIIth Century*. Cambridge, England: W. Heffer & Sons, 1940.

Cerone, Pedro. *El melopeo y maestro. Tractado de mvsica theorica y practica: en que se pone por extenso, lo que vno par hazerse perfecto musico ha menester saber: y por mayor facilidad, comodidad, y claridad del lector. Esta repartido en XXII libros. Va tan exemplificado y claro, que qualquiero de mediana habilidad, con poco trabajo alcancarà esta profesion*. Napoles: por Juan Bautista Gargano y Luccio Nucci, 1613. Facs. ed., Bibliotheca musica Bononiensis, sezione 2, no. 25. Bologna: Forni, 1969.

Chapman, Roger E. *Harmonie universelle: The Books on Instruments*. The Hague: M. Nijhoff, 1957.

Choquel, Henri Louis. *La musique rendue sensible par la méchanique, ou nouveau système pour apprendre facilement la musique soi-même*. Paris: Christophe Ballard, 1759. 2d ed. 1762. Facs. ed., Geneva: Minkoff, 1972.

Collins, Michael. "*Notes Inégales*: A Re-Examination." *JAMS* 20 (1967): 481–85.

———. "The Performance of Coloration, Sesquialtera, and Hemiolia (1450–1750)." Ph.D. diss., Stanford University, 1963.

Cooper, Grosvenor, and Leonard B. Meyer. *The Rhythmic Structure of Music*. Chicago: University of Chicago Press, 1960.

Cooper, Kenneth, and Julius Zsako. "Georg Muffat's Observations on the Lully Style of Performance." *Musical Quarterly* 53 (1967): 220–45.

Corrette, Michel. *L'Art de se perfectionner dans le violon*. Paris, 1782. Facs. ed., Geneva: Minkoff, 1972.

———. *L'Ecole d'Orphée; méthode pour apprendre facilement à joüer du violon dans le goût françois et italien; avec des principes de musique et beaucoup de leçons à I, et II violons: Ouvrage utile aux commençants et à ceux qui veulent parvenir à l'execution des sonates, concerto, pièces par accords et pièces à cordes ravalées . . . Oeuvre XVIIIe*. Paris: Chez l'Auteur, 1738.

———. *L'Ecole d'Orphée: Methode pour apprendre facilement à jouer du violon*. Paris, 1738. Facs. ed., Geneva: Minkoff, 1972.

———. *Le maître de clavecin pour l'accompagnement, méthode théorique et pratique*. Paris, 1753. Facs. ed., Bibliotheca musica Bononiensis, sezione 2, no. 135. Bologna: Forni, 1970.

———. *Methode pour apprendre aisement à jouer de la flute traversière*. Paris and Lyon, ca. 1740. Facs. ed., Hildesheim: Georg Olms Verlag, 1975

———. *Methode pour apprendre à jouer de la contrebasse à trois, à quatre, à cinq cordes*. Paris, 1781. Facs. ed., Geneva: Minkoff, 1977.

———. *Methode théorique et pratique pour apprendre en peu de temps le violoncelle dans sa perfection*. Paris, 1741. Facs. ed., Geneva: Minkoff, 1972.

———. *Le parfait maître à chanter. Méthode pour apprendre facilement la musique vocale & instrumentale*. Paris, [1758?].

Couperin, François. *L'Art de toucher le clavecin, 1716*. Ed. Maurice Cauchie. Oeuvres Complètes de François Couperin. Paris: Editions de l'Oiseau Lyre [1933]. Facs. ed., New York: Broude Bros., 1969. Trans. Margery Halford. Pt. Washington, N.Y.: Alfred Pub. Co., 1974.

Crocker, Richard L. "*Musica Rhythmica* and *Musica Metrica* in Antique and Medieval Theory." *Journal of Music Theory* 2 (April 1958): 2–23.

Crozier, Catherine. "The Principles of Keyboard Technique in *Il Transylvano* by Girolamo Diruta." M.A. thesis, Eastman School of Music, 1951.

Czerny, Carl. *Erinnerungen aus meinem Leben*. Ed. Walter Kolneder. Sammlung Musikwissenschaftlicher Abhandlungen, bd. 46. Strasbourg, Baden-Baden: Verlag Heitz GMBH, 1968.

Dahlhaus, Carl. "Zur Entstehung des modernen Taktsystems im 17. Jahrhundert." *Archiv für Musikwissenschaft* 18 (1961): 223–40.

———. "Zur Geschichte des Taktschlagens im frühen 17. Jahrhundert." In *Studies in Renaissance and Baroque Music in Honor of Arthur Mendel*, ed. Robert L. Marshall, pp. 117–23. Kassel: Bärenreiter Verlag, 1974.

———. "Zur Theorie des Tactus im 16. Jahrhundert." *Archiv für Musikwissenschaft* 17 (1960): 22.

Danoville. *L'art de toucher les dessus et basse de viole*. Paris, 1687.

Dard. *Nouveaux principes de musique*. Paris [1769].

Dart, R. Thurston. *The Interpretation of Music*. London: Hutchinson's University Library, 1954.

David, François. *Méthode nouvelle ou principes généraux pour apprendre facilement la musique, et l'art de chanter*. Paris: Vve. Boivin, 1737.

Démotz de la Salle, J. F. *Méthode de musique selon un nouveau système, très-court, très-facile & très-sûr, approuvés par messieurs de l'Academie Royale des Sciences, & par les plus habiles musiciens de Paris*. Paris: chez P. Simon, 1728.

Denis, Claude. *Nouveau système de musique pratique qui rend l'etude de cet art plus facile*. Paris, 1747.

———. *Nouvelle méthode pour apprendre en peu de temps la musique et l'art de chanter*. 2d ed. Paris, 1757.

Descartes, René. *Renatus Des-Cartes excellent compendium of musick: with necessary and judicious animadversions thereupon. By a person of honour*. [Trans. William Viscount Brounker.] London: T. Harper for H. Mosely, 1653.

Diruta, Girolamo. *Il Transylvano, dialogo sopra il vero modo di sonar organi, & istromento da penna* [5th ed.]. Venice: Alessandro Vincenti, 1625. Facs. ed., Bibliotheca musica Bononiensis, sezione 2, no. 132. Bologna: Forni, 1969.

Dolmetsch, Arnold. *The Interpretation of Music of the XVIIth and XVIIIth Centuries, Revealed by Contemporary Evidence*. London: Novello, 1914.

Donington, Robert. "Communication." *JAMS* 19 (1966): 112–14.

———. "A Problem of Inequality." *Musical Quarterly* 53 (1967): 513.

Douwes, Claas. *Grondig Ondersoek van de Toonen der Musijk* 1699. Ed. Peter Williams. Early Music Theory in the Low Countries, vol. 2. Amsterdam: Frits Knuf, 1970.

Dubos, l'abbé Jean-Baptiste. *Réflexions critiques sur la poésie et sur la peinture*. Paris: Chez Jean Mariette, 1719.

Du Cousu, Antoine. *La Musique universelle, contenant toute la pratique et toute la theorie*. Paris: Ballard, 1658. Facs. ed., Geneva: Minkoff, 1972.

Dumas, Antoine Joseph. *L'art de la musique*. Paris [1753].

Dupont, Pierre. *Principes de musique, par demande et par reponse, par lequel toutes personnes pourront aprendre d'eux même à connoître toutte la musique*. Paris: Chez l'hauteur, 1718.

Dupuits, Jean Baptiste. *Principes pour toucher de la vièle avec 6 sonates*. Paris [1741–42].

Dürr, Walther. "Auftakt und Taktschlag in der Musik um 1600." In *Festschrift Walter Gerstenberg zum 60 Geburtstag*, pp. 26–36. Wolfenbüttel: Bärenreiter Verlag, 1964.

Duval, l'Abbé. *Principes de la musique pratique, par demandes et par reponses*. Paris, 1764.

158 Bibliography

Duval, Pierre. *Méthode agréable et utile pour apprendre facilement à chanter juste, avec goût et precision.* Paris [1775]. Facs. ed., Geneva: Minkoff, 1972.

Egan, John B. *"Traité de l'harmonie universelle:* A Critical Translation of the Second Book." Ph.D. diss., Indiana University, 1962.

Eisel, J. P. *Musicus Autodidaktos oder der sich selbst informirende musicus, bestehende so wohl in Vocal- als üblicher Instrumental-Musique, welcher über 24 Sorten Instrumente beschreiber.* Erfurt: Funck, 1738.

Eisenhuet, R. D. Thomas. *Musikalisches Fundament/ So aufs denen berühmbt- und bewerthisten Authoribus eines Thails zusamen getragen; Andern Thails aber mit Vermeidung aller verdrüsslichen Weitläuffigkeit/ und schädlichen Auffenthaltung der Disciplen/ als sonderbarem Eyfer und affection gegen der edlen Music Liebhabern aignes Fleiss elaboriren/ auch in conformität dess iettzmahlig-Musikalischen Styli an Tag geben.* Campidonensi: Ex Ducali Typographia, 1682.

Engramelle, Marie-Dominique-Joseph. *La tonotechnie ou l'art de noter les cylindres, et tout ce qui est susceptible de notage dans les instruments de concerts méchaniques.* Paris: P. M. Delaguette, 1775. Facs. ed., Geneva: Minkoff, 1971.

Erhard, Lorenz. *Laurentii Erhardi Cantoris Gymnasii Francofurti Compendium Musices Latino-Germanicum, cui vecens nunc accederunt: 1o Tricinia, 2o Fugae, 3o Discursus musicalis, 4o Index terminorum-musicalium, 5o Rudimenta arithmetica, 6o Appendix nova ad arithmeticam pertinens.* Frankfurt, 1660.

Erig, Richard. *Italienische Diminutionen die zwischen 1553 und 1638 mehrmals bearbeiten sätze.* Herausgegeben von Richard Erig unter mitarbeit von Veronica Gutmann. Eng. trans. Anne Smith. Prattica Musicale 1. Zurich: Amadeus-Verlag, 1979.

Fajon, Robert. "Propositions pour une analyse rationalisé du récitatif de l'opéra lulliste." *Revue de Musicologie* 44 (1978): 55–75.

Falck, Georg. *Idea boni cantoris, das ist: getreu und gründliche Anleitung/ wie ein music-Scholar/ so wol im Singen/ als auch auf andern Instrumentis Musicalibus in kurzer Zeit so weit gebracht werden kan/ dass er eine Stück mit-zusingen oder zu spielen sich wird unterfangen dörffen; aus verschiedenen beruhmtem Musicis collegirt/ und der musik liebenden Jugend zu sonderbahrer Lust- Erweck- und nutzlichen Begreiffung zusammen geschrieben/ und hieraus gegeben von Georg Falcken dem Aelteren.* Nürnberg: Wolfgang Moritz Endter, 1688.

Farrar, Carol. *Michel Corrette and Flute Playing in the Eighteenth Century.* Brooklyn, 1970.

Fétis, François Joseph. *Biographie universelle des musiciens et bibliographie générale de la musique.* Deuxième edition. Paris: Firmin-Didot, 1883.

Frederici, Daniele. *Musica Figuralis, oder Newe/ und Klärliche Richtige/ und vorstentliche unterweisung/ der Singekunst. Mit gewissen Regulen, klaren und verstendigen Exemplen, neben vollkommener erklärung der Modorum Musicorum. Vor die Particular Schul zu Rostock zugerichtet.* Rostock: Joachim Fuess, 1619.

Freillon Poncein, Jean Pierre. *La veritable manière d'apprendre à jouer en perfection du hautbois, de la flûte, et du flageolet, avec les principes de la musique pour la voix et pour toutes sortes d'instruments.* Paris: Chez Collombat, 1700. Facs. ed., Geneva: Minkoff, 1974.

Frescobaldi, Girolamo. Preface to *Toccate e partite d'intavolatura di cimbalo.* Reprinted in Claudio Sartori, *Bibliografia della musica italiana stampata in Italia fino al 1700.* Florence: Olschki, 1952.

Frischmuth, Leonard. *Gedagten over de beginselen en onderwyzingen des clavicimbals.* Amsterdam: A. Olofsen [1758]. Reprint ed., Amsterdam: A. J. Heuwekemeijen, 1970.

Fuhrmann, Martin Heinrich. *Musikalischer Trichter/ dadurch ein geschickter Informator seinen Informandis die Edle Singe-Kunst nach heutiger manier bald und leicht einbringen kan/ darinn Vitiosa ausgemustert: Obscura Erläutert: Deficienta aber*

Erstattert/ mit einer Vorrede von der heutigen Music Vollkommenheit/ Kraffte/ Nutz und Nothwendigkeit/ herausgegeben durch ein mitglied der Singenden und Klingenden Gesellschafft. Franckfurt an der Spree, 1706.

Fuller, David. "Dotting, the 'French Style', and Frederick Neumann's Counter-Reformation." *Early Music* 5 (1977): 517–43.

———. *Mechanical Musical Instruments as a Source for the Study of 'Notes Inégales.'* Cleveland Heights: Divisions, 1979.

Galilei, Vincenzo. *Dialogo della musica antica et della moderna* Florence, 1581. Facs. ed., Milan, 1934.

Ganassi dal Fontego, Sylvestro. *Opera intitulata Fontegara, laquale insegna a sonare di flauto chon tutta l'arte opportuna a esso istromento, massime il diminuire il guale sara utile ad ogni instrumento di fiato et chorde: et anchora a chi si diletta di canto.* Venice, 1535. Facs. ed., Milan, 1934. Trans. Hildemarie Peter and Dorothy Swainson. Berlin: Lienau, 1959.

Geminiani, Francesco. *The Art of Accompaniment.* London, 1753.

———. *The Art of Playing on a Violin 1751.* Ed. David D. Boyden. London: Oxford University Press [1952].

———. *A Treatise of Good Taste in the Art of Musick.* London, 1749. Ed. Robert Donington. Facs. ed., New York: Da Capo Press, 1969.

Gengenbach, Nikolaus. *Musica Nova, Newe Singekunst so wol nach der alten Solmisation, als auch newen Bobisation und Bebisation der Jugend so leicht vorzugeben/ als zuvor noch nie an Tag kommen.* Leipzig: In Verlegung Eliae Rehefelds und Johan Grossen, Gedruckt bey Friedrich Lanckisch, 1626.

Gigault, André. *Livre de musique pour l'orgue 1685.* Ed. A. Guilmant and A. Pirro. Archives des maîtres de l'orgue des XVI. XVII. XVIII. siècles, vol 4. Paris, 1902.

Grassineau, James. *A musical dictionary being a collection of terms and characters as well ancient as modern: including the historical, theoretical and practical parts of music. Carefully abstracted from the best authors in the Greek, Latin, Italian, French and English Languages.* London: Wilcox, 1740.

Graves, Charles. "The Theoretical and Practical Method for Cello by Michel Corrette: Translation, Commentary and Comparison with Seven Other Eighteenth Century Methods." Ph.D. diss., Michigan State University, 1971.

Green, Robert. "Annotated Translation and Commentary of the Works of Jean Rousseau: A Study of Late Seventeenth-Century Musical Thought and Performance Practice." Ph.D. diss., Indiana University, 1979.

Gumpeltzhaimer, Adam. *Compendium musicae latino-germanicum Studio & operâ.* Trospergij: Iohannis Udalrici Schoenigij, 1632.

Haas, Robert. *Aufführungspraxis der Musik.* Handbuch der Musikwissenschaft, Band VI. Wildpark-Potsdam: Akademische Verlagsgesellschaft Athenaion, 1928–31.

Hanna, Ruth. "Cerone, Philosopher and Teacher." *Musical Quarterly* 21 (1925): 408–22.

Hase, Wolfgang. *Gründliche Einführung in die edle Music oder Singe-Kunst/ Anfangs der gemeinen Jugend zum besten/ und insonderheit für die Schule der Stadt Osteroda gestellet/ jetzto aber vermehret und verbessert/ und zum andern mal den Druck übergeben durch Wolfgangum Hasen.* Gosslar: Nicolao Dunckern in Verlagung des Autoris, 1657.

Hays, Elizabeth. "F. W. Marpurg's *Anleitung zum clavierspielen* 1755, and *Principes du clavecin* 1756: Translation and Commentary." Ph.D. diss., Stanford University, 1977.

Heckmann, Harald. "Der Takt in der Musiklehre des siebzehnten Jahrhunderts." *Archiv für Musikwissenschaft* 10 (1953): 116–40.

———. *W. C. Printz und seine Rhythmuslehre.* Dr. Phil. diss., University of Freiburg, 1952.

Heinichen, Johann David. *Der General-Bass in der Composition oder neue und grund-*

liche Anweisung, wie ein Music-Liebender mit besondern Vortheil, durch die Principia d. Composition, nicht allein d. General-Bass in Kirchen- Kammer- und Theatralischen Stylo . . . erlernen könne, nebst e. Einleitung oder musikalischen Raisonnement von der Musik überhaupt und vielen besonderen Materien der heutigen Praxeos. Dresden: bey dem Autor, 1728.

Herbst, Johann Andreas. *Musica Practica sive instructio pro symphoniacis.* Nürnberg, 1642; 2/1653.

Herman, Robert. "*Dialogo della musica antica et della moderna* of Vincenzo Galilei: Translation and Commentary." Ph.D. diss., North Texas State University, 1973.

Heyden, Sebald. *De arte canendi* 1540. Trans. Clement A. Miller. Musicological Studies and Documents, no. 26. Rome: American Institute of Musicology, 1972.

Hiller, Johann Adam. *Anweisung zum musikalisch-zierlichen Gesange.* Leipzig: J. F. Junius, 1780.

Holden, John. *An essay towards a rational system of music.* Glasgow: Rob. Urie for the Author, 1770.

Hotteterre, Jacques Martin. *Principes de la flûte traversière, ou flûte d'Allemagne, de la flûte à bec, ou flûte douce, et du Haut-bois.* Paris: C. Ballard, 1707. Facs. ed., Geneva: Minkoff, 1977. Trans. David Lasocki. New York: Praeger, 1968. Trans. Paul Douglas. New York: Dover, 1968.

Hsu, John. *A Handbook of French Baroque Viol Technique.* New York: Broude Brothers, 1981.

Jansen, Albert. *Jean-Jacques Rousseau als Musiker.* Berlin: Georg Reimer, 1884.

Jones, Rev. William of Nayland. *A treatise on the art of music, in which the elements of harmony and air are practically considered and illustrated by 150 examples in notes . . . as a course of lectures, preparatory to the practice of thorough-bass and musical composition.* Colchester: W. Keymer for the Author, 1784.

Jullien, Gilles. *Premier livre d'orgue 1690.* Ed. Norbert Dufourcq. Paris: Heugel et Cie, 1952.

Kalkbrenner, Christian. *Theorie der Tonkunst.* Berlin, 1789.

Kircher, Athanasius. *Musurgia Universalis sive ars magna consoni et dissoni in X libros digesta.* Rome: F. Corbeletti, 1650.

Kirkpatrick, Ralph. "On Re-reading Couperin's *L'Art de Toucher le Clavecin.*" *Early Music* 4 (January 1976): 3–11.

Kirnberger, Johann Philipp. *Die Kunst des reinen Satzes in der Musik aus sicheren Gründsatzen hergeleitet und mit deutlichen Beyspielen erlaütert.* 2 vols. Berlin und Königsberg, 1776–79. Facs. ed., Hildesheim: Georg Olms Verlagsbuchhandlung, 1968. Trans. David Beach and Jurgen Thym as *The Art of Strict Musical Composition.* Music Theory Translation series, 4. New Haven and London: Yale University Press, 1982.

Kite, Christopher. "The day has still to come when Mozart on a Steinway will be regarded . . . as necessarily a kind of transcription." *Early Music* 13 (February 1985): 54–56.

Koch, Heinrich Christoph. *Musikalisches Lexikon, welches die Theoretische und praktische Tonkunst, encyclopädisch bearbeitet, enthält, A-Z.* Franckfurt am Main: A. Hermann jun., 1802.

———. *Versuch einer Anleitung zur Composition.* Leipzig, 1782–93.

Kollmann, A. C. F. *An essay on musical harmony.* London: J. Dale, 1796.

Laborde, Jean-Benjamin de. *Essai sur la musique ancienne et moderne.* Paris: Ph.-D. Pierres, 1780.

Lacassagne, l'abbé Joseph de. *Traité générale des élémens du chant.* Paris: Chez l'Auteur, 1766. Facs. ed., Monuments of Music and Music Literature in Facsimile. 2d ser., Music Literature, 27. New York: Broude Bros., 1976.

L'Affilard, Michel. *Principes très-faciles pour bien apprendre la musique, qui conduiront promptement ceux qui ont du naturel pour le chant jusqu'au point de chanter toute sorte de musique proprement, & à livre ouvert.* 6ᵉ ed. Paris: C. Ballard, 1705. Facs. ed., Geneva: Minkoff, 1970.

Lampl, Hans. "A Translation of Syntagma Musicum III by Michael Praetorius." D.M.A. thesis, University of Southern California, 1957.

La Voye-Mignot, de. *Traité de musique, pour bien et facilement apprendre à chanter & composer, tant pour les voix que pour les instruments. Divisez en trois parties. Où se voyent tous les exemples des principales regles & observations pratiquées par les plus excellens Autheurs.* Paris: R. Ballard, 1656.

Le Blanc, Hubert. *Défense de la basse de viole contre les entreprises du violon et les prétentions du violoncel.* Amsterdam: Pierre Mortier, 1740. Eng. trans. by Barbara Garvey Jackson in *The Journal of the Viola da Gamba Society,* 1973–75.

Le Huray, Peter, and John Butt. "In Search of Bach the Organist." In *Bach, Handel, Scarlatti Tercentenary Essays,* ed. Peter Williams, pp. 185–207. Cambridge: Cambridge University Press, 1985.

Le Menu de Saint Philbert, Christoph. *Principes de musique courts et faciles.* Paris: Le Menu [1743].

Liliencron, Rochus von. "Die Chorgesänge des lateinisch-deutschen Schul-dramas im XVI Jahrhundert." *Vierteljahrschrift für Musikwissenschaft* (1890): 309–87.

———. "Die Horazischen Metren in deutschen Kompositionen des 16. Jahrhunderts." *Vierteljahrschrift für Musikwissenschaft* (1887): 26–91.

Lindley, Mark. "An Introduction to Alessandro Scarlatti's *Toccata prima.*" *Early Music* 10 (July 1982): 333–39.

———. "Keyboard Technique and Articulation: Evidence for the Performance Practices of Bach, Handel, and Scarlatti." In *Bach, Handel, Scarlatti Tercentenary Essays,* ed. Peter Williams, pp. 207–45. Cambridge: Cambridge University Press, 1985.

Löhlein, Georg Simon. *Clavierschule.* Dritte und verbesserte Auflage. Leipzig und Zullichau: Waisenhaus und Frommanischen Buchhandlung, 1779.

Lorenzoni, Antonio. *Saggio per ben sonare il flautotraverso.* Venice, 1779. Facs. ed., Bologna: Forni, 1969.

Loulié, Etienne. *Elémens ou principes de musique, mis dans un nouvel ordre & divisez en trois parties. La premiére pour les enfans. La seconde pour les personnes plus avancez en âge. La troisiéme pour ceux qui sont capable de raisonner sur les principes de la musique. Avec l'estampe, la description & l'usage du chronomètre . . . par le moyen duquel, les compositeurs de musique pourront desormais marquer le veritable mouvement de leurs compositions, & leurs ouvrages marquez par rapport à cet instrument, se pourront executer en leur absence comme s'ils en battoient eux-mesmes la mesure.* Paris: C. Ballard, 1696. Facs. ed., Geneva: Minkoff, 1971. *Elements or Principles of Music.* Trans. Albert Cohen. Musical Theorists in Translation, VI. Brooklyn: Institute of Medieval Music, 1965.

———. "Méthode pour apprendre à jouer la viole." Paris: Bibliothèque Nationale, MS fonds fr. n. a. 6355, fols. 210r–222r [ca. 1690].

Ludwig, Friedrich. "M. Mersenne und seine Musiklehre." *Beiträge zur Musikforschung* 4 (1935): 24.

Lussy, Mathis. *Le rythme musical, son origine, sa fonction et son accentuation.* Paris: Heugel et Cie., 1883.

Mace, Thomas. *Musick's Monument.* London, 1676. Facs. ed., Paris: Centre National de la Recherche Scientifique, 1958.

Maichelbeck, Franz Anton. *Die auf dem Clavier lehrende Caecilia.* Augsburg: J. J. Lotter, 1738.

Maier, Joseph Frederick Bernhard Caspar. *Museum musicum theoretico practicum, das ist neu-eröffneter theoretisch- und practischer Music-Saal, darinnen gelehret wird wie man sowohl die vocal- als instrumental-Musik grundlich erlernen auch die heut zu tag ublich und gewöhnlichste blasend/ schlagend und streichend instrumenten in kurzer Zeit und compendienser Application in besondern Tabellen mit leichter*

Mühe begreifen könne. Nebst einem Appendice derer anjetzo gebrauchlichst-Griechisch- Lateinisch- Italienisch- und Franzosisch-Musikalischen kunst Wörter nach alphabetischer Ordnung eingerichtet und erklaret. Nürnberg: Cremer, 1732.

Malcolm, Alexander. *A treatise of musick, speculative, practical and historical, containing . . . the nature and office of the scale of musick, the whole art of writing notes, and the general rules of composition, with a particular account of the ancient musick and a comparison thereof with the modern.* Edinburgh, 1721.

Malloch, William. "The Earl of Bute's Machine Organ, a Touchstone of Taste." *Early Music* 11 (April 1983): 172–84.

Manfredini, Vincenzo. *Regole armoniche o sieno precetti ragionati per apprendere i principi della musica, il portamento della mano, et l'accompagnamento del basso, sopra gli strumenti da tasto, come l'organo, il cembalo, ec..* Venice: Zerletti, 1775.

Mann, Elias. *The Northampton collection of sacred harmony.* Northampton, Mass., 1797.

Marcou, Pierre. *Elémens théoriques et pratiques de musique.* London and Paris: Ballard, 1782.

Marpurg, Friedrich Wilhelm. *Anleitung zum Clavierspielen.* Berlin: Haude & Spener, 1755. Facs. ed., Hildesheim: Georg Olms Verlag, 1970.

——. *Die Kunst das Klavier zu spielen.* Berlin: Haude & Spener, 1751–61.

Marshall, Robert L. "Tempo and Dynamic Indications in the Bach Sources: A Review of the Terminology." In *Bach, Handel, Scarlatti Tercentenary Essays,* ed. Peter Williams, pp. 259–76. Cambridge: Cambridge University Press, 1985.

Masson, Charles. *Nouveau traité des regles pour la composition de la musique, par lequel on apprend à faire facilement un chant sur des paroles: à composer à 2. à 3. à 4. parties, &c. Et à chiffrer la basse-continuë, suivant l'usage des meilleurs auteurs. Ouvrage très- utile à ceux qui joüent de l'orgue, du clavecin, & du théorbe.* 3d ed. rev. & cor. Paris: C. Ballard, 1705.

Mather, Betty Bang. *Interpretation of French Music from 1675 to 1775 for Woodwind and Other Performers.* New York: McGinnis and Marx, 1973.

Mattheson, Johann. *Critica musica, d.i. Grundrichtige Untersuch- und Beurtheilung/ Vieler/ theils vorgefassten/ theils einfaltigen Meinungen/ Argumenten und Einwürffe/ so in alten und neuen/ gedruckten und ungedruckten Musikalischen Schrifften zu finden. Zur müglichsten Ausräutung aller grossen Irrthümer/ und zur Beförderung eines bessern Wachsthums der reinen harmonischen Wissenschaft/ in verschiedene Theile abgefasset/ und Stuck-weise heraus gegeben von Mattheson.* Hamburg: auf ankosten des Autoris, 1722.

——. *Kleine General-Bass-Schule. Worin nicht nur lernende, sondern vornehmlich lehrende, aus den alleresten Anfangsgründen des Clavier-spielens durch verschiedene Classen und Ordnungen der Accorde zu mehrer Vollkommen-heit in dieser Wissenschaft angeführet werden.* Hamburg: Kissner, 1735.

——. *Das Neu-eröffnete Orchestre, oder Universelle und grundliche Anleitung wie ein Galant Homme einen Vollkommenen Begriff von der Hoheit und Würde der edlen Music erlangen . . . möge.* Hamburg: B. Schillers Witwe, 1713.

——. *Der vollkommene Capellmeister, das ist Gründliche Anzeige aller derjenigen Sachen, die einer wissen, konnen, und vollkommen inne haben muss, der einer Kapelle mit Ehren und Nutzen vorstehen Will: zum Versuch entworfen von Mattheson.* Hamburg: Verlegts Christian Herold, 1739. Faksimile-Nachdruck, ed. Margarete Reimann. Documenta musicologica. 1. Reihe: Druckschriften-Faksimiles, 5. Kassel: Bärenreiter-Verlag, 1953. Trans. Ernest C. Harriss. Ann Arbor: UMI Research Press, 1981.

Mercadier de Belesta. *Nouveau systeme de musique théoretique et pratique.* Paris, 1777.

Merck, Daniel. *Compendium musicae instrumentalis chelicae. Das ist: Kurzer Begriff/ welcher Gestalten die Instrumental-Musik auf der Violin, Pratschen/ Viola da*

Gamba, und Bass, gründlich und leicht zu erlernen seye. Der Jugend und andern Liebhabern zu Gefallen aufgesetzt/ und auf Begehren guter Freunde zu offentlichem Druck befördert/ von Daniel Mercken/ Stadt-Musico in Augspurg. Erster Theil. Augsburg: Druckts Johann Christoph Wagner, In Jahr Christi 1695.

Mersenne, Marin. *Harmonie universelle, contenant la théorie et la pratique de la musique, où il est traité de la nature des sons, et des mouvements, des consonances, des dissonances, des genres, des modes, de la composition, de la voix, des chants, et de toutes sortes d'instrumens harmoniques.* Paris: Gramoisy et Ballard, 1636–37. Facs. ed. edited by François Lesure. Paris: Centre National pour la Recherche Scientifique, 1975.

Metoyen, B. *Démonstration des principes de musique.* Paris [ca. 1730].

Mizler von Kolof, Lorenz Christoph. *Neu-Eröffnete Musikalische Bibliothek, oder Grundlichen Nachricht nebst unpartheyischem Urtheil von Musikalischen Schriften und Büchern.* Leipzig, 1739–54.

Momigny, Jérome-Joseph de. *Cours complet d'harmonie et de composition d'après une théorie neuve et générale de la musique.* Paris: Chez l'Auteur, 1803.

Montéclair, Michel Pignolet de. *Methode facile pour apprendre à jouer du violon* 1712. Facs. ed., Geneva: Minkoff, 1972.

———. *Nouvelle methode pour apprendre la musique par des demonstrations faciles, suivies d'un grand nombre de leçons à une et à deux voix, avec des tables qui facilitent l'habitude des transpositions et la conoissance des differentes mesures.* Paris: Chez l'Auteur, 1709.

———. *Principes de musique. Divisez en quatre parties. La première partie contient tout ce qui appartient à l'intonation. La IIme. partie tout ce qui regarde la mesure et le mouvement. La IIIe. la manière de joindre les paroles aux nottes et de bien former les agréments du chant. La IVe. partie est l'abregé d'un nouveau système de musique, par lequel l'auteur fait voir qu'en changeant peu de choses dans la manière de notter la musique, ou en rendoit l'étude et la pratique plus aisé.* Paris [1736]. Facs. ed., Geneva: Minkoff, 1972.

Morley, Thomas. *A plaine and easie introduction to practicall musicke, set down in forme of a dialogue: deuided into three partes, the first teacheth to sing with all things necessary for the knowledge of pricktsong. The second treateth of descante and to sing two parts in one upon a plainsong or ground, with other things necessary for a descanter. The third and last part entreateth of composition of three, foure, fiue or more parts with many profitable rules to that effect. With new songs of 2, 3, 4, and 5, parts.* London: imprinted by Peter Short dwelling on Breedstreet hill at the signe of the starre, 1597. Facs. ed., Westmead, Farnborough, Hants, England: Gregg International Publishers, 1971.

———. *A Plain and Easy Introduction to Practical Music* 1597. Ed. R. Alec Harman. New York: W. W. Norton, [1952].

Mozart, Leopold. *Versuch einer gründlichen Violinschule* [1756], Dritte vermehrte Auflage. Augsburg: Johann Jacob Lotter und Sohn, 1787. Facs. ed., Leipzig: VEB Deutscher Verlag für Musik, 1968. Trans. Editha Knocker. London: Oxford University Press, 1948.

Muffat, Georg. *Florilegium primum für Streichinstrumente, in Partitur mit unterlegtem Clavierauszug.* Ed. Heinrich Rietsch. Denkmäler der Tonkunst in Österreich, Band I, Zweite Hälfte. Wien: Artaria & Co., 1894.

———. *Florilegium secundum für Streichinstrumente in Partitur mit unterlegtem Clavierauszug.* Ed. Heinrich Rietsch. Denkmäler der Tonkunst in Österreich, II Band, Zweite Hälfte. Wien: Artaria & Co., 1895.

Münster, Joseph Joachim Benedict. *Musicis instructio.* Augsburg, 1748.

Murata, Margaret. "P. F. Valentini on Tactus and Proportion (Rome, 1643)." In *Proceedings of the Frescobaldi Quadricentennial Conference,* Madison, Wisconsin, ed. Alexander Silbiger. Madison, Wisconsin, forthcoming.

Mussard. *Nouveaux principes pour apprendre à jouer de la flütte traversiere.* Paris, 1779.

Neumann, Frederick. *Essays in Performance Practice.* Ann Arbor: UMI Research Press, 1982.

————. "External Evidence and Uneven Notes." *Musical Quarterly* 52 (1966): 448–64.

————. "The French *Inégales,* Quantz, and Bach." *Journal of the American Musico-logical Society* 18 (1965): 313–58.

A new and easie method to learn to sing by book: whereby one (who hath a good voice and ear) may, without other help learn to sing true by notes. London: Printed for Wm. Rogers, 1686.

Nivers, Guillaume Gabriel. *Livre d'orgue 1665.* Ed. Norbert Dufourcq. Paris: Editions Bornemann, 1963.

————. *Deuxième livre d'orgue 1667.* Ed. Norbert Dufourcq. Paris: Editions Borne-mann, 1956.

————. *Troisième livre d'orgue 1675.* Ed. Norbert Dufourcq. Paris: Pub. de la Société Française de Musicologie, 1958.

[North, Francis]. *A philosophical essay of musick directed to a friend.* London: W. Sill, 1677.

North, Roger. *Memoires of Musick.* In *Roger North on Music,* ed. John Wilson. London: Methuen, 1959.

Ornithoparcus, Andreas. *Andreas Ornithoparcus his micrologus, or introduction: con-taining the art of singing. Digested into foure bookes. Not onely profitable, but also necessary for all that are studious of Musicke. Also the Dimension and perfect use of the monochord, according to Guido Aretinus. By John Dowland Lutenist, lute-player, and Bachelor of Musicke in both the Universities.* London: Printed for Thomas Adams, dwelling in Paules Church-yard, at the Signe of the white Lion, 1609. Facs. ed., *A Compendium of Musical Practice.* Ed. Gustave Reese and Steven Ledbetter. AMS-MLA Reprint Series. New York: Dover Publications, 1973.

Ortiz, Diego. *Trattado de glosas sobre clausulas y otros generos de puntos en la musica de violones nuevamente puestos en luz, de Diego Ortiz tolledano 1553.* Ed. Max Schneider. Transcribed from the original edition. Kassel: Bärenreiter-Verlag, 1936.

Parkins, Robert. "Keyboard Fingering in Early Spanish Sources." *Early Music* 11 (July 1983): 323–32.

Parran, Antoine. *Traité de la musique théorique et pratique contenant les préceptes de la composition.* Paris: P. Ballard, 1636.

Pasquali, Niccolo. *The art of fingering the harpsichord.* Edinburgh: Robert Bremner, 1760.

Paulsmeier, Karin. "Temporelationen bei Frescobaldi." In *Alte Musik Praxis und Reflex-ion,* Sonderband der Reihe "Basler Jahrbuch für Historische Musikpraxis." Ed. Peter Reidemeister and Veronika Gutmann, pp. 187–203. Winterthur: Amadeus Verlag, 1983.

Penna, Lorenzo. *Li primi albori musicali. Per li principianti della musica figurata: dis-trinti in tre libri: dal primo spuntano li principij del canto figurato: dal secondo spiccano le regole del contrapunto: del Terzo appariscono li fondamenti per suo-nare l'organo ò clavicembalo sopra la parte.* Bologna: P. M. Monti, 4 impressione, 1684. Facs. ed., Bibliotheca musica Bononiensis, sezione 2, no. 38. Bologna: Forni, 1969.

Perrine [le Sieur]. *Livre de musique pour le lut. Contenant une méthode nouvelle et fa-cile pour apprendre à toucher le lut sur les notes de la musique, avec des regles pour exprimer par les même notes toutes sortes de pièces de lut dans leur propre mouve-ment. Une demonstration generale des intervalles qui se trouve dans la musique et sur le lut, avec leur diverse composition et division. Des cartes par lesquelles les proportions armoniques du lut sont expliquées et une table pour apprendre a tou-cher le lut sur la basse continuë pour accompagner la voix avec le regles generales et les principes de la musique.* Paris: Chez l'Auteur, 1679.

———. *Pieces de luth en musique avec des regles pour les toucher parfaitement sur le luth et sur le clavessin.* Paris, 1680.

Pisa, Agostino. *Battuta della musica dichiarata da Don Agostino Pisa, Dottore di Legge Canonica, & Ciuile, e Musico speculativo, & prattico. Opera nova utile, e necessaria alli professori della musica. Ristampata di novo, & Ampliata.* Rome: Zannetti, 1611. Facs. ed., Bibliotheca musica Bononiensis, sezione 2, no. 32. Bologna: Forni, 1969.

Playford, John. *A brief introduction to the skill of musick. In two books. The first contains the grounds and rules of musick. The second, instructions for the viol and also for the treble-violin.* London: John Playford, 1662.

———. *A brief introduction to the skill of musick: In three books. The first: the grounds and rules of musick . . . The second, instructions for the bass-viol, and also for the treble-violin: with lessons for beginners. By John Playford . . . The third: the art of descant, or composing musick in parts. By Dr. Tho. Campion. With annotations thereon by Mr. Chr. Simpson.* London: Wm. Godbid & J. Playford, 1670.

———. *An introduction to the skill of musick: in three books. By John Playford. Containing I. the grounds and principles of musick according to the gamut; being newly written and made more easie for young practitioners, according to the method now in practice, by an eminent master in that science. II. Instructions and lessons for the treble, tenor, and bass-viols; and also for the treble violin. III. The art of descant, or composing musick in parts; made very plain and easie by the late Mr. Henry Purcell. The thirteenth edition.* London: E. Jones for Henry Playford, 1697.

Portmann, Johann Gottlieb. *Leichtes Lehrbuch der Harmonie, Composition und des Generalbasses, zum Gebrauch für Liebhaber der Musik, angehende und fortschreitende musici und componisten.* Darmstadt: J. J. Will, 1789.

Pougin, Arthur. *Jean-Jacques Rousseau, Musicien.* Paris: Fischbacher, 1901.

Powell, Newman Wilson. "Early Keyboard Fingering and Its Effect on Articulation." M.A. thesis, Stanford University, 1954.

———. "Kirnberger on Dance Rhythms, Fugues, and Characterization." In *Festschrift Theodore Hoelty-Nickel.* Valparaiso, Indiana: Valparaiso University Press, 1967.

———. "Rhythmic Freedom in the Performance of French Music from 1650 to 1735." Ph.D. diss., Stanford University, 1958.

Praetorius, Michael. *Syntagma Musicum 1614–1619.* 3 vols. Faksimile-Nachdruck, ed. W. Gurlitt. Documenta musicologica. 1. Reihe: Druckschriften-Faksimiles, 14, 15, 21. Kassel: Bärenreiter-Verlag, 1958–59.

Prelleur, Peter. *The modern music-master or the universal musician, containing I: an introduction to singing, II: directions for playing on the flute, III: the newest method for learners on the German flute, IV: instructions on the hautboy, V: the art of playing on the violin, VI: the harpsichord . . . with sets of lessons for beginners . . . with a brief history of music, to which is added a musical dictionary.* London: Printing Office in Bow Church Yard, 1731. Facs. ed., Kassel: Bärenreiter-Verlag, 1965.

Printz, Wolfgang Caspar. *Compendium musicae signatoriae & modulatoriae vocalis, das ist: kurzer Begriff aller derjenigen Sachen, so einem, der die Vocal-Musik lernen will, zu wissen von nöthen seyn.* Dressden: Mieth, 1689.

———. *Musica Modulatoria Vocalis.* 1678.

———. *Phrynis mitilenaeus, oder Satyrischer Componist, welcher/ vermittelst einer Satyrischen Besicht/ die Fehler der ungelehrten/ selbgewachsegen/ ungeschickten/ und unverstandigen Componisten höflich darstellet/ und zugleich lehret/ wie ein Musikalisches Stück rein/ ohne Fehler/ und nach den rechten Grunde zu componiren und zu setzen sey/ worbey mancherley Musikalische Discurse/ als de Proportionibus, Variationibus, Basso-continuo, Generibus Modulandi, Temperaturâ, Musica Rhythmica, Variis Contrapunctis, von unterschiedlicher Prolation des textes und dergleichen/ w.f.s. auch eine Beschreibung eines Labyrinthi Musici, nebst eingemengten lustigen Erzehlungen gefunden werden.* Dressden und Leipzig: Verlegts J. C. Mieth und J. C. Zimmermann, Druckes Johann Riedel, 1696.

Pruitt, William. "Un traité d'interpretation du XVII siècle." *L'Orgue* 152 (1974): 99–111.

Purcell, Henry. *A choice collection of lessons for the harpsichord or spinnet.* London: Printed for Mrs. Frances Purcell . . . sold by Henry Playford, 1696.

Quantz, Johann Joachim. *Johann Joachim Quantzens, Konig. Preussischen Kammermusikus, Versuch einer Anweisung die Flöte traversière zu spielen; mit verschiedenen, zur Beförderung des guten Geschmackes in der praktischen Musik dienlich Anmerkungen begleitet, und mit Exempeln erläutert. Nebst XXIV kupfertafeln.* Berlin: Johann Friedrich Voss, 1752. Faksimile-Nachdruck of the 3d ed., ed. Hans-Peter Schmitz. Documenta musicologica. 1. Reihe: Druckschriften-Faksimiles, 2. Kassel: Bärenreiter-Verlag, 1953. *On Playing the Flute.* Trans. Edward R. Reilly. New York: The Free Press, 1966.

Quirsfeld, Johann. *Breviarum musicum oder kurzer Begriff, wie eine Knabe leicht und bald zur Singe-Kunst gelangen/ und die begreiffen und erlernen kan.* Dresden: Martin Gabriel Hübners, 1688.

Quitschreiber, Georg. *Musikbüchlein für die Jugend/ in deutschen und lateinischen Schulen zu gebrauchen. Daraus Jederman/ wer Deutsch verstehet/ und mit verstande lesen kan/ auch Lust zur Singekunst hat/ aus rechtem Grunde gar leichtlich Musicam verstehen und lernen kan.* Jehna: Doselbst zum andern mal gedrukt, 1607.

Rameau, Jean-Philippe. *Traité de l'harmonie reduite à ses principes naturels; divisé en quatre livres.* Paris: J. B. C. Ballard, 1722. *A treatise of musick, containing the principles of composition . . . by Mr. Rameau . . . translated into English from the original in the French language.* London: Robt. Brown for John Walsh, 1752. Trans. Philip Gossett. New York: Dover, 1971.

Raparlier. *Principes de musique, les agréments du chant et un essai sur la prononciation, l'articulation et la prosodie de la langue françoise.* Lille, 1772. Facs. ed., Geneva: Minkoff, 1972.

Ratner, Leonard. "Eighteenth-Century Theories of Musical Period Structure." *Musical Quarterly* 42 (1956): 439–54.

Ravenscroft, Thomas. *A briefe discourse of the true (but neglected) use of charact'ring the degrees, by their perfection, imperfection and diminution in measurable musicke, against the common practice and custom of these times. Examples whereof are exprest in the harmony of 4. Voyces, concerning the pleasure of 5. usual recreations: (1) hunting, (2) hawking, (3) dauncing, (4) drinking, and (5) enamouring.* London: Edw. Allde for Tho. Adams, 1614.

Reese, Gustave. *Music in the Renaissance.* New York: W. W. Norton, 1954.

Reilly, Edward R. *Quantz and His Versuch.* New York: American Musicological Society, 1971.

Riepel, Joseph. *Anfangsgrunde zur musikalischen Setzkunst . . . De Rhythmopoeia, oder von der Tactordnung.* Franckfort & Leipzig, 1752.

Rodgers, Julane. "Early Keyboard Fingering ca. 1520–1620." D.M.A. diss., University of Oregon, 1971.

Rollet. *Méthode pour apprendre la musique sans transposition.* Paris [1760].

Rosow, Lois. "French Baroque Recitative as an Expression of Tragic Declamation." *Early Music* 11 (July 1983): 468–79.

Rousseau, Jean. *Methode claire, certaine et facile, pour apprendre à chanter la musique, sur les tons transposez comme sur les naturels. A battre la mesure à toutes sortes de mouvemens ordinaires & extra-ordinaires. A faire les ports de voix & les cadences sur la musique avec regularité: et à connoître où il faut faire les tremblemens dans les livres où il ne sont pas marquez. Le tout expliqué & mis en ordre par Jean Rousseau.* Paris: Chez l'Auteur, 1683. Facs. ed., Geneva: Minkoff, 1976.

———. *Traité de la viole, qui contient une dissertation curieuse sur son origine, un démonstration générale de son manche en quatre figures, avec leurs explications.*

L'explication de ses jeux differents, & particulierement des pièces par accords, et de l'accompagnement à fond. Des regles certaines, pour connoître tous les agrémens qui se peuvent pratiquer sur cet instrument dans toutes sortes de pièces de musique. La veritable maniere de gouverner l'archet, & des moyens faciles pour transposer sur toutes sortes de tons. Paris: C. Ballard, 1688. Facs. ed., Amsterdam: Antiqua, 1965.

Rousseau, Jean-Jacques. *Dictionnaire de musique 1768.* Oeuvres Complètes de. J.-J. Rousseau, vols. XII and XIII. Paris: Dupont, 1824.

———. *Dissertation sur la musique moderne.* Oeuvres Complètes de J.-J. Rousseau, vol. XI, pp. 21–140. Paris: Dupont, 1824.

———. *Projet concernant de nouveau signes pour la musique.* Oeuvres Complètes de J.-J. Rousseau, vol. XI, pp. 1–17. Paris: Dupont, 1824.

Roussel, F. *Le guide musical ou théorie & pratique abrégées de la musique vocale & instrumentale.* Paris, 1775.

Rowley, Gordon. "*Le Maitre de clavecin pour l'accompagnement:* Michel Corrette's Method for Learning to Accompany from a Thoroughbass." Ph.D. diss., University of Iowa, 1979.

Sachs, Curt. *Rhythm and Tempo: A Study in Music History.* New York: W. W. Norton, 1953.

Saint Lambert, Michel de. *Nouveau traité de l'accompagnement du clavecin, de l'orgue, et autres instruments.* Paris, 1707. Facs. ed., Geneva: Minkoff, 1972.

———. *Les principes du clavecin, contenant une explication exacte de tout ce qui concerne la tablature & le clavier. Avec des remarques necessaires pour l'intelligence de plusieurs difficultées de la musique.* Paris: J. B. C. Ballard, 1702. Facs. ed., Geneva: Minkoff, 1972. *Principles of the Harpsichord by Monsieur de Saint Lambert.* Trans. Rebecca Harris-Warrick. Cambridge Musical Texts and Monographs. Cambridge: Cambridge University Press, 1984.

Saurin, Didier. *See* Borin.

Scaletta, Orazio. *Scala di musica molto necessaria fatta con ogni brevita.* Venice, 1592.

Scheibe, Johann Adolf. *Der critische Musikus. Neue, vermehrte und verbesserte Auflage.* Leipzig: Breitkopf, 1745.

———. *Ueber die musikalische Composition. Erster Theil: die Theorie der Melodie und Harmonie.* Leipzig: Schwickert, 1773.

Schunemann, Georg. *Geschichte des Dirigirens.* Leipzig: Breitkopf und Härtel, 1913.

Schwandt, Erich. "L'Affilard on the French Court Dances." *Musical Quarterly* 60 (1974): 389–400.

———. "L'Affilard's Published Sketchbooks." *Musical Quarterly* 63 (1977): 99–113.

Seares, Margaret. "Aspects of Performance Practice in the Recitatives of Jean-Baptiste Lully." *Studies in Music* 8 (1974): 8–16.

Simpson, Christopher. *A compendium of practical musick in five parts: teaching by a new and easie method. 1. The rudiments of song. 2. The principles of composition. 3. The use of discords. 4. The form of figurate descant. 5. The contrivance of canon.* London: W. Godbid for Henry Brome, 1667.

———. *A compendium: or introduction to practicall musick.* Eighth edition. London, 1732.

———. *The Division-Violist: or, an Introduction to the Playing upon a Ground.* London, 1659. Facs. of the 2d ed., London: J. Curwen, 1955.

Soderlund, Sandra. *Organ Technique, An Historical Approach.* Chapel Hill: Hinshaw Music, 1980. 2d ed. 1986.

Soehnlein, Edward John. "Diruta on the Art of Keyboard-Playing: An Annotated Translation and Transcription of *Il transilvano,* Parts I (1593) and II (1609)." Ph.D. diss., University of Michigan, 1975.

Speer, Daniel. *Grund-richtiger/ kurtz/ leicht/ und nöthiger Unterricht der musikalischen Kunst/ wie man fuglich und in kurtzer Zeit choral und figural Musik singen/ dem General-bass tractiren/ und componiren lernen soll. Denen lehr und lernenden zu beliebigem gebrauch/ herauss gegeben von Daniel Speeren.* Ulm: G. W. Kühne, 1687.

Sperling, Johann Peter. *Principia musicae, das ist Gründliche Anweisung zur Musik/ wie ein Musik-Scholar vom Anfang instruiret und nach der Ordnung zur Kunst oder Wissenschaft der Figural-Musik soll gefuhret und gwiesen werden.* Bautzen: bey Andreas Richter, 1705.

Steele, Joshua. *Prosodia rationalis or an essay towards establishing the melody and measure of speech.* 2d ed. London: J. Nichols, 1779.

Sternfeld, F. W. "Music in the Schools of the Reformation." *Musica Disciplina* 2 (1948): 98–122.

Stickney, John. *The gentleman and lady's musical companion.* Newbury-port, Mass.: Daniel Bayley, 1774.

Stillingfleet, Benjamin. *Principles and Power of Harmony.* London, 1771.

Strunk, Oliver. "Vergil in Music." *Musical Quarterly* 16 (1930): 482–97.

———. *Source Readings in Music History from Classical Antiquity through the Romantic Era.* New York: W. W. Norton [1950].

Sulzer, Johann-Georg. *Allgemeine Theorie der schönen Künste.* Neue vermehrte zweite Auflage. Leipzig, 1794.

Tans'ur, William Sr. *A new musical grammar: or the harmonical spectator. Containing all the useful theoretical, practical, and technical parts of musick. Being a new and correct introduction to all the rudiments, terms and characters and composition in all branches, etc.* London: Robinson, printed for the author and sold by him, 1746.

Tarade, Théodore-Jean. *Traité du violon, ou regles de cet instrument a l'usage de ceux qui veulent en jouer avec la parfaite connoisance de ton dans lequel on est.* Paris [1774]. Facs. ed., Geneva: Minkoff, 1972.

Tartini, Giuseppe. *Traité des agréments de la musique* (1752 or 1756?). Ed. E. R. Jacobi, with an English trans. by Cuthbert Girdlestone. New York: Hermann Moeck, 1961.

———. *Trattato di musica secondo la vera scienza dell' armonia.* Padova: Giovanni Manfrè, 1754.

Taylor, Ralph. "Georg Falck's *Idea boni cantoris;* Translation and Commentary." Louisiana State University thesis, 1971.

Tevo, Zaccaria. *Il musico testore.* Venice: Antonio Bortoli, 1706.

Thiémé, Frédéric. *Nouvelle théorie sur les différens mouvemens des airs, fondé sur la pratique de la musique moderne.* Paris, 1801.

Türk, Daniel Gottlob. *Klavierschule, oder Anweisung zum Klavierspielen für Lehrer und Lernende, mit kritischen Anmerkungen.* Leipzig und Halle: Auf Kosten der Verfassers, 1789. *School of Clavier Playing or Instructions in Playing the Clavier for Teachers and Students 1789.* Trans. Raymond H. Haggh. Lincoln: University of Nebraska Press, 1982.

Turner, William. *Sound anatomiz'd in a philosophical essay on musick.* London: Wm. Pearson, 1724.

Vague. *L'art d'apprendre la musique.* Paris, 1733.

Valentini, Pier Francesco. "Trattato della battuta musicale." Rome: Vatican Library Ms. Barb. lat. 4417, 1643.

———. "Trattato del tempo del modo e della prolatione." Rome: Vatican Library Ms. Barb. lat. 4419, 1643.

Villeneuve, Alexandre de. *Nouvelle methode tres courte, et tres facile avec un nombre de lecons pour apprendre la musique et les agréments du chant.* Paris, 1733.

Vion, P. F. C. X. *La musique pratique et theorique réduite à ses principes naturels.* Paris, 1742.

Vogel, Harald. Liner notes for *The Fisk Organ at Wellesley College, A Renewal of the Mean-Tone Tradition.* Organa Recording 3005.

Vossius, Isaac. *De poematum cantu et viribus rythmi.* Oxonii e Theatro Sheldoniano, Prostant Londini: apud Rob. Scot bibliop., 1673.

Vulpius, Melchior. *Musicae Compendium Latino germanicum M. Heinrici Fabri, pro Tyronibus hujus artis, in Schola Vinariensi, ad majorem discentium commoditatem aliquantulum variatum ac dispositum, cum facili brevique de Modis tractatu.* Jena: Excusum apud Johannem Weidnerum, Impensis Heinrici Birnstiels, 1608.

Walker, D. P. "The Aims of Baïf's Academie de Poésie et de Musique." *Journal of Renaissance and Baroque Music* 1 (1947): 91–100.

———. "Claude le Jeune and *Musique Mesurée.*" *Musica Disciplina* 3 (1949): 150–70.

———. "The Influence of *Musique Mesurée à l'Antique*, Particularly on the *Airs de Cour* of the Early 17th Century." *Musica Disciplina* 2 (1948): 141–63.

———. "Musical Humanism in the 16th and Early 17th Centuries." *Music Review* 2 (1941): 1–13, 111–21, 220–27, 288–308; 3 (1942): 55–71.

———. "Some Aspects of *Musique Mesurée à l'Antique*: The Rhythm and Notation of *Musique Mesurée.*" *Musica Disciplina* 4 (1950): 163–86.

Walther, Johann Gottfried. *Musikalisches Lexikon; oder, Musikalische Bibliothek.* 1732. Faksimile-Nachdruck, ed. Richard Schall. Documenta musicologica. 1. Reihe: Druckschriften-Faksimiles, 3. Kassel und Basel: Bärenreiter-Verlag, 1953.

———. *Praecepta der Musikalischen Composition 1708.* Herausgegeben von Peter Benary. Jenaer Beiträge zur Musikforschung, Band 2. Leipzig: Breitkopf und Härtel, 1955.

Westphal, Rudolph Georg Hermann. *Allgemeine Theorie der musikalischen Rhythmik seit J. S. Bach auf Grundlage der Antiken und unter Bezugnahme auf ihren historischen Anschluss an die Mittelalterliche mit besondere Berücksichtigung von Bach's Fugen und Beethoven's Sonaten.* Leipzig: Breitkopf und Härtel, 1880.

Widmann, Benedikt. "Die Kompositionen der Psalmen von Statius Olthof." *Vierteljahrschrift für Musikwissenschaft* (1889): 290–321.

Willems, Edgar. *Le rythme musical, étude psychologique.* Paris: Presses Universitaires de France, 1954.

Williams, C. F. Abdy. *The Aristoxenian Theory of Musical Rhythm.* Cambridge, England: At the University Press, 1911.

Williams, Peter. *The Organ Music of J. S. Bach.* Cambridge Studies in Music. Cambridge: Cambridge University Press, 1980–84.

Williams, R. F. "Marin Mersenne: An Edited Translation of the Fourth Treatise of the *Harmonie universelle.*" Ph.D. diss., University of Rochester, 1972.

Wolf, R. Peter. "Metrical Relationships in French Recitative of the Seventeenth and Eighteenth Centuries." *Recherches sur la Musique Française Classique* 18 (1978): 29–49.

Woodfield, Ian. *The Early History of the Viol.* Cambridge Musical Texts and Monographs. Cambridge: Cambridge University Press, 1984.

Yates, Frances A. *French Academies in the 16th Century.* London, 1948.

Zarlino, Gioseffo. *Le istitutioni harmoniche.* A facsimile of the 1558 Venice ed. Monuments of Music and Music Literature in Facsimile. 2d ser.: Music Literature, 1. New York: Broude Bros., 1965. Trans. of Part 3, *The Art of Counterpoint*, by Guy A. Marco and Claude V. Palisca. New York: W. W. Norton, 1976. Trans. of Part 4, *On the Modes*, by Vered Cohen. New Haven: Yale University Press, 1983.

INDEX